MasterChef
JUNIOR
BAKES!

Bold Recipes and Essential
Techniques to Inspire Young Bakers

FOREWORD BY
CHRISTINA TOSI

Clarkson Potter/Publishers
NEW YORK

Published in the United States by Clarkson Potter/Publishers,
an imprint of Random House, a division of Penguin Random
House LLC, New York.
clarksonpotter.com

CLARKSON POTTER is a trademark and POTTER with colophon
is a registered trademark of Penguin Random House LLC.

Library of Congress Cataloging-in-Publication Data
Title: MasterChef junior bakes! : bold recipes and essential
    techniques to inspire young bakers / MasterChef junior ;
    foreword by Christina Tosi.
Other titles: MasterChef junior.
Description: First edition. | New York : Clarkson Potter/
    Publishers, [2019]
Identifiers: LCCN 2018060756| ISBN 9781984822499 (trade
    pbk.) | ISBN 9781984822505 (ebook)
Subjects: LCSH: Baking. | LCGFT: Cookbooks.
Classification: LCC TX763 .M325 2019 | DDC 641.81/5--dc23 LC
    record available at https://lccn.loc.gov/2018060756

ISBN 978-1-9848-2249-9
Ebook ISBN 978-1-9848-2250-5

Printed in China

Book and cover design by Sonia Persad

10 9 8 7 6 5 4 3 2 1

First Edition

CONTENTS

FOREWORD

When I was a kid, I wanted to have my own bakery. The working name was Cookies, Cookies, Cookies. The idea stuck, but luckily the name didn't, and today, when I bounce between the kitchen and office of my bakery, Milk Bar, with flour in my hair, red Converse sneakers on my feet, and a notebook in hand, I feel like a kid again.

Growing up, my mom always told me to "be unapologetically yourself." I carry this advice with me everywhere I go, but the beauty of childhood is that for a while, you don't know how to be anything but yourself. Children are so wonderfully hopeful—they create, ideate, and express themselves freely, willing to try anything and everything that comes to mind. Their imaginations know no limit. The young home cooks of *MasterChef Junior* are just this, and when it comes to baking, I believe there is no better way to be.

A lot of cookbooks will tell you that baking is about science and precision. And that's true! But baking is also about experimentation, creativity, inspiration, and storytelling. Some of the recipes that I hold closest to my heart came out of baking sessions when I was a kid prancing barefoot in my grandmother's kitchen. Potato chips in cookies? Sure, why not. Mac and cheese in pancakes? Yes, please! I try to channel my kid-like spirit every time I turn the oven on, because at the end of the day, it's more fun that way.

The contestants on *MasterChef Junior* are young, but they are legit. These kids are champs—truly talented chefs with boundless passion and fresh ideas. One of the best parts about being a judge on the show is getting to watch and mentor this group of stunningly talented, blissfully curious kids coming into their own, as they discover what the world of food holds. They are old enough to know themselves, understand their palate, and taste nuances in flavor, but young enough to still be unapologetically fearless.

There are a lot of truly hysterical, outrageously fun, and downright thrilling moments that occur while filming *MasterChef Junior*. We surprised a couple of newlyweds by having our eight- to thrirteen-year-olds cook their three-course reception dinner. I've been dunked in enough frosting and sprinkles to coat thousands of birthday cakes (trust me—there's a reason we tie our hair up in the kitchen). It's an exciting, challenging, and rewarding job, and that's coming from someone who worked in fine-dining kitchens for a decade.

What thrills me the most, though, is watching the contestants in the pantry. In the first few minutes of a challenge, you can almost see the gears turning in each of their minds as they dash through the produce, thinking about the

ingredients, navigating the constraints of that particular challenge, balancing their big ideas against the racing clock. It's a fine wire-balancing act between what ingredients they are allowed to use, what ingredients they have to use, and what techniques they might try out. This is where the magic really happens. One moment, they are giggling over Gordon Ramsay's bad joke, and the next they are pulling picture-perfect macarons or blood orange cupcakes out of the oven.

This book is a compilation of some of the best outcomes of that process. There's the upscale (Green Tea Macarons with Strawberry Coulis, page 78) and the traditional (Classic Buttermilk Biscuits, page 28). There's a lot of sweet, the right amount of savory, and everything in between.

Above all, though, there's personality and perspective, a little bit of the chef's personal flair in each recipe. These kids inspire me, and I hope they inspire you, too.

xo.
TOSI

INTRODUCTION

MasterChef Junior is a unique cooking show that puts kids in the spotlight, inviting them to stretch their culinary muscles as well as their imaginations as they compete with—and cheer on—an amazing group of their peers. Savory cooking is certainly the main focus of the show, but because so many kids first fall in love with the kitchen by baking cookies, muffins, and cakes, no season would be complete without a chance for them to whip up something sweet, whether it's a showdown about homestyle cream pies or Parisian macarons. Baking's focus on precision is also a great way for the kids to discipline their kitchen habits and hone their techniques, just like the pros. Mentored by an esteemed group of judges—all masters in their fields—the incredible young *MasterChef Junior* contestants dream up an array of cakes, pies, cookies, and other delights that are every bit as polished as anything you'll find in a professional bakery or fancy restaurant—and have loads of fun doing it! The challenges they face are fast—and so are the friendships they make. When the kids are whipping up towering spiced ganache layer cakes (page 154), tender, chocolate-filled cream puffs (page 192), or pâtisserie-style green tea macarons (page 78), it's easy to forget that no one in the kitchen is more than thirteen years old. Talk about impressive!

Even though these young chefs are serious about baking, they still find plenty of ways to get creative—and crack each other up. Like the time in Season 3, when Jimmy won the lemon meringue pie challenge and got to throw his foamy pie right into judge Graham Elliot's face—and then the rest of the contestants grabbed pies and clobbered judges Gordon Ramsay and Joe Bastianich, too! Or in Season 6, after the three-legged doughnut-decorating challenge, when judge Christina Tosi, Joe, and Gordon all got soaked with a waterfall of frosting—followed by buckets of rainbow sprinkles!

Now, with this book to guide you, we hope you'll join in the fun, too. Whether you've been baking with your parents and grandparents since you were just big enough to hold a spoon or you're just starting out, the techniques and recipes in these pages offer a practical guide that will open up the wide world of baking and have you feeling like the master of your kitchen in no time. Packed with tips and recipes inspired by seven seasons of awesome *MasterChef Junior* contestants and challenges, you'll have all the tools you need to head to the oven with creativity and confidence. From new spins on all your family's favorite recipes, like gooey chocolate chip cookies, flaky buttermilk biscuits, and sticky banana bread, to towering sprinkle-strewn birthday cakes, tempting Sunday-morning doughnuts, fancy fruit tarts, buttery soft pretzels, and decadent cheese-filled quiches. You'll also hear from your favorite contestants as they share ideas and helpful skills they've learned along the way.

And that's not all. With dozens of pages devoted to important equipment and ingredients, detailed step-by-step photos, in-depth MasterChef Lessons that dive into the essential techniques, and ambitious Home Challenges that will push you to new limits, this book is a fun but practical primer designed to serve young bakers of all levels and ambitions. Get ready to learn the hows and whys of baking fundamentals, like how to measure ingredients (page 16), make meringue, decorate with spun sugar (page 122), frost towering layer cakes (page 146), melt chocolate, pipe pastries (page 188), and lots more cool techniques. For those of you who are ready to really to jump into the role of a *MasterChef Junior* baker, you'll find Home Challenges throughout the book—these are recipes that are especially challenging or involved. You'll also find tons of other practical hints about must-have ingredients, neat kitchen gear, and the science of baking. While some of the recipes in the collection are more complex than others, almost all of them can be broken down into easy pieces that are made to be mixed and matched any way you please. For instance, maybe you think the Butterscotch Budino with Salted Caramel and Crème Fraîche Whipped Cream (page 216) sounds amazing— but probably a little complicated for an after-school project? Save the caramel sauce and the whipped cream for another day and just make the pudding. It's delicious all on its own, takes less than 25 minutes to put together, and is guaranteed to wow everyone when you pull it out after family dinner!

Finally, beyond new recipes and techniques, we hope this cookbook encourages you to embrace the can-do spirit shared by so many of

the fantastic young chefs who have been a part of *MasterChef Junior*. So, jump in and get your hands dirty! Don't be afraid to try new ingredients and new flavors. Find inspiration in your family traditions and in exploring unfamiliar tastes and new corners of the world. Take a risk on a recipe you've never seen before. Trust yourself and all your abilities. Baking is a delicious adventure— and you're about to dive in!

GETTING PREPARED

Following a recipe is a great way to discover how to bake something you've never tried before and learn lots of cool new skills along the way. For the most delicious results, it's helpful to keep these few rules of thumb in mind as you prepare for any project.

1. **Read the whole recipe before you begin.** That way you'll know when you need to preheat the oven, if there are any unusual ingredients, or if any of the components need to rest overnight—because sometimes a recipe that looks like it will be done in 1 hour actually takes 2 days!

2. **Cook clean.** Real chefs are serious about cleanliness, and you should be, too. Always wash your hands before cooking and any time you get messy in the process. Keep your work surface clean and have a clean kitchen towel by your side. Keeping a metal bowl on your work surface can help, too—use it for trimmings, eggshells, or even dirty teaspoons and cup measures. Clean up little by little as you work through a recipe. That way, at the end, all that's left to do is taste test!

3. **Assemble your tools and ingredients.** After reading the recipe, make sure you have all the materials to start cooking. Find the tools, measure out your ingredients, let them come to the proper temperature, and set them out neatly on your workstation. The professional term for this is *mise en place*, which in French means "set in place."

4. **Use all your senses.** The best way to learn your way around the kitchen is to involve all your senses. Pay attention to scents and visual changes, like how fast a crust is browning or if something smells like it's burning. Every oven runs differently; stoves can cook faster or slower depending on whether they are gas or induction—even the material your skillets or cake pans are made from can impact how quickly or slowly something cooks or bakes. Using your senses will help you know when something is done, even if the recipe says you need 5 more minutes.

5. **When in doubt, ask for help.** Everyone is a beginner at some point, so don't be frustrated if you get confused by a direction or nervous about a new technique. Just ask a trusted adult to help you out—especially if it involves something tricky or a little dangerous, like making caramel or deep-frying.

6. **Remember, it's all practice.** Professional chefs never stop learning—and they know that even their biggest mistakes are just opportunities to improve. *MasterChef Junior* may be all about friendly competition, but at the end of the day, it isn't a test—it's a chance to try new things and have fun!

ESSENTIAL TOOLS

MEASURING CUPS AND SPOONS

Because baking recipes require precision, having a large liquid measuring cup and a variety of dry measuring cups and spoons is a must. Liquid measuring cups are usually clear and have a spout, which makes them perfect for measuring milk, orange juice, oil, and other pourables.

Dry measuring cups and spoons are ideal for measuring dry ingredients, like flour, sugar, or semisolid ingredients, like cream cheese, peanut butter, or jam. (For more on technique, see Measuring Ingredients, page 16.)

BOWLS

For prepping ingredients and mixing doughs, you'll want a set of bowls in a variety of sizes. Light, indestructible stainless steel bowls are a great option, and because they nest together, they won't take up too much room in your kitchen cabinets. Just make sure you have at least one that's *really* big—so you can whisk and knead with ease.

SPATULAS

These flat, handled kitchen tools come in a range of shapes, sizes, and materials. Thin metal spatulas are great for lifting brownies or pie squares from a baking dish; flexible silicone spatulas are perfect for mixing and folding delicate ingredients and smoothing batters into pans (and because they are heatproof, you can use them to stir sauces, too); and small offset spatulas are ideal for neatly frosting cupcakes and layer cakes.

WHISKS

The best whisks are stainless steel. Balloon whisks have large round wire heads and are perfect for whipping egg whites and whipped cream. Long, narrow whisks with rounded heads are also known as "French whisks" and are a great all-purpose option if you are going to buy just one. Flat whisks are useful for getting into the corners and sides of pans when making sauces.

WOODEN SPOONS

Sturdy wooden spoons are perfect for mixing thick batter and just get better with age. In fact, it's worth asking your grandma if she has any you can use!

KEY TO RECIPE LEVELS

★ ★ ★ Beginner: Simple ingredients and basic methods

★ ★ ★ Intermediate: Some multitasking and more involved techniques

★ ★ ★ Advanced: Elaborate instructions and challenging techniques

KEY TO BADGES

Recipes from or inspired by the show.

Classic recipes and contestant favorites.

PEELERS

A good peeler will help you prep a pie's worth of fruit in no time. Look for Y-shaped models with sharp blades and wide, comfy handles.

MICROPLANE ZESTER/GRATER

These tools have tiny sharp teeth, kind of like sandpaper, that are good for zesting citrus without getting any of the bitter white pith. You can also use them for grating whole spices like cinnamon and nutmeg, or for grating fresh ginger, garlic, or chocolate.

REAMER OR CITRUS PRESS

No need to get anything fancy—a simple reamer or handheld citrus press is great for when you need to get fresh juice from lemons, limes, or oranges.

PASTRY BRUSH

These small, flat brushes look kind of like mini paintbrushes and are used for brushing excess flour from pans, dabbing egg wash onto raw pie dough, or spreading melted butter over pastry. Silicone pastry brushes with flexible bristles, though not suited for delicate tasks like glazing fragile pastry, are much easier to clean and more durable than those with natural bristles—so it's always nice to have one of each kind on hand.

PASTRY BLENDER

This handled tool with curved metal blades helps cut cold butter into flour (page 32) quickly and easily. It's especially useful when making biscuits, scones, and pie and tart doughs.

BENCH SCRAPER

Also known as a dough scraper or a bench knife, this simple tool—essentially a flat rectangle (usually metal) with one curved, handled side—is surprisingly handy for a wide variety of kitchen tasks. Use it to scrape sticky bits of dough off your counter after rolling out pastry or cookie dough, to slice biscuits or scones, to trim the ends of logs of dough, or to scoop up and transfer loose ingredients from a work surface to a bowl.

ROLLING PINS

The best rolling pins are long and weighty enough to evenly roll out cookies, pie crusts, and other doughs. Though handles can be cute, most pastry chefs prefer tapered rolling pins (called French pins) because they're easier to control and don't have any little crevices for dough to get trapped in.

COOKIE CUTTER

Nowadays cookie cutters come in millions upon millions of different shapes and sizes. It's fun to build a collection, but if you're just starting out, simple shapes like stars, hearts, and graduated rounds (for cutting rolled cookies, biscuits, and doughnuts) are a good place to begin.

ICE CREAM SCOOPS

These utensils do much more than sling sundaes. Spring-loaded ice cream scoops are great for evenly portioning out cookie dough and cupcake and muffin batters.

PASTRY BAG

These cone-shaped bags can be made out of canvas, plastic, or nylon and have an opening at the narrow end to which you can attach decorative tips. Use them to pipe frostings, fillings, and light doughs like pâte à choux (page 188). If you don't have a pastry bag, you can improvise one by snipping off a small corner of a large zip-top storage bag.

To neatly fill a pastry bag, just place the bag inside a measuring cup for support, fold over the opening of the bag to create a collar, and spoon your frosting, filling, or dough into the opening.

Unfold the top of the bag and twist it closed while pressing on the top where the filling meets the plastic to release any air bubbles. Then, if necessary, use scissors to snip off the tip or a small corner of the bag and pipe away.

PARCHMENT PAPER

This heat-resistant, nonstick, disposable paper is the ultimate baker's helper. A sheet added to baking pans helps keep goodies, cookies, cake, and caramelized sugar from sticking. You can also roll pie dough between parchment layers to avoid using too much flour and to prevent sticking. Some bakers even lay a few sheets on their work surface to collect flour, spills, or frosting. It makes for much easier cleanup!

DIGITAL SCALE

The recipes in this book all use volume measurements, like cups and teaspoons, because they are the measurements most familiar to home bakers. But did you know that professional pastry chefs almost always measure their ingredients by weight, not volume? This is because weight measurements are the most accurate and because toggling between weight and volume measures can quickly get confusing. For example, 1 cup of sifted flour and 1 cup of milk weigh very different amounts! So, if you want to be really exact about your measurements, using a digital scale is the way to go. If you're just starting out, you'll be fine without one—but if you get serious about baking, you might want to put it on your wish list!

THERMOMETERS

Whether you're baking or cooking, the most accurate way to gauge the internal temperature of a sauce or syrup is with a thermometer. It comes in especially handy if you're making caramel (page 122), Swiss or Italian meringue (page 72), pastry cream (page 211), or crème anglaise (page 172). A glass-and-metal thermometer called a candy thermometer is used to measure the temperature of sugars, syrups, caramels, jams, and jellies. It is designed to clip onto the side of a saucepan and can also be used for deep-frying. It usually covers a range between 100° and 400°F. A digital instant-read thermometer has a long, thin probe that you can insert into whatever you are testing and a digital display that shows the temperature reading. Because instant-read thermometers are useful for taking the temperature of everything from a custard to a loaf of bread, they're the best all-purpose thermometer to have on hand in the kitchen—and higher-end models, whose temperature range reaches to 400°F and above, can even be used in candy making.

TIMER

Your oven or microwave may have a timer built right in; if it does, use it. If it doesn't, get yourself a simple kitchen timer to keep nearby while you bake, because no one wants to burn a batch of cupcakes just because they got a little distracted. That said, even though timers are great reminders, you should never rely on them completely. Always set your timer for 5 minutes less than the recipe recommends and check for doneness then, just in case!

IMPORTANT EQUIPMENT

BAKING SHEETS

Also called sheet pans, these rectangular rimmed pans are so handy, you can never have too many. Use them for baking cookies, scones, biscuits, sheet cakes, and small pastries. The most commonly used size is the half sheet (13 × 18 inches), but smaller quarter sheets (13 × 9 inches) are also great for toasting nuts, roasting or drying fruit, and organizing ingredients. Note that baking sheets with dark-colored surfaces tend to brown items more quickly, so your cookies or biscuits may brown on the bottom and be done before the recipe indicates.

BAKING PANS/DISHES

These deep pans can be made out of ceramic, glass, or metal and come in all kinds of shapes, from square to oval to rectangular. They're used for brownies, bars, crumbles, and lots of other baked goods. Two of the most common sizes are 8-inch square and 9 × 13 inches.

CAKE PANS

Usually round and made of metal, these pans come in a variety of sizes and are used for making cake layers as well as some yeasted pastries like sticky buns and cinnamon rolls. The most common sizes are 8- and 9-inch rounds.

BUNDT PANS

Bundts are a decorative type of cake pan with a hollow, tubular center and tall fluted sides. They're often used for pound cakes and other tea breads. Bundts come in lots of styles and sizes, but the most common has a 10- to 12-cup capacity.

LOAF PANS

These long, deep, narrow pans are most often used for making quick breads (like banana bread) and yeast breads. They can be made out of metal, glass, or ceramic. The most common size is 8½ × 4½ inches.

MUFFIN TINS

Most often used for muffins and cupcakes, these metal baking pans have small cups built in to hold individual portions of batter. Mini-muffin tins are great for making bite-size treats. Paper liners help prevent the batter from sticking to the pan and make cleanup easier.

PIE PANS AND TART PANS

Pie pans are deep rimmed dishes used for making all kinds of sweet and savory pies and quiches. They can be made out of metal, glass, or ceramic. The standard size is 9 inches; deep-dish pans are often 9½ inches (both sizes are used in these recipes). Tart pans are ideal for making delicate tarts and shortbread. They are made from metal and have shallow fluted edges and, usually, a removable bottom.

RAMEKINS

Perfect for puddings, custards, soufflés, and other delicate desserts, these are small, cuplike baking dishes, usually made from porcelain or glass. In this book, the most commonly used size is a 6-ounce straight-sided round.

WIRE RACKS

These raised wire stands are also known as bakers' racks or cooling racks. They're incredibly useful because they allow air to circulate around baked goods, cooling them quickly and preventing condensation from forming, which can cause sogginess.

USEFUL APPLIANCES

MIXER (HAND AND STAND)

Though you can cream butter, mix batters, and whip heavy cream by hand, it's quite a workout! Having an electric mixer to help makes the task a whole lot easier. Handheld mixers often come with both beater and whisk attachments and are good enough for most basic jobs, like whipping egg whites to stiff peaks. If you really get into baking, especially bread making, a big stand mixer with a dough hook, whisk, and paddle is definitely a worthwhile investment.

BLENDER

Like a tall pitcher with blades at the bottom and settings for pureeing, chopping, and mixing, a blender is great for quickly mixing batters and pureeing sauces. High-powered models, whose motors top 1,000 watts of power, can also be used to chop nuts or grind grains into flour.

FOOD PROCESSOR

With interchangeable blades that can slice, shred, chop, and mix, a food processor is handy for making pastry dough, chopping nuts or chocolate, and grinding bread, cookies, or crackers into crumbs. If you're making the investment, it's nice to look for one that has a small bowl insert to handle small quantities of ingredients (like combining sugar and citrus zest for scented sugar).

BASIC TECHNIQUES

MEASURING INGREDIENTS

Great bakers know the importance of being consistent. That's because consistency allows you to get the same (hopefully great!) results from a recipe again and again. One of the easiest ways to be consistent when you're baking is by measuring your ingredients carefully, so you can follow a recipe correctly every time.

Determining how to measure something depends on whether the ingredient is wet or dry, solid or sticky. Here are some examples:

FLOUR (all varieties, and larger amounts of dry ingredients in general)

Dry ingredients, like flour, cocoa powder, and cornmeal, are usually measured with dry measuring cups that come in graduated sizes from ¼ cup to 1 cup. (Advanced bakers and professionals may choose to use a digital scale to weigh their ingredients instead; see Digital Scale, page 13). But if you're using volume measures like cups, the most accurate way to measure flour (and the one used in this book) is what's known as the "spoon and level" method. This means spooning the flour into a measuring cup and leveling off the top with the straight edge of a spatula or knife. Doing it this way makes sure that the flour doesn't get too tightly packed into the measuring cup, which can cause you to add too much flour to a recipe, leading to dry and heavy results.

SUGAR

For granulated sugar, use a dry measuring cup to scoop up the ingredient. Level the top flat with the edge of a spatula or knife. For brown sugar, spoon the sugar into the cup and then press it firmly into the cup (this is called *packing*) until it is level with the edges (you may need to add more sugar after packing the first time). Because it is powdery, confectioners' sugar should be measured using the spoon-and-level method, just as you do for flour.

BUTTER

Butter usually comes in 4-ounce sticks that have a wrapper printed with measurement marks for tablespoons, ¼ cup, ⅓ cup, and ½ cup. Use a knife to slice the butter into the amount you need. If a recipe calls for "⅓ cup butter, melted" you should measure out the quantity of butter first and then melt it.

LIQUIDS

You can measure small amounts of liquid—like a teaspoon or 2 tablespoons—using measuring spoons. If you need more than ¼ cup liquid, it's best to use a clear liquid measuring cup with a pouring spout. Make sure the cup is on a level surface when you fill it and check your measurements by bending down to look straight on at the volume markings on the side of the cup.

SEMISOLIDS AND THICK, STICKY STUFF

For semisolid and sticky ingredients, like honey, molasses, and peanut butter, use the same dry measuring cups you'd use for flour and sugar. Having trouble getting something completely out of the cup? Coat the measuring cup lightly with nonstick pan spray before measuring, and even the stickiest ingredient will slide right out.

STIRRING VS. BEATING VS. WHISKING VS. FOLDING

When making doughs, pastries, and batters, recipes often use the terms *stir*, *beat*, *whisk*, and *fold* to describe the way ingredients are combined. It may seem confusing, but it's important to understand the distinctions between them, because each method has a different effect.

- *Mixing* is the most basic: It simply means moving a spoon or a spatula in a circular direction through two or more ingredients until the ingredients are combined.
- *Beating* and *stirring* are similar, except that beating indicates that you should be more forceful, or stir for a longer amount of time.
- *Whisking* is a type of stirring that can have two effects: It can introduce air and increase volume (like whipping egg whites or heavy cream), or it can be used as an alternative to sifting to evenly combine and distribute dry ingredients.
- *Folding* is a method of incorporating a light, aerated ingredient (like whipped egg whites) into a heavier ingredient (like a soufflé batter) with the goal of deflating the batter as little as possible. It is done by spooning the lighter ingredient on top of the heavier one, then very gently using a rubber spatula (or a whisk) to slice down through the middle of the mixture to the bottom, then lightly moving the spatula up and back on top of itself to "fold" the ingredients together. Continue, making small slices and scoops, turning the bowl as you work, until the mixtures are fully incorporated but still fluffy.

KNIFE SKILLS

Sharp knives can be intimidating, but a basic set will make all your work in the kitchen easier—and safer, too, since you don't put as much pressure on a sharp knife to cut through something as you do on a dull one. Have an adult teach you how to hold them safely and then start practicing. The grip that will give you the most control over your knife is called the "blade grip." This is done by wrapping your bottom three fingers around the knife's handle while using your index finger and thumb to pinch the blade where it flares out and meets the handle. (This can feel awkward at first, but will start to seem natural in no time.) When you're cutting food, for the most stability, always position the ingredient with a flat side down against your cutting board. Protect the fingertips on the hand holding the food in place by curling them under as you cut (this is called the "claw grip"), then use your free hand to guide your knife. Using the claw grip ensures that even if your knife accidentally slips, it will only hit your knuckles or your fingernails, and not slice off a fingertip! You don't need to rush out and spend your whole allowance on a fancy knife. Here are the knives you'll reach for most often when baking:

- A *chef's knife* is an all-purpose knife with a large, long, sharp blade. Use it for slicing and dicing, and for chopping ingredients like chocolate and nuts. Chef's knives come in different sizes; professionals sometimes use ones that are as large as 12 inches—but for most home cooks (especially younger ones with smaller hands) a shorter blade, in the 6- to 8-inch range, should do the trick. If you're not sure what to get, go to the store and hold a few different knives to help figure out which feels the most comfortable.

- A *paring knife* is a small, pointed knife that fits neatly in the palm. Use it for smaller tasks like trimming fruit.
- A *serrated knife/bread knife* is a long knife with a saw-toothed blade. Use it for slicing cakes, breads, and ingredients like melons or pineapples that have especially tough skins.

Ever wonder what the difference is between *chop*, *mince*, *slice*, and *dice*? It's simple:

- To *chop* means to cut food into pieces of even size, but not of even shape. If a recipe says to "finely chop," the pieces should be small; if a recipe says to "coarsely chop," the pieces should be on the bigger side.
- To *mince* means to chop into *very* small pieces of even size.
- To *slice* means to cut into thin pieces of even width.
- To *dice* means to cut into small cubes of even size. If a recipe asks for "fine dice," the pieces should be especially small.

PREPARING YOUR PAN

There's nothing sadder than baking a beautiful cake, only to watch it crumble because it got stuck in the pan! Your best insurance against such tragedy is to properly prepare your bakeware. Recipes usually tell you the best approach—either greasing the pan with butter, oil, or nonstick spray; sprinkling with flour or cocoa; lining with parchment paper; or some combination of these methods—but here are some rules to keep in mind:

- For cookies and pastries prepared on baking sheets, line the sheets with parchment paper.
- For brownies and bars, and for cakes and breads made in loaf pans, line the bottom and long sides of the pan with a parchment paper "sling." Grease any sides not covered by parchment with butter, oil, or nonstick pan spray.
- For cake layers, line the bottom of the pan with a round of parchment paper and generously grease the sides with butter, oil, or nonstick pan spray.
- For specialty pans like Bundt, madeleine, and doughnut pans, grease the inside of the pan with butter, oil, or nonstick pan spray, making sure to get in every cranny. For extra protection, after greasing the pan, sprinkle in a bit of flour and rotate the pan so the flour evenly coats it, then tap out any excess. For a chocolate cake, use a little bit of cocoa powder instead of flour so that the cake doesn't wind up with white streaks on it.

THE BAKER'S PANTRY

The *MasterChef Junior* pantry is the stuff of legend—but you don't need a kitchen full of exotic ingredients to begin your baking adventures. Most recipes start with the same few staples, so the most important things are to get the basics and to know how to use them. With these ingredients on hand, you'll always be able to whip up a little something sweet!

FLOUR

In baking, flour is used to hold batters and doughs together and give baked goods structure. That structure is a result of activating *gluten*—a protein that's found in all wheat, rye, and barley flours that gets stretchy when kneaded.

Though all-purpose flour is the most common type, these days lots of interesting whole-grain and alternative flours like whole wheat flour and buckwheat flour are available in grocery stores. Almond flour, which is made from almonds that have been ground to a fine, flour-like consistency, is another type that you may encounter often. It can be fun to experiment with them (and we include some ideas in this book). But just remember that because they all behave a little differently, they can't all be substituted for one another—for example, almond flour may be fine-textured and flour-like, but it doesn't have any gluten, so it won't work in a recipe as a clean swap for wheat flour. Cake flour is a fine-grained wheat flour that has less protein (gluten) in it—which makes it bake up a little lighter and tenderer than all-purpose flour. Bread flour is the opposite: a protein-rich wheat flour that's especially designed to increase the elasticity of a dough, making it strong enough to be kneaded and shaped. Self-rising flour is just all-purpose flour to which a small amount of salt and baking powder has already been added.

Flour has a long shelf life, but there are still a few things you can do to keep it as fresh as possible. All-purpose flour should be stored in an airtight container in a cool, dry place and used within 12 to 18 months of purchase. Because whole-grain and nut flours contain more oil—and oil goes rancid fast—it's best to store them in an airtight container in the freezer and use them within 1 year.

BAKING POWDER AND BAKING SODA

Both baking powder and baking soda are *leaveners*—which means they make baked goods rise. Although they do similar jobs, they can't be used interchangeably. Baking powder's rising powers start working when it is combined with a liquid, and it gets a second boost when it is exposed to the oven's heat (which is why it's called "double-acting"). Baking soda's rising powers need an acidic ingredient—like buttermilk, yogurt, sour cream, molasses, or lemon juice—in

order to be activated. Both baking powder and baking soda do lose their strength after 6 to 12 months, so it's important make sure yours is fresh (see Tip, page 28), or else you're liable to end up with cakes and cookies that are short and squat!

BUTTER

Butter is a fat used to bind batters, create browning, and add tenderness and flavor. It comes in two varieties—salted and unsalted. Most baking recipes (including the ones in this book) call for unsalted butter, so that you can add salt separately according to your own taste. Butter usually comes packaged in 1-pound boxes made up of four 4-ounce (8-tablespoon) sticks.

Besides salted or unsalted, the other factor to keep in mind when using butter is its temperature. Recipes usually indicate whether the butter should be ice cold, room temperature, or melted—and it's really important to pay attention to those descriptions, because butter temperature can have a huge effect on how a recipe works (or doesn't!). For instance, when you make biscuits, pie crusts, or any other baked goods that have a "short" flaky texture, you'll want to use ice-cold butter that can be combined with the dry ingredients in coarse, pebbly chunks. (This is called "cutting in" butter; see the MasterChef Lesson, page 32, for more on that technique.) On the other hand, for cakes and cookies with a light texture and a fine crumb, you'll want to use room-temperature butter, which is easily "creamed" together with sugar to make a light, fluffy batter or dough. (For more on this technique, see the MasterChef Lesson, page 54.) Room-temperature butter should be slightly soft and almost plastic-y in texture, not melty or greasy; to get the right texture, take the butter out of the refrigerator at least 30 minutes before you plan to use it.

EGGS

Eggs do so many things that they seem kind of magical. In baking, they're used to add structure to cakes and cookies, richness to custards and ice cream, and strength and color to pastries. When you're standing in front of the egg case at the grocery store, the options may seem overwhelming. Should you get organic or free-range eggs? Large or jumbo? White or brown?! It's simple, really: Most recipes (including the ones in this book) are written for large eggs, so that's the size you should buy unless a recipe says otherwise. The color of an egg doesn't matter—it just has to do with the kind of chicken it comes from, and won't change the way the egg performs or how it tastes. Similarly, whether or not you buy conventional, free-range, or organic eggs is a personal choice that won't affect how the recipe works.

Some recipes call for separating the egg yolks from the egg whites so both of them can be used in different ways. That's because egg whites and egg yolks have very different properties and behave dramatically differently during baking. Egg yolks are a fat, so they're mostly used to add richness, creaminess, and smoothness to doughs, batters, and custards. Because the proteins in egg yolks gel when heated, they're also sometimes used as a thickener or binder in puddings and sauces. Egg whites are a combination of protein and water. Whipping egg whites, as you do when making a meringue (see the MasterChef Lesson, page 72), sponge cake, or soufflé (page 199), turns them into a foam filled with millions of tiny air bubbles—and those bubbles expand when they are exposed to oven heat, causing whatever batter they've been folded into to rise and lift.

To crack an egg without tears, you don't have to be too forceful, just tap the side of the egg gently against a flat surface, then open it with both hands and let the egg fall into a bowl (cracking an egg against the edge of a bowl can cause shells to get into the egg). The more you do it, the more natural it will feel—after a while you might even be able to do it with just one hand!

If a bit of shell gets in the bowl, don't try to scoop it out with your fingers—eggs are super slippery and hard to grasp! Instead, use some of the broken eggshell as a scoop to pull the shard out—it's a neat little trick that works perfectly every time.

Egg whites and yolks are easiest to separate when they're cold, so when separating is called for in a recipe, pull them right out of the refrigerator and give it a try. Crack the egg over a bowl, using your hands to slowly open it. As you do, let the yolk fall into one half of the shell like a little cup, while the whites drip over the side of the shell into the bowl. Pass the yolk back and forth between the two sides of the shell until all the whites have fallen into the bowl—then pour the yolk into a separate bowl.

When they're kept refrigerated, eggs stay fresh for 3 to 5 weeks; if you're not sure how long your eggs have been lying around, you can check their freshness by placing one in a container of cold water. If the egg gently falls to the bottom, it's fresh enough to eat; if it floats at the top, it's not.

SUGAR

Baking simply wouldn't be as sweet without sugar! The most common sweetener used in the kitchen, sugar tenderizes baked goods and helps develop golden, caramelized crusts. There are lots of different varieties, and these days you can even find many alternative sugars, like maple sugar, coconut sugar, and date sugar, at grocery stores. But the three types that are most often used in baking are granulated sugar, brown sugar, and confectioners' (or powdered) sugar.

Granulated (or white) sugar is a refined sugar that is pure white because the natural molasses has been removed. Unrefined sugar can generally be used in place of refined granulated sugar, but it still has a tinge of brownness from the molasses. It is usually coarser as well, so substituting it for refined sugar in a recipe may slightly change the texture. Brown sugar is refined sugar that has some of the molasses left in. There are two types of brown sugar—light and dark. If a recipe calls for brown sugar, you can use either one, but dark brown sugar will give whatever you are baking a deeper caramel/molasses flavor and a denser consistency. Confectioners' sugar is just refined sugar that has been ground until light and powdery and mixed with a tiny amount of cornstarch to keep it from clumping together. Some recipes in this book also call for turbinado, or raw, sugar as a finishing sugar. With its light molasses flavor and coarse crystals, a sprinkle of turbinado is a nice way to add a lovely crunch and sparkle to the tops of muffins, quick breads, cookies, pies, and pastries.

To keep brown sugar soft and fresh, it should be stored in an airtight container in a cool, dry place. If you go to make a batch of cookies and discover your brown sugar has dried out into a hard brick, you can soften it by placing it in a microwave-safe bowl, covering it with a damp paper towel, and microwaving it for 20 to 30 seconds.

SALT

Because not all salts are interchangeable, using the wrong type can spell disaster for a recipe. Unless otherwise noted, all the recipes in this book call for Diamond Crystal kosher salt, which dissolves quickly and has a nice neutral flavor, making it a great all-purpose salt for everything from baking to grilling.

If you want to substitute table salt for kosher salt, make sure to halve the amount you're using, because table salt is much finer and more densely packed than kosher salt. So if you don't adjust the amount, the finished dish will be much too salty! Flaky sea salts, such as Maldon, are often used as finishing salts to add a pop of salinity and crunch to a dish. Try flaky salt in a compound butter or as a finishing touch on chocolate chip cookies.

CHOCOLATE

You can bake without chocolate—but why would you want to? From brownies to soufflés, chocolate is one of the most essential flavors in the world of baking. Most recipes call for chocolate in one of three forms: cocoa powder, chocolate bars (or baking bars), or chocolate chips. Sweetened cocoa is fine for hot chocolate, but for baking, the cocoa powder you buy should always be unsweetened. Most of the cocoa powder you find in stores falls into two categories: natural or Dutch process. Dutch-process cocoa powder tends have a darker color and a slightly more intense flavor than natural. Because it has been treated to reduce its acidity, Dutch-process cocoa powder won't react properly with alkaline leaveners like baking soda; that's why recipes that include Dutch-process cocoa powder usually use baking powder instead.

If a recipe calls for "dark" chocolate, that generally means chips or bars that have more than 70% cacao and an intense flavor verging on bitter. "Semisweet" or "bittersweet" chocolate is slightly milder, falling in the 60 to 70% cacao range. White chocolate, on the other hand, is just cocoa butter, sugar, and (usually) milk solids. Unsweetened baking chocolate, which doesn't contain sugar or other additives, is the purest chocolate you can bake with and can

be useful when you want to add flavor without increasing the sweetness. But beware: because of its bitter taste, it's definitely not for nibbling! Store chocolate in an airtight container in a cool, dry place (65° to 70°F is ideal). Older chocolate sometimes takes on a powdery white film, called a "bloom," as a result of a change in temperature or humidity. It may not look pretty, but don't worry, it's still fine for eating and baking. (For more on melting chocolate and making ganache, see the MasterChef Lesson, page 108.)

MILK, HEAVY CREAM, AND OTHER DAIRY PRODUCTS

In general, using dairy—like heavy cream, milk, buttermilk, yogurt, or sour cream—is a way to add moistness and tenderness to cakes, cookies, and other baked goods. Milk is sold in a variety of fat contents, with whole milk being the highest in fat percentage and fat-free milk being the lowest. Most baking recipes (including the ones in this book) are written using whole milk. If you don't have whole milk, you can use low-fat milk in some cases—but be prepared to lose some tenderness. Traditionally, buttermilk was the liquid left over after churning cream into butter—

they are also very expensive, so they are usually saved for special recipes when you want to see flecks of vanilla seeds. Depending on where they are grown, vanilla beans may have subtly different characteristics. Madagascar Bourbon beans tend to have the most classically sweet, mild vanilla flavor. Tahitian vanilla beans are often a little bit fruitier. And Mexican beans usually have a little extra warmth and spice. To get the vanilla seeds out of a vanilla bean pod, use the tip of a paring knife to split the pod in half lengthwise from tip to tip. Use the tip of the knife to open the pod (like a book) and then hold the knife against the sticky insides (those are the seeds) and scrape from top to bottom on both sides of the pod to get the seeds out. But don't throw that empty pod away! Stash it in a glass jar along with some granulated sugar, and in 2 weeks you'll have a batch of vanilla sugar that's lovely for sprinkling on cookies or oatmeal or stirring into tea.

Vanilla extract is made by soaking vanilla beans in alcohol. The effect of extract is less powerful, but still adds lovely flavor and fragrance to cookies, cakes, custards, and much more. Just make sure you read the label on the bottle when you're shopping and always buy "pure" vanilla extract, not "imitation," which is made from synthetic ingredients and can have a funny fake flavor.

but these days, most buttermilk is commercially fermented by warming low-fat milk and adding live bacterial cultures (like those that live in yogurt). Like milk, yogurt comes in a variety of fat contents; Greek yogurt is just plain yogurt that has been drained to remove whey, which makes it thicker. Sour cream is cream that has been fermented by adding live bacterial cultures—which are also what gives it its signature tang. Crème fraîche is similar to sour cream but has an even higher fat content, which makes it extra decadent. Of course, a dollop of freshly whipped cream makes just about everything you bake taste better—good thing it's so simple to make! All you need is a cold, clean bowl, a whisk, and a cupful of heavy cream (see page 88 for more on whipping cream).

VANILLA

Most bakers use vanilla in one of two forms: vanilla beans or vanilla extract. Of the two, vanilla beans have the more potent flavor, but

SPICES

If baking is an art, spices are like the colors on your palette—a delicious way to bring color and complexity to even the simplest recipes. The spices used most frequently in American baking are cinnamon, ginger, nutmeg, cloves, and allspice. These are the spices that you probably associate with the holidays, because their combined scent is so reminiscent of pumpkin pie and apple pie (not to mention pumpkin spice doughnuts, gingerbread, and dozens of other fall treats!). There are a lot of other spices that are great for baking, too, like cardamom, lavender, coriander, and saffron. Exploring new spices can be a wonderful way to liven up your baking routine and explore unfamiliar tastes.

Spices can be bought in either whole or ground form. Most recipes (including the ones in this book) are written for ground spices—but keep in mind that after they are ground, spices quickly begin to lose strength. For that reason, it's best to purchase them in small quantities, replace them after about 6 months, and always store them in airtight containers in a cool, dry place. Or buy them whole and use a spice mill (or coffee grinder) to grind them yourself for the freshest, most fragrant flavor.

YEAST

It may not look like much, but inside tiny yeast granules there are billions of living organisms! Yeast is a living thing and is used to help doughs rise and to create tall, airy breads and pastries. There are three kinds of yeast: active dry yeast and instant (Rapid Rise) yeast, both of which are usually sold in packets; and fresh or "cake" yeast, which is sold in small squares. Active dry yeast needs to be dissolved in a lukewarm liquid before it is added to a dough, whereas instant (Rapid Rise) yeast can be mixed directly into the dry ingredients. Cake yeast is much more fragile than active dry or instant yeast—it needs to be stored in the refrigerator and only stays fresh for a couple of weeks.

To work, yeast needs to be "activated" by a warm liquid and "fed" by a sugar or another sweetener—which is why at least a small quantity of those things usually appear in most yeast dough recipes. When the yeast eats the sugar, it converts it into alcohol and carbon dioxide, which creates air bubbles in the dough and makes it rise. Fresh yeast activates more quickly and stays active longer than dry yeast, so it can be good for projects that call for a slow, extended rising time, like sourdough breads. And some bakers believe fresh yeast lends baked goods a slightly more complex taste. But all the recipes in this book work perfectly well with dry yeast.

Many recipes call for letting dough rise once, then "punching it down" to remove some of the gas before letting it rise a second time (either as the whole dough or as small pieces shaped into rolls, twists, or knots). This second rise is also known as "proofing."

Most yeast doughs also involve kneading to strengthen, smooth, and help develop gluten. This is easily done with a stand mixer fitted with a dough hook attachment, but you can also do it by hand. (For a how-to, see the MasterChef Lesson, page 234.)

FOOD COLORING, SPRINKLES, SANDING SUGAR, AND OTHER DECORATIONS

These colorful accents may not be essentials, but they are a big part of what makes baking so fun! The most common varieties of food coloring are the traditional liquid—which is what you'll find in most grocery stores—and gel liquid, which is thicker, produces more vivid colors, and can be bought online or in craft and baking supply stores. There are all sorts of decorative sugars, including nonpareils (tiny sugar balls), sprinkles (thin, cylindrical sugar bits), confetti (flat colorful sugar rounds), and sanding sugars (bright, crystal-like sugar sparkles).

BISCUITS, MUFFINS,

AND OTHER BREAKFAST TREATS!

Lemon–Poppy Seed
Muffins with Citrus
Drizzle, page 39

CLASSIC
BUTTERMILK BISCUITS

In Season 6, Cade showed off his Southern heritage—and some serious baking skills—by preparing a batch of golden, flaky buttermilk biscuits to serve alongside okra and blackened shrimp. One way to get extra flakes in your biscuits is by folding the dough in a stack before cutting it. This helps to create lots of flaky layers in the biscuit that let you split the biscuit open easily—and are perfect for slathering with extra butter and jam! These biscuits are big enough for breakfast sandwiches, but you can cut them into smaller squares before baking if you want to serve them as a side.

MAKES 6 LARGE BISCUITS

3 cups all-purpose flour, plus more for shaping

2 teaspoons baking powder

½ teaspoon baking soda

1 teaspoon sugar

1 teaspoon kosher salt

1½ sticks (6 ounces) ice-cold unsalted butter, cubed

¾ cup plus 2 tablespoons buttermilk

1 large egg, beaten

TIP To test the freshness of baking powder, sprinkle a half spoonful into a small cup of hot water: If it fizzes and bubbles, you're good to go. For baking soda, sprinkle half a spoonful into a small cup of something acidic, like lemon water: Again, if it starts bubbling, you're all set.

1. Preheat the oven to 400°F. Line a baking sheet with parchment paper.

2. In a large bowl, whisk together the flour, baking powder, baking soda, sugar, and salt. Add the butter to the bowl. Use your fingertips to cut the butter into the flour until the mixture is the texture of coarse crumbs and a few pea-size pieces of butter are still visible. (To learn more about this technique, see the MasterChef Lesson, page 32.) Add the buttermilk to the bowl and stir gently with a fork just until a shaggy dough forms.

3. Transfer the dough to a lightly floured work surface and use your hands to press it into an 8-inch square. Fold the square in half and then in half again in the other direction. Gently press the folded dough with your hands, then use a rolling pin to roll it into a 9-inch square. Use a sharp knife or a bench scraper to slice the dough horizontally in half, then slice each square into 3 equal strips to create 6 large rectangles. Transfer the rectangles to the prepared baking sheet, leaving 2 inches of space between them. Chill in the freezer for 15 minutes. (Or refrigerate for at least 1 hour or up to overnight.)

4. Brush the tops of the biscuits with beaten egg. Bake until they are tall, golden, and crisp around the edges, 20 to 22 minutes. Serve warm. Leftover biscuits will keep for 2 days and can be wrapped in foil and reheated in a 350°F oven.

BASIC CREAM BISCUITS

Cream biscuits are a simple style of biscuit that has just four ingredients: flour, baking powder, salt, and heavy cream. You might be wondering how you can make rich, tender biscuits without butter. The key is the heavy cream, which works in the recipe as both a fat and a liquid! Here's one more thing to love about cream biscuits: Not only are they super quick and easy to make, they're also endlessly adaptable. Stir in some cheese for a savory suppertime side; add some sugar to the dough and you have a shortcake (page 36). In fact, if you are going to memorize only one recipe in this book, this should be it. It's only four ingredients . . . that's easy!

MAKES 6 LARGE BISCUITS

2 cups all-purpose flour, plus more for shaping

1 tablespoon baking powder

¾ teaspoon kosher salt

1¼ cups plus 2 tablespoons heavy cream

1. Preheat the oven to 425°F. Line a baking sheet with parchment paper.

2. In a large bowl, whisk together the flour, baking powder, and salt. Add 1¼ cups of the cream and stir the mixture with a fork just until the dough looks shaggy and holds together when squeezed.

3. Use an ice cream scoop or large spoon to drop 2½- to 3-inch knobs of dough onto the baking sheet, leaving 1½ to 2 inches between them. Chill in the freezer for 15 minutes. (Or refrigerate for at least 1 hour or up to overnight.)

4. Brush the tops of the biscuits with the remaining 2 tablespoons cream. Bake until the biscuits are pale golden and slightly puffed, 20 to 22 minutes. Wait until they are just cool enough to handle, then serve warm. Leftover biscuits will keep for 2 days and can be wrapped in foil and reheated in a 350°F oven.

VARIATION

Herb and Cheese Biscuits: Add ½ cup shredded hard cheese (such as sharp cheddar, Manchego, or provolone) and 2 tablespoons minced fresh herbs (such as rosemary, thyme, or basil) to the flour mixture before stirring in the cream, then proceed with the rest of the recipe as instructed.

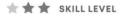
SWEET POTATO BISCUITS
WITH MARSHMALLOW-HONEY BUTTER

These biscuits are gently sweet and moist, thanks to the addition of cooked sweet potato. They get served with a smear of salty-sweet marshmallow-honey butter—kind of like the brûléed marshmallow-topped sweet potato biscuit that Kade made in Season 4. It's the ultimate finishing touch, and the flavor combo should be familiar to anyone who looks forward to digging into an ooey-gooey marshmallow-topped sweet potato casserole during the holidays!

MAKES 10 SMALL BISCUITS

SEASON 4

KADE

SWEET POTATO BISCUITS

10 ounces sweet potatoes (about 2 small) or 1 cup canned unsweetened pumpkin puree

¾ cup plus 1 tablespoon buttermilk

2½ cups all-purpose flour, plus more for shaping

3 tablespoons light brown sugar

2½ teaspoons baking powder

½ teaspoon baking soda

1 teaspoon kosher salt

1 stick (4 ounces) ice-cold unsalted butter, cubed

1 large egg, beaten

MARSHMALLOW-HONEY BUTTER

1 stick (4 ounces) unsalted butter, at room temperature

1 cup marshmallow crème (such as Fluff)

2 tablespoons honey

⅛ teaspoon kosher salt

1. Make the sweet potato biscuits: Pierce the sweet potatoes all over with a fork and place them on a microwave-safe plate. Microwave the potatoes until they are soft and starting to leak some juices from the holes from the fork, 10 to 12 minutes. Set aside to cool. Once the potatoes are cool, make a lengthwise slit from end to end, squeeze them open, scoop the flesh into a small bowl, and mash until smooth. (Discard the skins . . . or eat them!)

2. Measure out 1 cup of the sweet potato mash (save the leftovers for a snack) and add it to a bowl along with the buttermilk. Whisk the mixture until smooth and set aside.

3. In a large bowl, whisk together the flour, brown sugar, baking powder, baking soda, and salt. Add the butter to the bowl. Use your fingertips to cut the butter into the flour until the mixture is the texture of coarse crumbs and a few pea-size pieces of butter are still visible. (To learn more about this technique, see MasterChef Lesson, page 32.) Add the sweet potato mixture to the bowl and stir gently with a fork just until a sticky, shaggy dough forms.

4. Preheat the oven to 400°F. Line a baking sheet with parchment paper and set aside.

5. Transfer the dough to a generously floured work surface and use your hands to press it into an 8-inch square. (The dough will be quite sticky: Don't be afraid to generously flour the top of the

dough and your hands, too.) Fold the square in half, gently pat it out a bit, then fold it in half again crosswise. Gently press the dough into an approximately 5 × 10-inch rectangle with your hands. Use a sharp knife or a bench scraper to slice the dough horizontally in half, then slice each rectangle crosswise into 5 even strips to create 10 small rectangles. Transfer the biscuits to the baking sheet, leaving 2 inches of space between them. Chill in the freezer for 15 minutes. (Or refrigerate for at least 1 hour or up to overnight.)

6. Brush the tops of the biscuits with beaten egg. Bake until they are tall, golden, and crisp at the edges, about 17 minutes. Remove biscuits from the oven and set aside to cool slightly (they are best served warm).

7. While the biscuits bake, make the marshmallow-honey butter: In a large bowl, using an electric mixer, beat the butter until smooth, about 1 minute. Add the marshmallow crème and continue beating. Add the honey and salt and beat until smooth, about 20 seconds more. Spoon the butter into a small bowl. The butter will keep, covered, in refrigerator for 1 week.

8. Serve the warm biscuits with the marshmallow-honey butter. Leftover biscuits will keep for 2 days and can be wrapped in foil and reheated in a 350°F oven.

MAKING THE FLAKIEST PASTRIES AND DOUGHS

How do pastry chefs turn out perfectly flaky biscuits, scones, and pie crusts every time? The secret isn't a magic spell—it's how they handle the flour and butter when they're preparing the dough.

Unlike recipes for cookies and cakes, which usually involve "creaming" butter and sugar (see MasterChef Lesson, page 54) to produce a light, fine-textured interior, recipes for so-called "short" flaky pastries tell the baker to "cut in" the butter. No, this doesn't involve scissors! It just means adding the butter to the flour so that the mixture is crumbly, like coarse sand with a few large pebbles of butter left in. Some chefs like to get their hands dirty by simply rubbing the flour and chilled butter between their fingertips. Another option is to use a pastry blender, which is a tool with curved metal blades that helps press the butter into the flour without it absorbing the heat from your hands. Other bakers like to use a food processor because it keeps their fingers clean and the ingredients cold—plus, it's fast! There's a reason you want to leave some of the butter in big bits—but more on that in a minute!

First, let's talk temperature. Did you know that whether you use butter that's warm or cold makes a huge difference in the texture of your baked treats? The reason is simple: When chilly butter inside dough hits the heat of an oven, it lets off a burst of steam. The bigger the chunk of butter is, the more powerful the burst will be. Those steam bursts create pockets of air that push up inside the dough and create light, flaky layers within.

So, if it's flakes you're after, before you start making biscuits or scones, both your flour and your butter should be icy cold. One simple way to make sure that everything is at the right temperature is to pop your butter into the freezer for a few minutes before you begin. (This is especially useful if it's summer and your kitchen is really hot.) Some bakers even freeze their flour—think of it as extra insurance for a super-flaky finish. Once you've finished shaping your dough, pop the pan in the refrigerator or freezer: This gives the butter one more chance to cool down and ensures that the dough will spring up nicely once it hits the oven's heat.

Finally, there's just one more rule: Like all the other ingredients, any liquid you add to dough should always be very cold. Drizzle it in just a teaspoon at a time, mixing (or pulsing) while the liquid is added. If, while adding the water, the dough clumps together when you squeeze it in your palm but doesn't feel sticky, you'll know you've hit the right spot. If the dough still seems powdery, it might need an extra spoonful of water.

Indeed, like so much of baking, getting a feel for the proper texture of dough is just a matter of practice, practice, practice. That's why, especially if you're just starting out, doing things the simplest way—by hand—can be a great place to begin. Sure, it's a little messy, but isn't that part of the fun?

Step 1: Combine the dry ingredients and ice-cold butter.

Step 2: Process until the mixture is sandy with a few pea-size chunks of butter still visible.

Step 3: Stir in cold water just until a shaggy dough forms; it should hold together when squeezed.

Step 4: Divide the dough into 2 equal halves and press and shape each into a disc, then chill until ready to use.

CURRANT SCONES
WITH JAM AND CLOTTED CREAM

Avani from Season 5 fell in love with flaky scones on a family trip to England, where they're served with tea. She soon discovered that they're delicious any time of day—especially when you slather them with strawberry jam and clotted cream, a thick spread that's kind of like a soft, slightly sweet cream cheese! Dried currants are essentially little raisins—they give the scones small pops of texture and sweetness. You can leave them out if you prefer, or make one of the variations on page 35.

MAKES 8 SCONES

3 cups all-purpose flour, plus more for shaping

⅓ cup granulated sugar

1 tablespoon baking powder

½ teaspoon kosher salt

6 tablespoons (¾ stick) ice-cold unsalted butter, cubed

1¼ cups heavy cream

½ cup dried currants

1 large egg, beaten

2 tablespoons turbinado sugar (such as Sugar In the Raw)

Strawberry jam, for serving

Clotted cream or crème fraîche, for serving

TIP Because it is coarse, turbinado sugar is a great "finishing" sugar that's often used to add sparkle, sweetness, and crunch to baked goods. If you can't find it or don't have any on hand, it's also fine to leave it off.

1. Preheat the oven to 375°F. Line a baking sheet with parchment paper and set aside.

2. In a large bowl, whisk together the flour, granulated sugar, baking powder, and salt. Add the butter and, using your fingers, cut the butter into the flour mixture until it is crumbly and a few pea-size pieces of butter are still visible. (For more on this technique, see MasterChef Lesson, page 32.)

3. Make a well in the middle of the flour mixture and pour in the heavy cream. Stir the flour gently into the cream with a fork until a shaggy dough begins to form and pulls away from the sides of the bowl. Stir in the currants. Use your hands to lightly knead the dough once or twice to bring it together.

4. Transfer the dough to a lightly floured work surface. Use your fingers to pat it out into a 10-inch round that is about 1¼ inches thick. Using a sharp knife, slice the round into 8 wedges (like a pizza). Transfer the wedges to the prepared baking sheet, leaving about 1 inch of space between them. Chill for 15 minutes. (Or refrigerate for at least 1 hour or up to overnight.)

5. Lightly brush the tops of the scones with the beaten egg and sprinkle each with a pinch of turbinado sugar. Bake the scones until they are golden and beginning to brown at the edges, about 30 minutes. Serve warm, with strawberry jam and clotted cream.

VARIATIONS

Lemon-Ginger Scones: Rub 1 tablespoon grated lemon zest and ½ teaspoon ground ginger into the sugar until fragrant, then mix with the other dry ingredients. Omit the currants and add ¼ cup minced candied ginger.

Mixed Berry Scones: Omit the currants and add ¾ cup mixed fresh or frozen blueberries, raspberries, or cranberries.

Maple-Pecan Scones: Replace ⅔ cup of the all-purpose flour with oat flour. (To make your own oat flour, pulse rolled oats in a high-speed blender, food processor, or spice grinder until they are finely ground and powdery.) Omit the currants and add ¼ cup chopped toasted pecans. Brush the tops of the scones with maple syrup and sprinkle with turbinado sugar.

ROASTED STRAWBERRY-RHUBARB
SHORTCAKES
WITH ORANGE CHANTILLY CREAM

These roasted strawberry and rhubarb filled shortcakes are just like Avery's in the Season 4 finale that judge Christina Tosi called "light, buttery, and flaky in all the right ways." Roasting the fruit amps up its sweetness (even when strawberries are out of season) and makes the mixture extra juicy. For the brightest, most fuchsia-toned filling, pick the reddest rhubarb you can find. Chantilly cream is just another name for whipped cream that has been generously sweetened; here a splash of orange blossom water (which is a flavor extract that comes from the blossoms of the bitter orange tree) adds a subtle, floral flavor that complements the jammy fruit.

MAKES 6

SEASON 4

AVERY

SHORTCAKES

2 cups all-purpose flour, plus more for shaping

1 tablespoon baking powder

2 teaspoons granulated sugar

¾ teaspoon kosher salt

1¼ cups plus 2 tablespoons heavy cream

1 tablespoon turbinado sugar (such as Sugar In the Raw), for sprinkling

ROASTED STRAWBERRY-RHUBARB FILLING

1 quart strawberries, hulled and halved (quartered if large; about 4 cups)

4 stalks very pink or red rhubarb, cut into 1-inch pieces (about 4 cups)

3 tablespoons granulated sugar

2 tablespoons fresh lemon juice

ORANGE CHANTILLY CREAM

1 cup heavy cream

3 tablespoons confectioners' sugar

1 teaspoon pure vanilla extract

½ teaspoon orange blossom water or ¼ teaspoon orange extract

1. Make the shortcakes: In a large bowl, whisk together the flour, baking powder, granulated sugar, and salt. Slowly add 1¼ cups of the cream and stir the mixture with a fork just until a shaggy dough forms. Use your hands to press the dough into a ball in the bowl, then transfer it to a lightly floured work surface.

2. Line a baking sheet with parchment paper and set aside. Using a rolling pin, gently roll the dough into an 8 × 10-inch rectangle. Slice the dough in half horizontally and then cut each rectangle into thirds vertically so you are left with 6 rectangles. Transfer the biscuits to the prepared baking sheet, leaving 1½ to

2 inches between them. Chill for 15 minutes. (Or refrigerate for at least 1 hour or up to overnight.)

3. Preheat the oven to 425°F.

4. Brush the tops of the shortcakes with the remaining 2 tablespoons cream and sprinkle with the turbinado sugar. Bake until golden and puffed, 20 to 22 minutes. Remove from the oven and reduce the temperature to 375°F. Transfer the shortcakes to a wire rack to cool.

5. Make the roasted strawberry–rhubarb filling: In a large baking dish, toss together the strawberries, rhubarb, granulated sugar, and lemon juice and spread them into an even layer. Bake until the fruit is soft and juicy, about 25 minutes, stirring once halfway through. Set aside to cool for at least 30 minutes. (The filling can be made up to 3 days ahead of time and refrigerated, covered, until ready to use.)

6. Make the orange Chantilly cream: In a medium bowl, using an electric mixer fitted with the whisk, beat the cream, confectioners' sugar, vanilla, and orange blossom water until it forms soft peaks, 2 to 3 minutes. (If you do not have an electric mixer, you can also beat the cream by hand using a balloon whisk.)

7. To serve, split the cooled shortcakes in half. Top each bottom half with a spoonful of the cooled fruit filling, top with a dollop of chantilly cream, and cover with the top half of the shortcake.

TENDER TREATS: BISCUITS, SCONES, AND SHORTCAKES

They're called by different names and their ingredients vary slightly, but recipes for biscuits, scones, and shortcakes have a lot of elements in common. Each one is just a mixture of a flour, a fat (usually butter), a leavener that helps give the dough lift (like baking powder and/or baking soda), and a liquid (often buttermilk or heavy cream). It's how those ingredients are combined and handled that makes all the difference.

For instance, traditional buttermilk biscuits (like the ones on page 28) get their signature layers from a process called *lamination*, which is a technique of rolling and folding the butter-flecked dough so that it bakes in flaky, peel-apart pieces. Cream biscuits (page 29) get their tenderness from heavy cream and don't contain any butter at all! These are sometimes called "drop biscuits" since you can stir the dough together with a wooden spoon and then drop them right onto a baking sheet before baking—no rolling required.

Scones contain many of the same ingredients as biscuits, but have an egg and some sugar added to the mix, which make them sweeter and denser. They are also usually patted instead of rolled and folded. And shortcakes are basically a sweetened type of biscuit, usually split and served topped with fresh fruit and whipped cream.

MASTERING MUFFINS

A fresh-baked muffin is always a thing of beauty, but paying attention to the details can take your next batch from good to great. Here are a few of our favorite tips.

Preparing the batter: If you want light, tender muffins with textbook-perfect domes on top, it's best to take a "less is more" approach when mixing the batter. That's because overmixing activates the gluten in the dough, which produces muffins that are dense and heavy and more bready than cakey. How much mixing is enough? When combining wet and dry ingredients, use a rubber spatula to gently fold the two together, just until the floury streaks have disappeared. Yes, there will still be lumps (like pancake batter)—but trust us, that's a good thing!

Adding mix-ins: Heavier muffin mix-ins like blueberries or chocolate chips have a habit of falling toward the bottom of the muffin batter during baking. Here's a neat way to stop the sink: Before you fold any mix-ins into your batter, scoop out a small bowlful of plain batter and set it aside. Later, when you're filling the muffin tin, put a small spoonful of the plain batter into each cup first, before filling them the rest of the way with the flavored batter. The plain batter acts as a buffer during baking and—voilà!—the mix-ins stay evenly distributed.

DIY muffin liners: Paper liners help shape the muffins during baking, make it easy to remove them from the pan once they're done, and, of course, are just plain pretty. But if you don't have any in your cupboard, take heart! It's easy to make café-style muffin liners using just a sheet of parchment paper. Here's how: Cut the parchment into 5-inch squares until you have one square for every cup in your muffin tin. Find a jar or can that sits snugly in the muffin tin—a small juice glass or a can of tomato paste is usually a good fit. One by one, wrap the parchment squares around the bottom of the glass so that they form a cup shape, then place the squares into the cupcake pan with their frilly edges sticking up. Fill each cup three-quarters full with batter, as you would a regular paper liner, and bake!

Storage: Most muffins are best the day they are made, but they also freeze very well. Just wrap cooled, unglazed muffins securely in plastic wrap and stash them in a zip-top freezer bag; they will keep well for up to 1 month. When you want to eat them, the muffins can be thawed at room temperature or wrapped in foil and reheated in a 350°F oven for 10 minutes.

LEMON-
POPPY SEED MUFFINS
WITH CITRUS DRIZZLE

Evan from Season 6 loves the sunny taste and subtle crunch of lemon-poppy seed muffins. Rubbing the sugar and lemon zest together in a bowl before mixing it into the batter is a neat way to activate the citrus oils in the zest and bring out big lemon fragrance and flavor. Sour cream adds tang and tenderness, and a lemon glaze adds a bright citrus essence. One storage note: Because they're high in fat, poppy seeds lose their freshness fast. To make sure they taste their best, store them in the freezer. After six months, toss them and buy a fresh batch.

MAKES 12 MUFFINS • **See photograph on page 27**

MUFFINS

¾ cup granulated sugar

2 tablespoons grated lemon zest (from 2 lemons)

2 cups all-purpose flour

1 teaspoon baking powder

1 teaspoon baking soda

¼ teaspoon kosher salt

¼ cup fresh lemon juice (from 2 lemons)

¾ cup sour cream

2 large eggs

1½ teaspoons pure vanilla extract

1 stick (4 ounces) unsalted butter, melted and cooled

¼ cup poppy seeds

GLAZE

1 cup confectioners' sugar

2 tablespoons fresh lemon juice

1. Preheat the oven to 400°F. Line a 12-cup muffin tin with paper liners.

2. Make the muffins: In a large bowl, combine the granulated sugar and lemon zest. Use your fingertips to rub the sugar and bits of zest together until the sugar looks pale yellow and smells lemony. Stir in the flour, baking powder, baking soda, and salt.

3. In another bowl, whisk together the lemon juice, sour cream, eggs, vanilla, and melted butter. Pour the wet ingredients into the dry ingredients and stir gently until just combined. Stir in the poppy seeds. Divide the batter evenly among the muffin cups, filling each one three-quarters full.

4. Bake until the muffins are puffed and golden and a toothpick inserted into the center of the largest one comes out clean, about 18 minutes. Let the muffins rest in the muffin tin for 5 minutes, then transfer them to a wire rack to cool completely.

5. Make the glaze: In a small bowl, combine the confectioners' sugar and lemon juice and whisk until smooth.

6. Use a spoon to drizzle the glaze over the cooled muffins. Let rest for 20 minutes to allow the glaze to set, then serve. (See Mastering Muffins, opposite, for storage tips.)

BLUEBERRY MUFFINS
WITH BROWN SUGAR STREUSEL

Blueberry muffins are an American breakfast classic and a favorite of many *MasterChef Junior* contestants. Avani from Season 5 especially likes fresh-from-the-oven blueberry muffins that deliver a pop of warm, jammy blueberry with every bite. In this version, acidic buttermilk lends a pleasant tangy flavor and keeps the muffins tender. Ground ginger adds some gentle spice, and a crumbly topping of brown sugar streusel is a simple but dramatic way to give the muffins a bakery-quality finish.

MAKES 12 MUFFINS

MUFFINS

2 cups all-purpose flour

1½ teaspoons baking powder

1 teaspoon baking soda

½ teaspoon ground ginger

¼ teaspoon kosher salt

1¼ cups buttermilk

1 large egg

½ cup granulated sugar

2 teaspoons pure vanilla extract

¼ cup canola oil

1¼ cups fresh or frozen blueberries

STREUSEL

½ cup packed dark brown sugar

⅓ cup all-purpose flour

½ teaspoon ground cinnamon

⅛ teaspoon kosher salt

4 tablespoons (½ stick) unsalted butter, melted

2 tablespoons chopped toasted pecans (optional)

1. Preheat the oven to 350°F. Line a 12-cup muffin tin with paper liners.

2. Make the muffins: In a large bowl, whisk together the flour, baking powder, baking soda, ginger, and salt.

3. In another bowl, whisk together the buttermilk, egg, granulated sugar, vanilla, and oil. Pour the wet ingredients into the dry ingredients and use a rubber spatula to gently fold them together until just combined. Fold in the blueberries. Divide the batter evenly among the muffin cups, filling each three-quarters full.

4. Make the streusel: In a medium bowl, whisk together the brown sugar, flour, cinnamon, and salt. Stir in the melted butter and pecans (if using). Use your fingers to pinch the mixture into large crumbs. Sprinkle the streusel mixture over the muffins.

5. Bake until the muffins are tall and golden and a toothpick inserted into the center of the largest one comes out clean, 25 to 30 minutes. Let the muffins rest in the muffin tin for 5 minutes, then transfer them to a wire rack to cool completely. (See Mastering Muffins, page 38, for storage tips.)

YOGURT BREAKFAST MUFFINS
WITH CHIA SEEDS AND RASPBERRIES

Competing on *MasterChef Junior* takes a lot of stamina and focus. These fruit-studded treats are like a cross between energy bars and morning muffins, and are a great way to fuel up when you're on the go. The keys to their chewy texture and bright flavor are a sneaky scoopful of omega-3 fatty acid- and protein-packed chia seeds and a splash of orange juice. Raspberries add nice tartness to the mix, but you could substitute an equal amount of any berry (or dried fruit) in their place.

MAKES 12 MUFFINS

2½ cups rolled oats

1 cup whole wheat flour

⅓ cup chia seeds

¾ cup packed light brown sugar

2 teaspoons baking powder

½ teaspoon baking soda

2 teaspoons ground cinnamon

½ teaspoon kosher salt

1 large egg, beaten

1 cup plain whole-milk yogurt

½ cup canola oil

½ cup orange juice, preferably fresh

1 teaspoon pure vanilla extract

1½ cups fresh or frozen raspberries

1. Preheat the oven to 350°F. Line a 12-cup muffin tin with paper liners

2. In a large bowl, whisk together the oats, flour, chia seeds, brown sugar, baking powder, baking soda, cinnamon, and salt. Stir in the egg, yogurt, oil, orange juice, and vanilla. Use a rubber spatula to gently fold the ingredients together until just combined. Fold in the raspberries.

3. Divide the batter evenly among the muffin cups, filling each cup nearly to the top. Bake until the muffins are golden and springy and a toothpick inserted into the center of the largest muffin comes out clean, about 25 minutes. Let the muffins rest in the muffin tin for 5 minutes, then transfer them to a wire rack to cool completely. (See Mastering Muffins, page 38, for storage tips.)

FUDGE-SWIRL
PUMPKIN BREAD

Shayne from Season 5 remembers learning how to bake pumpkin bread with his grandma, and he still looks forward to making it each autumn. A blend of warm spices gives this tempting version a wonderful scent and a decadent ribbon of melted chocolate marbled into the batter helps keep the cake moist for days.

SERVES 10

Nonstick pan spray

1½ cups all-purpose flour

1⅓ cups sugar

1½ teaspoons baking powder

1 teaspoon baking soda

1 teaspoon ground cinnamon

½ teaspoon ground cardamom

½ teaspoon ground ginger

½ teaspoon nutmeg, preferably freshly grated

½ teaspoon kosher salt

⅓ cup canola oil

½ cup buttermilk

2 large eggs

1 cup canned unsweetened pumpkin puree (see Tip)

1 teaspoon pure vanilla extract

½ cup bittersweet chocolate chips

3 tablespoons unsweetened Dutch process cocoa powder

TIP Pumpkin puree usually comes in 15-ounce cans, which means you'll have some left over after making this recipe. Add the extra to a banana and almond milk smoothie or to a basic pancake or waffle batter for a breakfast treat that really tastes like fall.

1. Preheat the oven to 350°F. Coat an 8½ × 4½-inch loaf pan with pan spray and line with parchment paper, leaving a few inches of overhang on both of the long sides. (This will help you lift the loaf out of the pan after baking.)

2. In a large bowl, whisk together the flour, sugar, baking powder, baking soda, cinnamon, cardamom, ginger, nutmeg, and salt. In a medium bowl, whisk together the oil, buttermilk, eggs, pumpkin puree, and vanilla. Pour the wet ingredients into the dry ingredients and stir with a rubber spatula until just combined. Set aside.

3. Put the chocolate chips in a microwave-safe bowl and microwave on medium for 40 seconds. Stir, then microwave for another 15 to 20 seconds, until completely smooth. Set aside.

4. Pour half of the batter into a separate bowl. Add the cocoa powder and melted chocolate to one of the bowls. Stir just until smooth.

5. Spoon large scoops of each batter into the pan, alternating between pumpkin and chocolate. Once the pan is filled, insert a butter knife and gently swirl the batters together, moving from one end of the pan to the other. (Be careful not to overswirl, or the cake will become all chocolate!)

6. Bake until the cake is springy to the touch and a toothpick inserted into the center comes out clean, about 1 hour. If the cake begins to look a little dark on top, tent the top with foil. Transfer pan to a wire rack to cool completely. Store, wrapped in plastic wrap at room temperature, for 3 to 4 days.

CORNMEAL-AND-BACON
WAFFLES
WITH BLACK PEPPER–MAPLE BUTTER

Cade came out on top of the Season 6 "chicken and waffles" challenge thanks to a killer recipe for cornmeal waffles that he paired with Cajun fried chicken and bacon salsa. Inspired by those flavors, these bacon-studded cornmeal waffles strike a perfect balance between sweet and savory. Homemade black pepper–maple butter is an ideal complement—but these waffles would also be equally delicious topped with poached eggs or a drizzle of maple syrup.

MAKES 6 TO 8 WAFFLES (USING A STANDARD WAFFLE IRON)

BLACK PEPPER–MAPLE BUTTER

4 tablespoons (½ stick) unsalted butter, at room temperature

2 tablespoons maple syrup

¼ teaspoon freshly ground black pepper

1 teaspoon kosher salt

CORNMEAL-AND-BACON WAFFLES

5 thick-cut slices bacon (about 6 ounces), diced

2 large eggs

1¾ cups buttermilk

1 tablespoon molasses

1 cup coarse yellow cornmeal

1 cup all-purpose flour

2 teaspoons baking powder

½ teaspoon baking soda

½ teaspoon kosher salt

4 tablespoons (½ stick) unsalted butter, melted

Maple syrup (optional)

1. Make the black pepper–maple butter: In a medium bowl, combine the butter, maple syrup, pepper, and salt. Place a sheet of plastic wrap on a clean work surface and the spoon the butter onto it in a strip. Use the plastic wrap to roll the butter into a cylinder. Chill until firm and ready to use.

2. Make the waffles: In a medium skillet, cook the bacon over medium heat until crispy, about 6 minutes. Transfer to paper towels to drain.

3. Preheat a standard waffle iron (a Belgian waffle iron makes thicker waffles and will yield fewer servings) according to the manufacturer's instructions.

4. In a large bowl, whisk together the eggs, buttermilk, and molasses. In another large bowl, stir together the cornmeal, flour, baking powder, baking soda, and salt. Pour the wet ingredients into the dry ingredients and fold gently to combine. Fold in the bacon. Add the melted butter and stir until just incorporated.

5. Spoon about ½ cup of the batter onto the hot waffle iron. Cook until the iron stops steaming and the waffle is golden and crisp all over, about 6 minutes. Serve the waffle immediately or transfer it to a wire rack while you make the rest. Repeat with the remaining batter (don't stack them on top of each other or the steam will make them lose their crunch.) Top the waffles with a pad of the black pepper–maple butter and more maple syrup, if desired.

SKILLET CORN BREAD
WITH FRESH CORN

Baking this recipe in a cast-iron skillet not only looks cool, it helps give the corn bread a wonderfully golden, crispy crust. (If you don't have a cast-iron skillet, don't sweat it: A 9-inch square baking pan is a fine substitute.) Typically Southern-style corn bread is unsweetened, while northern-style ones include sugar. Mikey from Season 6 likes to split the difference, spiking the batter with just a little bit of maple syrup and stirring in a cupful of whole corn kernels for texture. Pair it with butter and jam at breakfast—or with a big pot of chili at dinner!

SERVES 8

Nonstick pan spray

2 cups yellow cornmeal

1 teaspoon baking powder

1 teaspoon baking soda

1 teaspoon kosher salt

2 large eggs

1 cup buttermilk

¼ cup maple syrup, plus more for serving

4 tablespoons (½ stick) unsalted butter, melted, plus more for serving

1 cup fresh or frozen corn kernels

1. Preheat the oven to 425°F. Coat a 10-inch cast-iron skillet with pan spray.

2. In a large bowl, whisk together the cornmeal, baking powder, baking soda, and salt. In another bowl, whisk together the eggs, buttermilk, and maple syrup. Add the wet ingredients to the dry ingredients and mix until just combined. Stir in the melted butter and fold in the corn kernels.

3. Scrape the batter into the skillet and bake until golden brown around the edges and a toothpick inserted into the center comes out clean, about 20 minutes. Let cool for 10 minutes before slicing. Serve warm, with additional butter on the side and maple syrup for drizzling. Leftover slices will keep, wrapped tightly in plastic wrap for 2 days, and can be wrapped in foil and reheated in a 350°F oven for 10 minutes.

SPICED APPLE DUTCH BABY
WITH BROWN BUTTER

Whether you call this a skillet pancake, a Dutch baby, or a Bismarck, there is one thing everyone agrees on—it's delicious! Using room-temperature ingredients and working quickly while the pan is hot are the keys to making sure the pancake puffs up tall and golden. Adding spiced sliced apples to the pan before baking gives the Dutch baby a lovely fall flavor.

SERVES 4

1 large tart apple (such as Granny Smith), peeled, halved, cored, and thinly sliced

1 tablespoon fresh lemon juice

2 tablespoons light brown sugar

½ teaspoon kosher salt

¾ teaspoon ground cinnamon

½ teaspoon ground cardamom

4 tablespoons (½ stick) unsalted butter

4 large eggs, at room temperature

1 cup whole milk, at room temperature

1 teaspoon pure vanilla extract

1 tablespoon granulated sugar

1 cup all-purpose flour

Confectioners' sugar, for serving

1. Place a 10-inch ovenproof skillet (preferably cast-iron) on the center rack of the oven and preheat the oven to 450°F.

2. In a medium bowl, toss together the apple, lemon juice, brown sugar, salt, ½ teaspoon of the cinnamon, and ¼ teaspoon of the cardamom.

3. In a large skillet, melt the butter over medium heat. Cook, stirring often, until the butter foams and smells nutty, about 5 minutes. Pour into a small bowl and set aside to cool.

4. In a blender or food processor, combine the eggs, milk, vanilla, granulated sugar, flour, and remaining ¼ teaspoon cinnamon and ¼ teaspoon cardamom. Process on medium-high until the batter is frothy and smooth, about 1½ minutes. (It will look thinner than a typical pancake batter.)

5. Using an oven mitt, carefully remove the skillet from the oven. (The pan will be hot: You may want to ask an adult for help!) Pour the butter into the skillet and evenly scatter half the spiced apple slices over the bottom of the skillet. Pour in the batter and top with the remaining apple slices. Immediately return the skillet to the oven. Bake until the pancake is puffed, golden around the edges, and set at the center, 20 to 22 minutes. (Resist the temptation to open the oven during cooking—this will cause the pancake to deflate!)

6. Remove the skillet from the oven, sprinkle the hot pancake with confectioners' sugar, and serve immediately.

BROWN SUGAR-ROASTED
BANANA BREAD
WITH TOASTED COCONUT

Love banana bread but hate having to wait until your bananas turn brown before you can make it? Problem solved! This tropical-accented toasted coconut and brown sugar banana bread is inspired by a technique Cydney from Season 5 shared for roasting firm bananas *before* mashing them into the batter. It might sound odd, but the high heat brings out the amazing caramel and nutty flavors in the fruit. And there's no waiting required!

SERVES 10

Nonstick pan spray

4 large barely ripe bananas (mostly yellow—a couple of brown flecks are okay), whole and unpeeled

½ cup plus 1 tablespoon unsweetened coconut flakes

2 cups all-purpose flour

2 teaspoons baking powder

½ teaspoon kosher salt

1 stick (4 ounces) butter, at room temperature

1 cup packed dark brown sugar

2 large eggs, beaten

2 tablespoons robust molasses

1½ teaspoons pure vanilla extract

1 teaspoon turbinado sugar (such as Sugar In the Raw)

TIP "Robust" molasses is darker and has a deeper, more concentrated flavor than mild molasses; depending on the brand, it may also be called "full flavor" molasses, so make sure to check the label.

1. Preheat the oven to 350°F. Coat an 8½ × 4½-inch loaf pan with pan spray and line with parchment paper, leaving a few inches of overhang on both of the long sides. (This will help you lift the loaf out of the pan after baking.)

2. Line a baking sheet with parchment paper and place the bananas on top. Bake, flipping the bananas once, until their skin is deeply blackened on both sides but not split, about 25 minutes. Set the bananas aside to cool. Once the bananas are cool, remove the soft flesh from the skins (discard the skins) and spoon it into a bowl. Mash the flesh roughly with a fork, leaving some lumps. Set aside.

3. Meanwhile, in a large, dry skillet, spread ½ cup of the coconut out into single layer. Cook over medium-low heat, stirring frequently, until the flakes smell toasty and are golden brown, about 5 minutes. Remove the skillet from the heat, spoon the toasted coconut into a bowl, and set it aside to cool.

4. In a large bowl, whisk together the flour, baking powder, and salt and set aside.

5. In a large bowl, using an electric mixer, beat the butter and brown sugar on medium-high speed until light, fluffy, and pale, about 5 minutes. Reduce the speed to medium-low and add the eggs, one at a time, beating well after each addition

and scraping down the sides of the bowl as needed. Beat in the molasses and vanilla. Add the mashed bananas and beat until just combined.

6. Using a rubber spatula, fold in the flour mixture and ½ cup of the toasted coconut flakes until just combined.

7. Scrape the batter into the prepared pan. Sprinkle the top with the remaining 1 tablespoon coconut flakes and the turbinado sugar. Bake until the loaf is domed and deeply golden and a toothpick inserted into the tallest part of the center comes out clean, about 1 hour 10 minutes. Let the loaf rest in the pan for 15 minutes, then use the parchment sling to lift the loaf out of the pan and transfer it to a wire rack to cool completely. Once cool, the banana bread will keep at room temperature, wrapped in plastic wrap, for 3 to 4 days.

VARIATION

Chocolate Chip Banana Bread: Replace the toasted coconut with ½ cup bittersweet chocolate chips stirred into the batter.

COOKIES

Earl Grey Madeleines with Grapefruit Glaze, page 66

VANILLA
CUT-OUT COOKIES

Don't be fooled: These simple sugar cookies pack some big, buttery vanilla flavor. Easy to put together with mostly pantry ingredients, they're a great family project—just ask Mikey from Season 6, who has been making cut-out cookies like these with his grandmother since he was two years old. The best part: Every time she comes to visit, she brings a surprise new cookie cutter. (What a fun way to start a new collection!) Sturdy and sweet, these cookies are a perfect blank canvas for decorating (bring on the icing) or all on their own, with a mug of cocoa.

MAKES ABOUT 36 (3- TO 4-INCH) COOKIES

2½ cups all-purpose flour, plus more for rolling

¼ teaspoon kosher salt

2 sticks (8 ounces) unsalted butter, at cool room temperature

1 cup granulated sugar

2 large egg yolks

1 tablespoon pure vanilla extract

Sanding sugar, sprinkles, or icing (see Royal Icing, page 63) to decorate (optional)

1. In a large bowl, whisk together the flour and salt.

2. In another large bowl and using an electric mixer with the paddle attachment, beat the butter and granulated sugar on medium-high speed until light and fluffy, about 5 minutes. Add the egg yolks and vanilla and beat to combine, about 1 minute more. Reduce the mixer speed to low, scrape down the sides of the bowl, and gradually add the flour, mixing until just combined.

3. Divide the dough into 2 equal portions and press each into a 1-inch-thick disc. Wrap the discs tightly in plastic wrap and refrigerate until firm, about 30 minutes.

4. Position the racks in the upper and lower thirds of the oven and preheat the oven to 375°F. Line two baking sheets with parchment paper.

5. On a lightly floured work surface, roll out one disc of dough into an even ⅛-inch-thick sheet. Cut the dough into shapes using the cookie cutter of your choice. Gather any scraps, press them into a ball, re-roll, and continue cutting out more shapes. (If at any point the dough gets warm or feels limp and sticky, pop it into the refrigerator to chill for a few minutes before continuing.) After re-rolling once, discard the remaining scraps.

6. Arrange the cookies on the prepared baking sheets, leaving at least 1 inch between them. (If you are decorating with

sanding sugar, sprinkle it onto the cookies now, before baking, and press it gently to adhere.) Transfer the baking sheets to the refrigerator and chill until the cookies are firm, about 20 minutes.

7. Bake the cookies, switching the pans from top to bottom rack and rotating the pans front to back once halfway through, until there is just a hint of golden color at the edges, about 10 minutes. Let the cookies rest on the baking sheets for 5 minutes, then transfer them to a wire rack to cool completely. Repeat the process with the remaining disc of dough. Cool the cookies completely before decorating with icing and sprinkles. Store the cookies in an airtight container for up to 1 week.

HOW TO CREAM BUTTER

Butter is one of baking's most elemental ingredients—and how it is used in a recipe is one of the factors that has the biggest effect on how a cookie, cake, or pie turns out. Earlier we saw how the process of "cutting in" cold butter to flour produces light, flaky biscuits, scones, and pastry crusts (see MasterChef Lesson, page 32). Here we're going to look how "creaming" softened butter and sugar results in light, airy cakes and tender cookies.

In a nutshell, "creaming" butter and sugar just means beating room-temperature butter and sugar until the sugar granules get evenly suspended throughout the mixture. The movement of the sugar forces air into the butter, lightening it in color. This helps baked goods rise and gives them a fine, fluffy texture.

When creaming, many recipes call for "room-temperature" butter—but what does that really mean? Ideally, it should be soft but not greasy. If you press firmly on the butter with a fingertip, it should leave an impression, like pressing your finger into very soft clay—it should *not* squish right into it. (If you wind up with a cake that is too dense and squat, overly warm butter may be the culprit!) If you want to be super-accurate, you can check the temperature of the butter with an instant-read thermometer: Between 64° and 68°F is the sweet spot. The easiest way to get that is to take the butter out of the refrigerator about 30 minutes before you plan to use it.

Though it's certainly possible to cream butter and sugar by hand, the most effective (and arm-friendly!) way to do it is to use an electric hand mixer or stand mixer with the paddle attachment. Begin by putting the butter in the bowl and beating it on low speed until smooth, about 30 seconds to 1 minute. Then increase the speed to medium-high and slowly add the sugar. Continue beating, pausing to scrape down the sides and bottom of the bowl occasionally, until the butter-sugar mixture has lightened considerably and is smooth and fluffy. This usually takes about 5 minutes—or longer, if you're doing it by hand!

GLUTEN-FREE
PEANUT BUTTER COOKIES

Bursting with peanut butter goodness, these classic cookies have such big old-fashioned flavor that you'd never guess they're gluten-free! Even better: The recipe is so simple you can do it all in one bowl. Any store-bought creamy peanut butter without a layer of oil on top (in other words, not "natural") works as a base—or, if you're feeling creative, you can try swapping in chunky peanut butter for a bit of crunch or almond or cashew butter for a different take. Chilling the dough well before baking makes it easier to handle and helps the cookies hold their shape. And don't skip making the classic fork-press crisscross design on top before baking—Cydney from Season 5 says you can't have *real* peanut butter cookies without it!

MAKES ABOUT 18 (3-INCH) COOKIES

2 cups creamy peanut butter (not "natural," which has oil on top)

1½ cups packed light brown sugar

½ teaspoon baking soda

½ teaspoon kosher salt

2 large eggs

2 teaspoons pure vanilla extract

1. In a bowl, using an electric mixer with the paddle attachment, beat the peanut butter, brown sugar, baking soda, and salt on medium speed until smooth and well combined, about 3 minutes. Add the eggs, one at a time, beating between additions to incorporate, followed by the vanilla. Beat briefly until just combined. Transfer the bowl to the refrigerator and chill the dough for 30 minutes.

2. Position the racks in the upper and lower thirds of the oven and preheat the oven to 350°F. Line two baking sheets with parchment paper.

3. Shape the dough into balls (about 1½ tablespoons each) and divide them among the prepared baking sheets, leaving about 2 inches between them. Gently press down on the center of each ball with the tines of a fork, creating a crisscross pattern.

4. Bake the cookies, switching the pans from top to bottom rack once halfway through, until they are just golden and slightly crinkled on top, about 15 minutes. Let the cookies cool on the baking sheets for 10 minutes, then transfer them to a wire rack to cool completely. Store the cookies in an airtight container for up to 5 days.

JAMMY
ALMOND THUMBPRINTS

Many of the *MasterChef Junior* children say they made their first foray into baking while helping their families make holiday cookies— and no festive cookie tray would be complete without a few classic jam-filled thumbprints. Buttery and crumbly, with a lovely warm, nutty flavor from the toasted almond flour, these are seriously hard to resist. Bright-red raspberry and golden apricot jams make lovely fillings, but feel free to swap in any other flavor preserves if you prefer. Just don't skip rolling the rounds in coarse sugar before baking—it gives the cookies a lovely sparkle and crunch.

MAKES ABOUT 36 COOKIES

1½ cups almond flour

2 sticks (8 ounces) unsalted butter, at cool room temperature

½ cup granulated sugar

1 large egg

1 teaspoon pure vanilla extract

1 teaspoon pure almond extract

1½ cups all-purpose flour

1½ teaspoons baking powder

½ teaspoon kosher salt

½ cup turbinado sugar (such as Sugar In the Raw)

1 cup fruit preserves, such as raspberry jam, apricot jam, or orange marmalade

1. Preheat the oven to 350°F.

2. Line a baking sheet with parchment paper and spread the almond flour on it in an even layer. Toast, stirring often, until the flour is lightly golden and fragrant, about 8 minutes. Remove the pan from the oven and set the almond flour aside to cool. Increase the oven temperature to 375°F and position the racks in the upper and lower thirds of the oven.

3. In a large bowl, using an electric mixer with the paddle attachment, beat the butter and granulated sugar on medium-high speed until light and fluffy, about 5 minutes. Reduce the speed to low, then add the egg, vanilla, and almond extract and beat until combined, scraping down the bowl as needed, about 1 minute. In a large bowl, whisk together the cooled almond flour, all-purpose flour, baking powder, and salt. Gradually add the flour mixture to the butter mixture and stir with a rubber spatula until just combined. Cover the bowl with plastic wrap and refrigerate for 30 minutes.

4. Line two baking sheets with parchment paper. Spread turbinado sugar on a plate or in a bowl. Use a tablespoon to scoop the dough and roll it into 1-inch balls. Roll the balls in the turbinado sugar (you may need to press slightly to get the sugar to adhere) and transfer them to the prepared baking sheets, leaving 2 inches between them.

5. Gently press an indentation into the top of each ball with your finger. (Try to make the indentation deeper than it is wide, as the opening will expand during baking—you may want to use your pinky finger!) Fill each indentation with a small spoonful of preserves.

6. Bake the cookies, switching the pans from top to bottom rack once halfway through, until the cookies are golden around the edges, 15 to 17 minutes. Let the cookies rest on the baking sheets for 5 minutes, then transfer to a wire rack to cool completely. Store in an airtight container for up to 5 days.

CHOCOLATE-COVERED
OATMEAL RAISIN COOKIES
WITH **WHITE CHOCOLATE DRIZZLE**

Raisins and chocolate are both awesome additions to old-fashioned oatmeal cookies, and the best part of this moist, chewy version—inspired by one of Ben's favorite cookie combinations—is that you don't have to choose just one. Using melted butter and oil, rather than creaming butter and sugar together, means that the batter can be assembled quickly and easily with just two bowls—and makes these cookies perfect for when you need a quick pick-me-up.

MAKES ABOUT 22 COOKIES

2 cups rolled oats

1 cup all-purpose flour

½ teaspoon kosher salt

¼ teaspoon baking soda

½ cup sugar

1½ teaspoons ground cinnamon

4 tablespoons (½ stick) unsalted butter, melted

⅓ cup maple syrup

¼ cup canola oil

1 teaspoon pure vanilla extract

1 large egg

1 cup chocolate-covered raisins

1 cup white chocolate chips

1. Position racks in the upper and lower thirds of the oven and preheat the oven to 375°F. Line two baking sheets with parchment paper.

2. In a large bowl, whisk together the oats, flour, sugar, cinnamon, salt, and baking soda. In a small bowl, whisk together the melted butter, maple syrup, oil, vanilla, and egg. Pour the butter mixture into the flour mixture and stir with a rubber spatula until it forms a sticky dough. Cover the bowl with plastic wrap and refrigerate for 30 minutes.

3. Use a tablespoon to scoop the dough onto the prepared baking sheets, leaving at least 1½ inches between them.

4. Bake the cookies, switching from top to bottom rack once halfway through, until they have spread and are golden and crisp around the edges, about 15 minutes. Let the cookies rest on the baking sheets for 5 minutes, then transfer them to a wire rack to cool completely.

5. Place the white chocolate chips in a microwave-safe bowl and microwave on medium for 40 seconds. Stir, then microwave until completely smooth, 15 to 20 seconds longer.

6. Use a spoon to drizzle melted white chocolate over each cookie. Return the cookies to the rack to cool until the white chocolate is set, about 20 minutes. Store in an airtight container for up to 5 days.

SNICKERDOODLE
SNOWBALLS

Instead of buying store-bought presents for the holidays, every year Quani from Season 6 makes big batches of homemade cookies to share. Talk about sweet! His snowball cookies and snickerdoodles are always everyone's favorites—so here they're combined in one buttery, crumbly, spicy treat. Think of it as the best of both worlds!

MAKES ABOUT 36 COOKIES

SEASON **6**

1½ cups all-purpose flour

1 teaspoon cream of tartar

½ teaspoon baking soda

¼ teaspoon kosher salt

½ teaspoon nutmeg, preferably freshly grated (see Tip)

2 teaspoons ground cinnamon

1 stick (4 ounces) unsalted butter, at cool room temperature

¾ cup granulated sugar

1 large egg

1 teaspoon pure vanilla extract

1 cup confectioners' sugar

TIP If a recipe calls for nutmeg, buy the nutmeg whole and grate the amount you need yourself using a Microplane zester/grater (page 12) for the purest, brightest flavor. Just remember to remove the outer shell first.

1. In a medium bowl, whisk together the flour, cream of tartar, baking soda, salt, nutmeg, and 1 teaspoon of the cinnamon.

2. In a bowl, using an electric mixer with the paddle attachment, beat the butter and granulated sugar on medium-high speed until light and fluffy, about 5 minutes. Add the egg and vanilla and beat until combined, about 30 seconds, using a rubber spatula to scrape down the sides and the bottom of the bowl as needed. Reduce the mixer speed to low and add the flour mixture, mixing until just combined. Cover the bowl with plastic wrap and refrigerate for 30 minutes.

3. Preheat the oven to 350°F. Line two baking sheets with parchment paper.

4. In a wide, shallow bowl, whisk together the confectioners' sugar and remaining 1 teaspoon cinnamon. Set aside.

5. Roll the dough into 1-inch balls and arrange them on one of the baking sheets, leaving about 2 inches between them. (Return any remaining dough to the refrigerator to chill until ready to shape the next batch.) Bake, switching the pans from top to bottom rack once halfway through, until the cookies are puffed and lightly golden around the edges, about 15 minutes. Let the cookies rest on the baking sheet until just cool enough to handle.

6. While the cookies are still warm, toss each one in the cinnamon-confectioners' sugar mixture until well coated on all sides. Transfer the coated cookies to a wire rack to cool completely.

7. Meanwhile, repeat the process with any remaining dough. Store the cookies in an airtight container for up to 2 weeks.

CHOCOLATE
CHUNK COOKIES

For Cory, chocolate chip cookies are not only an all-American classic—they're big business! Before he impressed the judges with his skills on Season 3 of *MasterChef Junior*, the enterprising young baker started his own company. While his original recipe is a secret, his cookies, like these, are known for being packed with bittersweet chocolate. We adore the crispy texture of this take on the classic, and think the sprinkle of salt on top gives them a sophisticated edge.

MAKES ABOUT 20 COOKIES

2 cups all-purpose flour

1 teaspoon baking soda

½ teaspoon kosher salt

2 sticks (8 ounces) unsalted butter, at cool room temperature

1½ cups packed dark brown sugar

½ cup granulated sugar

2 teaspoons pure vanilla extract

2 large eggs

2 (4-ounce) bittersweet chocolate bars, coarsely chopped, or about 1½ cups bittersweet chocolate chunks

Flaky sea salt (such as Maldon), for finishing (optional)

1. Position racks in the upper and lower thirds of the oven and preheat the oven to 350°F. Line two baking sheets with parchment paper.

2. In a medium bowl, whisk together the flour, baking soda, and kosher salt.

3. In a bowl, using an electric mixer with the paddle attachment, beat the butter, brown sugar, and granulated sugar on medium-high speed until fluffy and pale, about 5 minutes. Reduce the mixer speed to medium-low and add the vanilla and eggs, one at a time, beating well after each addition and scraping down the sides of the bowl as needed. Add half the flour mixture and use a rubber spatula to stir until just a few dry streaks remain. Add the remaining flour and stir until just combined. Stir in the chocolate chunks.

4. Drop large spoonfuls of dough (about the size of a walnut) onto the prepared baking sheets, leaving at least 2½ inches between them. Sprinkle each mound with a small pinch of flaky sea salt, if desired. (Place any remaining dough in the refrigerator to chill until ready to shape.)

5. Bake the cookies, switching the pans from top to bottom rack once halfway through, until the cookies are golden brown, nearly flat, and crispy at the edges, 12 to 15 minutes. Let rest on the baking sheet for 5 minutes, then transfer to a wire rack to cool completely. Repeat with the remaining dough. Store the cookies in an airtight container for up to 5 days.

SPICY GINGERBREAD FOLKS
WITH ROYAL ICING

When Cydney and Peyton won the team gingerbread-house-decorating challenge in Season 5, judges Gordon Ramsay and Christina Tosi praised their precise, steady work with the icing and their attention to detail. Bring the same skills to these deliciously dark gingerbread cookies and you'll have little edible works of art! Gingerbread men are traditional, of course, but this adaptable dough can be rolled and cut into whatever shape you like. And the icing is super versatile, too; try using it to decorate Vanilla Cut-Out Cookies (page 52). Avani from Season 5 even likes to make little holes in her gingerbread cookies and hang them as ornaments on her family's Christmas tree! Black pepper might seem like an odd addition, but the heat from the pepper gives the cookies a wonderfully warm bite. Note that the dough needs to chill for at least 2 hours before you roll, cut, and bake the cookies, so plan accordingly!

MAKES 24 TO 36 (3- TO 4-INCH) GINGERBREAD PEOPLE

SEASON 5

GINGERBREAD

4½ cups all-purpose flour, plus more for rolling

1½ teaspoons baking soda

1 tablespoon ground cinnamon

1 tablespoon ground ginger

1 teaspoon ground cloves

1 teaspoon nutmeg, preferably freshly grated

1 teaspoon freshly ground black pepper

¼ teaspoon kosher salt

2 sticks (8 ounces) unsalted butter, at cool room temperature

1 cup granulated sugar

1 large egg

¾ cup robust molasses (see Tip, page 48)

ROYAL ICING

2 cups confectioners' sugar, plus more if needed

2 tablespoons meringue powder (see Tip)

1 teaspoon light corn syrup

½ teaspoon pure vanilla extract

Sprinkles, sanding sugar, dragées, or gel colors (optional)

TIP Meringue powder is an egg white substitute that's often used in icing to provide stability and is a great alternative for anyone who is worried about eating raw eggs.

1. Make the gingerbread: In a large bowl, whisk together the flour, baking soda, cinnamon, ginger, cloves, nutmeg, pepper, and salt until combined.

2. In a bowl, using an electric mixer with the paddle attachment, beat the butter and granulated sugar on medium-high speed

recipe continues

cutters of your choice. Slide a metal spatula under the cutouts and transfer them to the prepared baking sheets, leaving 1½ inches between them. Gather any scraps, press them into a ball, re-roll, and continue cutting out more shapes. (If at any point the dough gets warm or feels limp and sticky, pop it into the refrigerator to chill for a few minutes before continuing.) After re-rolling once, discard the remaining scraps. (Keep the other discs of dough in the refrigerator until ready to roll and cut.) Transfer the cookies to the freezer and chill for 10 minutes.

5. Bake the cookies, switching the pans from top to bottom rack once halfway through, until firm but not dark, about 14 minutes. Let the cookies rest on the baking sheets for 5 minutes, then transfer them to a wire rack to cool completely before icing. Repeat with the remaining dough.

6. Make the royal icing: In a medium bowl, whisk together the confectioners' sugar, meringue powder, corn syrup, vanilla, and ¼ cup water until smooth, about 3 minutes. (The consistency of the icing should be like thick honey. If it's runny, beat in a bit more confectioners' sugar; if it's thin, add more water, 1 tablespoon at a time.) Use a rubber spatula to transfer the icing to a squeeze bottle or a pastry bag fitted with a very small plain tip.

7. Ice the cookies and decorate them with sprinkles, sanding sugar, dragées, or gel colors as desired. After decorating, let the cookies set completely, about 2 hours, before serving. Store the cookies in an airtight container for up to 1 week.

until light and fluffy, about 5 minutes. Reduce the mixer speed to medium-low and beat in the egg and molasses until just combined, using a rubber spatula to scrape down the sides and bottom of the bowl as needed. Reduce the mixer speed to low and add the flour mixture 1 cup at a time, mixing until the dough is just combined, about 45 seconds. Divide the dough into even thirds, then press each piece into a 1-inch-thick disc and wrap tightly in plastic wrap. Refrigerate for at least 2 hours or up to 2 days.

3. Position racks in the upper and lower thirds of the oven and preheat the oven to 375°F. Line two baking sheets with parchment paper.

4. On a lightly floured work surface, roll one disc of dough to a ⅛-inch thickness, reflouring as needed to keep the dough from sticking. Cut the dough into shapes using the cookie

HONEY-LAVENDER
SHORTBREAD

Avani from Season 5 says that one of the best lessons she learned from Chef Ramsay is that it's important to push outside your comfort zone, and this shortbread is a perfect example of the delicious things that can happen when you do. Dried lavender can be tricky to bake with—but when balanced with salty butter and honey, it adds up to sophisticated cookie perfection.

MAKES 8 PIECES

2 sticks (8 ounces) plus 1 tablespoon salted butter (preferably European, like Kerrygold or Lurpak; see Tip, page 67), at cool room temperature

¾ cup confectioners' sugar

1 tablespoon finely grated lemon zest (from 1 lemon)

3 teaspoons crushed culinary lavender

2 cups all-purpose flour

1½ tablespoons honey

2 teaspoons turbinado sugar (such as Sugar In the Raw)

1. Use 1 tablespoon of the butter to grease the bottom and sides of a 10-inch fluted tart pan or springform cake pan.

2. In a bowl, using an electric mixer with the paddle attachment, beat the remaining 2 sticks butter on medium-low speed until smooth, about 2 minutes. In a small bowl, whisk together the confectioners' sugar, lemon zest, and 2 teaspoons of the lavender. Add the sugar mixture to the butter and increase the speed to medium-high. Beat until very pale and fluffy, about 3 minutes more, scraping bowl as needed. Reduce the mixer speed to low and slowly sprinkle in the flour, mixing until just combined.

3. Transfer the dough into the prepared pan and press it into an even layer, using the back of a spoon to smooth the surface. Place the pan in the refrigerator and chill the dough until firm, at least 30 minutes.

4. Meanwhile, preheat the oven to 300°F.

5. In a small saucepan, warm the honey over low heat until runny. In a small bowl, combine the remaining 1 teaspoon lavender and turbinado sugar. Brush the surface of the chilled dough with the honey and sprinkle it with the lavender-sugar mixture. Score the dough into 8 wedges and prick the surface all over with the tines of a fork.

6. Bake the shortbread until it is pale golden and firm in the center, about 1 hour. Recut the wedges, then transfer the pan to a wire rack to cool completely. Store the cookies in an airtight container for up to 1 week.

EARL GREY MADELEINES
WITH GRAPEFRUIT GLAZE

Just as a batch of perfectly baked citrus-scented madeleines helped Logan clinch the win during the finale of Season 2, these buttery little two-bite French cakelets are guaranteed to delight anyone who is lucky enough to have a taste. Though madeleines have a reputation for being tricky, the recipe is quite forgiving since it involves no creaming of butter or complicated techniques. Stirring a few tablespoons of finely ground citrusy Earl Grey tea into the batter adds a lovely floral fragrance that perfectly complements the bright, tangy grapefruit glaze. The signature scallop-shaped pans are the only special equipment it requires.

MAKES ABOUT 18 MADELEINES

MADELEINES

1 tablespoon Earl Grey tea (from about 3 teabags)

⅔ cup all-purpose flour

1 teaspoon baking powder

⅛ teaspoon kosher salt

⅓ cup granulated sugar

1 tablespoon finely grated grapefruit zest

2 large eggs

1½ teaspoons pure vanilla extract

6 tablespoons (¾ stick) unsalted butter, melted and cooled to room temperature

3 tablespoons whole milk

Nonstick pan spray

GLAZE

1¼ cups confectioners' sugar

2 to 3 tablespoons fresh grapefruit juice

1. Make the madeleines: Pulse the tea in a spice grinder until finely ground. (If you do not have a spice grinder, you can use a coffee grinder, a small food processor, or a mortar and pestle; the aim is just to break down the tea so that it is not in large pieces.) In a medium bowl, whisk together the ground tea, flour, baking powder, and salt.

2. In a large bowl, using an electric mixer fitted with the whisk attachment, beat the granulated sugar and grapefruit zest on low speed until the mixture is fragrant and sandy looking, about 30 seconds. Add the eggs and beat on medium-high until the mixture is light and has begun to thicken, 3 to 4 minutes. With the mixer running, beat in the vanilla. Using a rubber spatula, gently fold in the flour mixture by hand until just combined. Stir in the melted butter and the milk. Cover the bowl with plastic wrap and refrigerate for at least 1 hour or up to overnight.

3. Thirty minutes before you plan to bake the madeleines, place a 12-cavity madeleine pan into the freezer to chill (if you have 2 madeleine pans, chill them both) and preheat the oven to 400°F (if using two madeleine pans, adjust the oven racks to the upper and lower thirds of the oven).

4. Remove the madeleine pan(s) from the freezer and evenly coat them with pan spray. Spoon the batter evenly into the molds, filling each cavity three-quarters full. Tap the pan gently on the counter once or twice to release any air bubbles. Bake until the cookies are golden around the edges, about 15 minutes. Let the madeleines rest in the pan for 2 minutes, then gently nudge them out of the pan with your fingers or the rounded end of a spoon and transfer them to a wire rack to cool until just cool to the touch.

5. Immediately make the glaze: In a small bowl, whisk together the confectioners' sugar and grapefruit juice until smooth. (Start with 2 tablespoons of grapefruit juice; if the glaze seems a little stiff, add a bit more juice.)

6. When the madeleines are just cool to the touch, dip each one lightly into glaze, ridged-side down. Let any excess glaze run off the madeleine and back into the bowl. Return the glazed madeleines to the rack, glazed-side up, and set aside until the cookies have cooled completely and the glaze is set, about 15 minutes. Though they will keep in an airtight container for up to 3 days, madeleines are best the day they are made—and are preferably eaten while still a little warm!

TIP Not all butters are created equal, so when you're in the dairy aisle, look closely at the labels. American-style butters (like Land O'Lakes) are required to have at least 80% butterfat and tend to have a balanced, neutral flavor. "European"-style butters (like Kerrygold and Lurpak) are made with "cultured" cream that has been lightly fermented with live cultures and churned longer than American butters, which gives them a higher butterfat content (upward of 82%), a deeper, yellowy hue, and an intense "buttery" taste. How do bakers know which type to use and when? Because of their gentle flavor, American-style butters work well in recipes like brownies and cupcakes, where butter plays a part but isn't the star. European-style butters, on the other hand, are ideal for recipes like the sugar cookies (page 52) or shortbread (page 65), where you want the bold, rich butter flavor to shine through.

MINI
S'MORES WHOOPIE PIES

It's no surprise that the combo of sweet, nutty graham crackers, melty chocolate, and gooey marshmallow is a favorite inside the *MasterChef Junior* kitchen. After all, what kid doesn't love s'mores? In Season 5, Jasmine decided to go with s'mores cupcakes with seven-minute frosting as her entry in the blowtorch challenge. This take on the campfire classic shows off the flavors in mini whoopie pie form, with tender brown sugar and cinnamon-scented graham cracker-inspired cakelets sandwiched with a rich chocolate ganache and fluffy marshmallow crème—no blow torch needed!

MAKES 16 TO 18 SMALL WHOOPIE PIES

GRAHAM CAKES

1½ cups all-purpose flour

1 cup whole wheat flour

1 cup packed dark brown sugar

1 teaspoon baking soda

½ teaspoon ground cinnamon

¼ teaspoon kosher salt

½ cup plain whole-milk yogurt

⅓ cup canola oil

2 teaspoons pure vanilla extract

3 large eggs

GANACHE

¾ cup milk chocolate chips

¼ cup heavy cream

MARSHMALLOW FILLING

1 stick (4 ounces) unsalted butter, at room temperature

1 cup confectioners' sugar

1½ cups marshmallow crème (such as Fluff)

1 teaspoon pure vanilla extract

1. Make the graham cakes: In a medium bowl, whisk together the all-purpose flour, whole wheat flour, brown sugar, baking soda, cinnamon, and salt.

2. In a bowl, using an electric mixer with the paddle attachment, beat the yogurt, oil, vanilla, and eggs on medium-high speed until smooth and slightly thickened, about 3 minutes. Use a rubber spatula to mix the flour mixture into the egg mixture in two parts, stirring just to combine after each addition. Cover the bowl with plastic wrap and transfer it to the refrigerator to chill for 30 minutes.

3. Preheat the oven to 350°F. Line two baking sheets with parchment paper.

4. Spoon the chilled dough onto the prepared baking sheets in rounded tablespoons, leaving 1½ inches between them (you will have about 36 rounds total.) Bake until golden and springy, about 10 minutes. Let the graham cakes rest on the baking sheets for 2 minutes, then transfer them to a wire rack to cool completely.

5. Make the ganache: Place the chocolate chips in a heatproof medium bowl. In a small saucepan, bring the cream to a simmer over medium heat (watch it closely—cream likes to come to a boil really fast and then bubble over the rim of the saucepan!). Pour the hot cream over the chocolate chips and set aside for 1 minute, then whisk until smooth. Cool until spreadable, about 1 hour.

6. Make the marshmallow filling: In a large bowl, with an electric mixer, beat the butter, confectioners' sugar, marshmallow crème, and vanilla on medium speed until fluffy, smooth, and spreadable, about 4 minutes.

7. To assemble the whoopie pies, spread a layer of ganache on the flat side of half the graham cakes. Spread a thick layer of marshmallow filling onto the flat side of each of the remaining cookies. Sandwich the two sides together. Serve the whoopie pies immediately, or store in an airtight container in the refrigerator for up to 24 hours. Let the whoopie pies come to room temperature before serving.

CANNELÉS

Cydney from Season 5 loves to explore new baking recipes, especially pâtisserie classics, and lately, she says, her obsession has been cannelés—small French pastries with custardy vanilla-flavored centers and dark, chewy, caramelized sugar shells. Heads up—the cannelé batter is best after a day of resting in the fridge (this allows the flour to completely absorb the liquid)—so be prepared to make the batter the day before you plan to bake. But once you've got that ready, the rest of the process is a snap.

MAKES 16 CANNELÉS

2 cups whole milk

⅓ cup heavy cream

1 vanilla bean, split lengthwise (see page 24)

1 cup sugar

1 cup all-purpose flour

2 large eggs

2 large egg yolks

2 tablespoons unsalted butter, melted

1½ teaspoons rum extract

Nonstick pan spray

1. In a small saucepan, bring the milk and cream to a simmer over low heat, then remove from the heat. With the tip of a paring knife, scrape the vanilla seeds out of the vanilla bean and add to the milk mixture. Let cool for 10 minutes.

2. In a large bowl, gently whisk together the sugar, flour, whole eggs, and egg yolks until the mixture is smooth but pasty. Slowly drizzle in the warm milk mixture and the melted butter and whisk until it comes together. Stir in the rum extract to combine. (The consistency should now be similar to a loose pancake batter.) Transfer the batter to a 4-cup measuring cup, cover with plastic wrap, and refrigerate for at least 12 hours or up to (and preferably) 24 hours.

3. Remove the chilled batter from the refrigerator an hour before you plan to bake the cannelés and let it come to room temperature. (If the batter has separated, lightly whisk it until smooth and tap the measuring cup against the counter once or twice to release any air bubbles.)

4. Preheat the oven to 450°F. Lightly coat the inside of two 8-cavity silicone cannelé molds with pan spray and place each one on a baking sheet (if you only have one mold, then bake half the batter at a time).

5. Pour the batter into the molds, filling each cavity three-quarters full. Bake for 10 minutes, then reduce the oven temperature to 400°F and bake until the cannelés are a deep mahogany

brown, 50 to 60 minutes more. (Don't panic if they seem burned: That is actually how they are supposed to look!) Let the cannelés cool inside the molds for 10 minutes, then carefully unmold them using the rounded back of a spoon to push them up and out of the silicone molds (they stay hot!) and place them, domed-side up, on a wire rack to cool completely. The cannelés will keep in an airtight container for up to 3 days.

MERINGUE

It's the mile-high cloud-like topping on a lemon meringue pie, it's the fluffy base that you fold into mousses and soufflé batters to make them airy and light—it's meringue! As delicate as snowflakes, meringue feels a little bit like magic every time you make it, with the most amazing thing about it, being how simple it is to prepare!

Changing the way you combine the sugar and eggs produces different styles of meringue: There is French meringue, Italian meringue, and Swiss meringue. French meringue is the most straightforward style—and the one that appears most often on *MasterChef Junior* in delicate macarons and on top of tall, white-peaked pies. To make French meringue, you simply beat egg whites vigorously with sugar and, usually, a pinch of cream of tartar (which is an acid that stabilizes the meringue) until the mixture becomes thick, frothy, and full of air bubbles. From there you can spoon or pipe the meringue into shapes or dollop it onto a pie. While this meringue is the easiest kind to make, it's also the most delicate and prone to deflating—so it needs to be baked right away. After baking, French meringues are pale and crisp on the outside and light and airy inside.

For Italian meringue, sugar is melted on the stovetop in a saucepan until it becomes a syrup, which is then slowly drizzled into egg whites while they are being beaten into glossy peaks. Italian meringue is the most stable but also the toughest kind to make!

Swiss meringue is a nice compromise between the two. Like Italian meringue, it uses cooked sugar—but instead of combining it with water to make a syrup, the sugar is added directly to the egg whites and the two are cooked together in a bain-marie (a bowl set over a saucepan of simmering water) until it reaches 140°F and then transferred to a mixer and whipped to stiff peaks. After whipping, both Italian and Swiss meringues have a shiny, soft, fluffy, marshmallow-like consistency.

MAKING FRENCH MERINGUE

Since French meringue is the simplest style for beginners to master and is the most popular method used by the young bakers on *MasterChef Junior*, it's worth diving into a little more detail on how to get it just right. Before the lemon meringue pie challenge in Season 3, judges Graham Elliot and Gordon Ramsay gave the contestants a few rules to remember when making French meringues.

1. Make sure your bowl and whisk (or mixer attachment) are completely clean and dry. Fat is the enemy of meringue—and even a dribble of water or a smudge of butter can contaminate the egg whites and make them much harder to whip (some bakers even whip vinegar around

Soft peaks: The meringue has begun to firm up but is still soft and falls quickly.

Medium peaks: The meringue is stiff. When you invert your whisk, the meringue holds a peak but the tip curls over.

Stiff peaks: The meringue is very thick. When you invert your whisk, the peak holds its shape without collapsing.

the inside of their bowl and their whisk to make sure there is no fat remaining before whipping egg whites). It's also the reason you should be really careful when separating the egg whites from the egg yolks. Egg yolks have fat, and even a drop will prevent your whites from whipping to peaks. Another tip: Use a glass or metal bowl, because plastic is more porous and more likely to trap residue that could get in the way of firm and glossy peaks.

2. Let the egg whites come to room temperature before you begin, because warmer eggs whip faster than cold ones.

3. Start whisking on a low speed, then increase the speed gradually, so you don't have to worry about overbeating (yes, egg whites can be overwhipped—when they are, they go from smooth and glossy to bumpy and broken looking).

4. Add the sugar gradually as you're beating the whites so it has time to dissolve during whipping—or else the result will be a gritty meringue. Nobody wants that!

5. Finally, bake the meringues low and slow in a cool oven so that they stay pale and light without a hint of sogginess. This is critical if you are baking Meringue "Ghosts" (page 75), or baking the meringues in larger discs to make a Pavlova (like the one on page 197).

CUSTOMIZE YOUR MERINGUE

You can use any kind of sugar when making a French meringue. Granulated sugar is standard, but confectioners' sugar is a bit easier to dissolve (and has cornstarch in it so that it doesn't form clumps). Brown sugar produces meringues that are a pale tan color instead of pure white—it also gives the meringue a gentle caramel flavor. You can also try dressing up meringue by flavoring it with a splash of extract (vanilla, peppermint, almond, and lemon are all nice) or tint it with a drop or two of food coloring to make pink, lavender, blue, or really any shade you can think of. To make pretty meringue bites, use a pastry bag fitted with a decorative tip to pipe the meringue onto baking sheets in decorative swirls before baking. The little crisp treats are easy, elegant, and cute as can be—not to mention naturally gluten-free.

MERINGUE "GHOSTS"

These ghoulishly cute treats are one of Cydney's (from Season 5) most beloved Halloween traditions. "My mom started baking these for our family when I was a little kid," she says. "And now we love to make them together!" Because the process is as simple as making a basic meringue (see MasterChef Lesson, page 72), it's a great way for young bakers to practice their whipping and piping skills.

MAKES ABOUT 24 GHOSTS

6 large egg whites, at room temperature

½ teaspoon cream of tartar

½ teaspoon pure almond extract (optional)

¼ teaspoon kosher salt

1½ cups confectioners' sugar, sifted

48 mini chocolate chips

TIP You will have yolks left over after you separate the eggs; for ways to use them up, try Key Lime Pie Bars (page 84) or Malted Milk Crème Brûlée (page 212).

1. Preheat the oven to 200°F. Line two baking sheets with parchment paper.

2. In a large, clean, dry bowl, combine the egg whites, cream of tartar, and almond extract (if using). Beat, using an electric mixer with the paddle attachment, on medium speed until soft peaks form, about 2½ minutes. With the mixer running, add the salt and then the sugar, 2 tablespoons at a time, and beat until the meringue forms stiff, glossy peaks, about 3 minutes more.

3. Spoon the meringue into a pastry bag fitted with a ½-inch plain tip (see page 12). Pipe the meringue onto the baking sheets in tall conical swirls, 2 inches in diameter at the base and 3 inches tall, that taper as they come to a point at the top, spacing them 1 inch apart. Once they are all piped, place two mini chocolate chips onto each swirl to create eyes.

4. Carefully place the pan in the oven and bake until the meringues are pale, dry, and crisp to the touch, about 1½ hours. Turn off the oven and let the meringues rest in the oven until completely dry and cool to the touch, about 2 hours. Store the meringues in an airtight container at room temperature for up to 1 week.

~ MASTER *THIS* ~

MACARONS

These delicate French meringue cookies are a perennial favorite on *MasterChef Junior* and were the focus of exciting competitions in Seasons 5 and 6. When introducing the young bakers to the challenges, judge Christina Tosi explained that macarons require a tremendous amount of technical skill to get just right. What makes a perfect one? Look for a smooth, hollow shell with a ruffled edge (sometimes called a "foot") and a rich, thin filling of jam, buttercream, or ganache. This recipe is a starting place—use it to play with all sorts of flavors and fillings (see the variations opposite).

MAKES ABOUT 36 MACARONS

1 cup almond flour

2 cups confectioners' sugar

4 large egg whites

⅛ teaspoon kosher salt

⅛ teaspoon cream of tartar

¼ cup superfine sugar (see Tip)

¾ cup jam or ganache (page 108), for filling

TIP Superfine sugar is a type of granulated sugar that has been ground into very fine crystals so that it dissolves quickly. You can find superfine sugar in the baking aisle of most grocery stores, but it's also simple to make your own in a pinch: Just put granulated sugar in a food processor or blender (it's best to use a little bit more than the amount of superfine sugar you need so you can measure it out), then process on high speed for about 1½ minutes, until the sugar is finely ground.

1. In a large bowl, whisk together the almond flour and 1 cup of the confectioners' sugar until combined. Set aside.

2. Put the eggs whites in a large bowl. Sprinkle in the salt and cream of tartar and, using an electric mixer fitted with the whisk attachment, beat on medium-high speed until light and foamy, 1 to 1½ minutes. Reduce the speed to medium-low and slowly sprinkle in the remaining 1 cup confectioners' sugar and the superfine sugar. Beat until the meringue forms glossy peaks, about 4 minutes more. (If adding food coloring or flavoring, stir it in now; see the variations opposite.)

3. Using a clean rubber spatula, gently fold the almond flour mixture into the meringue until there are no streaks visible.

4. Line two baking sheets with parchment paper. Working in two batches, transfer the batter to a pastry bag fitted with a ¼-inch plain tip. Hold the tip perpendicular to the parchment so that it is nearly touching and gently squeeze the batter onto the parchment in 1½-inch rounds, leaving at least 1 inch of space between them. (Tip: For even mounds, before piping, use a pencil to lightly trace circles onto the parchment as a template, then flip the parchment so the marks face the baking sheet.) Tap the baking sheets firmly against the counter to release any air bubbles.

5. Transfer the baking sheets to a cool, dry place. Let the macarons rest until the tops dry out a bit and form a delicate skin, about 1½ hours.

6. Position a rack in the center of the oven and preheat the oven to 325°F. When ready to bake, reduce the oven temperature to 300°F.

7. Bake the macarons, one sheet at a time, until the tops are firm and smooth and set, about 12 minutes. Remove the macarons from the oven and set aside to cool on the baking sheet for 15 minutes, then transfer them to a wire rack to cool completely.

8. Before serving, spread the flat side of half of the macarons with jam, ganache, or the filling of your choice and top with the remaining rounds, domed-side up.

VARIATIONS

Chocolate-Hazelnut Macarons: Add 1 tablespoon unsweetened cocoa powder and 4 or 5 drops brown gel food coloring to the batter along with the confectioners' sugar. To assemble the cookies, spread half the rounds with chocolate-hazelnut spread and top with the remaining halves.

Peanut Butter and Jelly Macarons: Stir 1 tablespoon finely ground freeze-dried raspberries and 4 or 5 drops purple gel food coloring into the batter once the meringue has formed stiff, glossy peaks. Make peanut butter buttercream by blending 1 cup creamy peanut butter, 4 tablespoons (½ stick) softened unsalted butter, and 1¼ cups confectioners' sugar until smooth. To assemble the cookies, spread half the rounds with the peanut butter buttercream. Dot a small spoonful of raspberry jelly in the center of the buttercream and top with the remaining halves.

GREEN TEA MACARONS
WITH STRAWBERRY COULIS

SEASON
6

REMY

When Remy presented these sophisticated little cookies during the Season 6 macaron challenge, judge Christina Tosi called them "incredibly delicious and unique" and praised Remy for her careful technique. Matcha, which is a powder made from finely ground green tea leaves, gives the shells and the buttercream filling a delicate, earthy flavor that's a perfect complement to the bright sweetness of the strawberry coulis—and the pale-green-and-pink color combination couldn't be any prettier.

MAKES ABOUT 36 MACARONS

MACARONS

Macaron batter (page 76) made through step 2

4 or 5 drops green gel food coloring

2 tablespoons finely ground freeze-dried strawberries

STRAWBERRY COULIS

1 cup sliced strawberries

1 tablespoon fresh lemon juice

¼ cup granulated sugar

1 tablespoon cornstarch

GREEN TEA BUTTERCREAM

10 tablespoons unsalted butter, at room temperature

2 cups confectioners' sugar

1 tablespoon pure vanilla extract

1 tablespoon matcha powder (green tea powder)

1. Make the macarons: Make the macaron batter as directed on page 76. Once the meringue forms shiny, glossy peaks in step 2, add the green food coloring and beat on high for 30 seconds to combine. Using a clean rubber spatula, gently fold the almond flour mixture into the meringue until the batter is streak-free.

2. Pipe the macaron batter onto lined baking sheets as described. Using a fine sieve, sprinkle each round with a fine dusting of the ground freeze-dried strawberries. Transfer the baking sheets to a cool, dry place. Let the macarons rest until the tops dry slightly and form a delicate skin, about 1½ hours.

3. Meanwhile, make the strawberry coulis: In a small saucepan, combine the strawberries, lemon juice, sugar, and 2 tablespoons water. Bring to a simmer over medium heat and cook, stirring frequently, until the strawberries begin to break down, 10 to 12 minutes. Whisk in the cornstarch and return to a simmer until thickened, 2 to 3 minutes, using a wooden spoon to break up any large pieces of strawberry that remain. Remove from the heat and scrape the mixture into a small bowl. (You should have about ½ cup.) Set aside to cool completely.

4. Make the green tea buttercream: In a bowl, using an electric mixer with the paddle attachment, beat the butter on high speed until light and creamy, about 2 minutes. Reduce the

speed to medium and add the confectioners' sugar ½ cup at a time, beating well after each addition. Add the vanilla and matcha powder and beat on high until the buttercream is smooth, 20 to 30 seconds. Spoon the buttercream into a pastry bag fitted with a ¼-inch plain tip and refrigerate until ready to use.

5. Bake and cool the macarons as directed in the recipe.

6. When ready to assemble, remove the buttercream from the refrigerator and let it come to cool room temperature (this could take up to 30 minutes depending on how firm the buttercream is when you remove it from the fridge). Spread a scant ½ teaspoon of the coulis over the flat side of half the macarons. Pipe the buttercream onto the flat sides of the remaining macarons. Sandwich the two sides together and arrange the macarons on a baking sheet. Lightly cover the sheet with plastic wrap and refrigerate for 30 minutes or until ready to serve. Let the macarons come to room temperature for 15 minutes before serving. Store the macarons in an airtight container in the refrigerator for up to 3 days or in the freezer for up to 3 months.

BARS AND BITES

Fudgy Brownies with Chocolate Chips and Cacao Nibs, page 82

FUDGY BROWNIES
WITH CHOCOLATE CHIPS AND CACAO NIBS

Justise from Season 5 says that the secret to spectacular brownies is a fudgy center and a mix of different kinds of chocolate. This version uses brown sugar alongside granulated sugar, which keeps the brownies moist. Crunchy cacao nibs, which are dried, roasted, and crushed bits of the cacao bean, can be found in most major grocery stores or ordered online; if you have leftovers, they are delicious mixed into Easy Vanilla Ice Cream (page 220) or used in Compost Cookie Bites (page 86).

MAKES 24 BROWNIES · **See photograph on page 81**

2 sticks (8 ounces) unsalted butter, cubed

1½ cups plus 3 tablespoons bittersweet chocolate chips

1 cup packed dark brown sugar

¾ cup granulated sugar

1¼ cups all-purpose flour

½ teaspoon kosher salt

4 large eggs

2 teaspoons pure vanilla extract

2 tablespoons cacao nibs

1. Preheat the oven to 350°F. Line a 13 × 9-inch metal or glass baking pan with parchment paper, leaving a few inches of overhang on both of the long sides. (This will help you lift the brownies out of the pan after baking.)

2. In a heatproof medium bowl set over a pan of simmering water (make sure the bottom of the bowl doesn't touch the water), combine the butter, 1½ cups of the chocolate chips, the brown sugar, and the granulated sugar. Stir occasionally until the butter has completely melted and the mixture is smooth. Using oven mitts, remove the bowl from the pan and set aside to cool slightly.

3. In a small bowl, whisk together the flour and salt. In a large bowl, using an electric mixer with the whisk attachment, beat the eggs until slightly thickened, about 1½ minutes. Reduce the speed and beat in the vanilla and the melted chocolate mixture. Using a rubber spatula, fold in the dry ingredients until just combined, taking care not to overmix.

4. Use the spatula to evenly spread the batter in the prepared pan and scatter the surface with the remaining 3 tablespoons chocolate chips and the cacao nibs. Bake until the brownies are glossy on top and the center resists light pressure when pressed, about 35 minutes. Let the brownies cool completely in the pan on a wire rack. Use the parchment to lift the brownies out onto a cutting board and cut into 24 pieces. Store the brownies in an airtight container for up to 4 days.

BUTTERSCOTCH
CHAI BLONDIES

Think of these rich, chewy blondies as brownies' delectable vanilla-and-butterscotch-infused cousins. Avani from Season 5 says that she likes to play around in the kitchen with spices that reflect her Indian heritage. Here the use of chai—a warm blend of spices including cardamom, cinnamon, and ginger that is traditionally brewed into a warm, sweetened milk tea—follows that inspiration and lends the bars a heady aroma and an added dimension of complexity. These are lovely just the way they are, but if you wanted to dress them up even more, you could sprinkle the surface with a handful of chopped toasted pistachios or white chocolate chips before baking.

MAKES ABOUT 24 BLONDIES

Nonstick pan spray
1½ cups all-purpose flour
1 teaspoon baking powder
1 teaspoon ground cardamom
¼ teaspoon ground allspice
¼ teaspoon ground aniseed
¼ teaspoon ground cinnamon
¼ teaspoon ground ginger
¼ teaspoon kosher salt
1½ sticks (6 ounces) unsalted butter, melted
1½ cups packed dark brown sugar
2 large eggs
1½ tablespoons pure vanilla extract

1. Preheat the oven to 350°F. Line a 9 × 13-inch metal or glass baking pan with parchment paper, leaving a few inches of overhang on both of the long sides. (This will help you lift the blondies out of the pan after baking.) Coat the pan and the parchment with pan spray.

2. In a medium bowl, whisk together the flour, baking powder, cardamom, allspice, aniseed, cinnamon, ginger, and salt. Set aside.

3. In a large bowl, using an electric mixer with the whisk attachment, beat the melted butter and brown sugar on medium-high speed until thick and smooth, about 1 minute. Add the eggs, one at a time, and then the vanilla, using a rubber spatula to scrape down the sides of the bowl as needed. Fold the dry ingredients into the butter mixture until just combined, taking care not to overmix.

4. Spoon the batter into the prepared pan, using the spatula or the back of a spoon to smooth the surface. Bake until the blondies are golden brown and resist light pressure when pressed, about 25 minutes. Let the brownies cool completely in the pan on a wire rack, about 1 hour. Use the parchment to lift the blondies out of the pan onto a cutting board and cut into 24 pieces. Store the blondies in an airtight container for up to 4 days.

KEY LIME PIE BARS

Mikey from Season 6 says he's crazy about Key lime pie, particularly the way the bold citrus flavor cuts through the creamy sweetness of the filling. A riff on the classic, these bars are great for sharing at picnics and potlucks. (They need to chill before serving, so remember to plan ahead!) For a spicy twist, swap in gingersnaps for the graham crackers. Real Key limes are smaller and tarter than regular (also known as Persian) limes—but it's fine to use regular supermarket limes instead.

MAKES 16 BARS

SEASON 6

CRUST

Nonstick pan spray

5 ounces graham crackers (about 30 squares, or the equivalent of 1 sleeve), broken into large pieces

¼ cup pecan halves

⅓ cup packed light brown sugar

¾ teaspoon kosher salt

6 tablespoons (¾ stick) unsalted butter, melted

FILLING

4 ounces cream cheese, at room temperature

3 large egg yolks

1 (14-ounce) can sweetened condensed milk

2 tablespoons finely grated lime zest (4 or 5 regular limes)

½ cup fresh lime juice (12 to 14 Key limes, from 4 or 5 regular limes)

¼ teaspoon kosher salt

WHIPPED CREAM

½ cup heavy cream

1 tablespoon confectioners' sugar

1 teaspoon pure vanilla extract

1. Make the crust: Preheat the oven to 325°F. Line an 8-inch square baking pan with parchment paper, leaving a few inches of overhang on two sides. (This will help you lift the bars out of the pan after baking.) Coat the pan and the parchment with pan spray.

2. In a food processor, pulse the graham crackers and pecans until they form fine crumbs, about 1 minute. Add the brown sugar and salt and pulse to combine. Drizzle in the melted butter and pulse until the mixture moistens and begins to clump together, about 1 minute.

3. Spoon the graham cracker mixture into the prepared pan and press it into an even layer. Bake until golden, about 15 minutes. Transfer the pan to a wire rack to cool.

4. Meanwhile, make the filling: In a large bowl, using an electric mixer with the paddle attachment, beat the cream cheese until smooth, about 2 minutes. Beat in the egg yolks one at a time, then add the condensed milk, lime zest, lime juice, and salt and beat until combined.

5. Pour the filling over the crust and smooth out the surface. Bake until the edges have set and begun to pull away slightly from the pan, about 16 minutes. Let cool to room temperature in the pan on a wire rack, about 1 hour. Cover and refrigerate until completely chilled, at least 1½ hours or up to overnight.

6. When ready to serve, make the whipped cream: In a medium bowl, using an electric mixer with the whisk attachment, beat the cream, confectioners' sugar, and vanilla on medium-high speed until it forms soft peaks, 2 to 3 minutes.

7. Lift the bars out of the pan and cut them into 16 (2-inch) squares. The bars can be stored, covered, in the refrigerator for up to 2 days. Before serving, top each one with a teaspoon of whipped cream.

TIP To get the most juice out of a lime, before squeezing make sure the fruit is at room temperature, not chilled, and roll it against the counter or between your palms to get the juices flowing.

COMPOST COOKIE BITES

These jam-packed morsels are a two-bite take on judge Christina Tosi's famous compost cookies. You can make lots of different versions of "compost dough" with whatever yummy odds and ends you have in your snack cabinet—pretzels, graham crackers, potato chips, peanut butter chips, mini marshmallows, or just about anything else you can think of!

MAKES ABOUT 40 COOKIE BITES

1¼ cups all-purpose flour

2 tablespoons cornstarch

1 teaspoon baking powder

½ teaspoon kosher salt

1½ sticks (6 ounces) unsalted butter, at cool room temperature

¼ cup granulated sugar

¾ cup packed light brown sugar

1½ teaspoons pure vanilla extract

2 large eggs

½ cup rolled oats

3 tablespoons ground coffee

½ cup crushed pretzels

½ cup crushed potato chips

¼ cup peanut butter chips

¼ cup mini chocolate chips

1. In a medium bowl, whisk together the flour, cornstarch, baking powder, and salt.

2. In a large bowl, using an electric mixer, beat the butter, granulated sugar, and brown sugar on medium-high speed until lightened and fluffy, about 5 minutes. Beat in the vanilla and eggs until just combined, using a rubber spatula to scrape down the bowl as needed. Fold in the flour mixture until just combined. Fold in the oats, ground coffee, crushed pretzels, potato chips, and peanut butter and chocolate chips.

3. Line two baking sheets with parchment paper. Scoop out the dough by the heaping teaspoon and gently roll it between your palms to form small balls. You should have about 40 total. Transfer the balls to the prepared baking sheets and chill until firm, about 30 minutes.

4. Preheat the oven to 350°F. Line two 24-cup mini-muffin tins with paper liners.

5. Place a dough ball into each cup. Bake until the cookie bites are golden brown, about 15 minutes. Let rest in the pan for 2 minutes, then transfer to a wire rack to cool completely. Store the cookie cups in an airtight container for up to 4 days.

OLIVE OIL GRANOLA
WITH CHERRIES, ALMONDS, AND PUMPKIN SEEDS

Although it's perfect for a quick nutritious breakfast, granola is also a hearty nibble on the go, making it a staple in lots of family pantries. Store-bought brands can be packed with processed sugar and less-than-wholesome fillers—so why not make your own? This easy homemade version—inspired by the Season 6 mystery box challenge that asked contestants to craft desserts using all natural sweeteners—includes no refined sugar and is chockablock with yummy nuts, seeds, and fruit. And it's still addictively delicious! Stirring in egg whites before baking is a clever way to make sure you get lots of snackable clusters. Note: If date sugar is hard to find, the recipe does work just as well with an equal amount of brown sugar.

MAKES ABOUT 6 CUPS

½ cup extra-virgin olive oil

½ cup honey

⅓ cup date sugar (or packed light brown sugar)

1 teaspoon pure vanilla extract

1 teaspoon pure almond extract

1 teaspoon ground cinnamon

½ teaspoon kosher salt

3 cups rolled oats

1 cup pumpkin seeds

¾ cup unsalted dry-roasted almonds, coarsely chopped

2 large egg whites, lightly whisked until frothy

1 cup dried cherries (preferably unsweetened)

1. Preheat the oven to 325°F.

2. In a 4-cup measuring cup or small bowl, whisk together the olive oil, honey, date sugar, vanilla, almond extract, cinnamon, and salt until smooth.

3. In a large bowl, combine the oats, pumpkin seeds, and almonds. Use a rubber spatula to scrape the olive oil mixture into the oat mixture and stir to combine, making sure everything is completely moistened. (The best way to do this is with your hands; yes, it's messy—but easy to wash up afterward!) Add the egg whites and stir with a rubber spatula until well combined.

4. Spread the granola over a rimmed baking sheet and press firmly into a single layer. Bake, stirring once halfway through, until the granola is golden brown, about 40 minutes. Set the granola aside to cool to room temperature (it may seem soft when you remove it from the oven, but will get crunchier as it cools).

5. Transfer the cooled granola to a large bowl, breaking any large clumps into bite-size pieces. Stir in the cherries. The granola will keep in an airtight container for 2 to 3 weeks.

BROWN SUGAR
APPLE CRISP
WITH MAPLE WHIPPED CREAM

Few desserts are as comforting as an apple crisp made from fresh fall apples. Evan from Season 6 was lucky to learn that lesson early: When he was young, his family always picked apples from the trees on his grandparents' ranch and used their haul to bake together.

SERVES 8

APPLE FILLING

¼ cup granulated sugar

2 teaspoons cornstarch

1 teaspoons ground cinnamon

2¼ pounds (about 6) mixed apples (such as McIntosh, Granny Smith, or Golden Delicious), cored and cut into ¼-inch-thick slices

⅔ cup golden raisins

3 tablespoons fresh lemon juice

1 teaspoon pure vanilla extract

CRUMBLE TOPPING

2 cups rolled oats

¾ cup packed dark brown sugar

½ cup granulated sugar

1 teaspoon ground cinnamon

½ teaspoon nutmeg, preferably freshly grated

½ teaspoon kosher salt

1 stick (4 ounces) unsalted butter, melted

MAPLE WHIPPED CREAM

1 cup heavy cream

1½ tablespoons maple syrup

½ teaspoon pure vanilla extract

1. Preheat the oven to 400°F.

2. Make the apple filling: In a small bowl, whisk together the granulated sugar, cornstarch, and cinnamon. In a large bowl, toss together the apples, raisins, lemon juice, and vanilla. Add the sugar-cornstarch mixture and toss to combine. Scrape the apple mixture and any juices into a 9-inch square baking dish and smooth it into an even layer.

3. Make the topping: In a food processor or high-powered blender, pulse 1 cup of the oats on high until broken down into fine crumbs. Transfer to a bowl and add the remaining 1 cup rolled oats, the brown sugar, granulated sugar, cinnamon, nutmeg, and salt. Whisk in the melted butter until the mixture moistens and forms small clumps. Spoon the crumble topping evenly over the apples, completely covering them.

4. Bake until the crumble is golden brown on top and the fruit is bubbling around the edges of the pan, about 1 hour. Transfer the pan to a wire rack to cool for 30 minutes.

5. Make the maple whipped cream: In a medium bowl, using an electric mixer, beat the cream, maple syrup, and vanilla on medium-high speed until the cream holds soft peaks, 2 to 3 minutes.

6. To serve, spoon the warm crisp into bowls and serve with a dollop of maple whipped cream. Leftovers will keep, covered and chilled, for up to 5 days. Reheat in the microwave, or in a 325°F oven for 15 minutes.

CRANBERRY-OATMEAL
CRUMBLE BARS

Quani from Season 6 says he likes to work fresh fruit into his baked goods whenever possible because of the bright sweetness it can bring to a dish. These rustic cranberry-oat bars are a prime example: Full of jammy goodness, lightly spiced, and topped with a chunky oatmeal streusel, they strike a perfect balance between tart and sweet.

MAKES 9 BARS

Nonstick pan spray

1 cup all-purpose flour

1 cup rolled oats

¾ cup granulated sugar, divided

¼ cup plus 1 tablespoon packed light brown sugar

½ teaspoon ground cinnamon

½ teaspoon kosher salt

1 stick (4 ounces) unsalted butter, melted

1 teaspoon pure vanilla extract

1 large egg, beaten

2 cups fresh or frozen cranberries

2 teaspoons cornstarch

1. Preheat the oven to 350°F. Line an 8-inch square baking pan with parchment paper, leaving a few inches of overhang on two sides. (This will help you lift the bars out of the pan after baking.) Coat the pan and the parchment with pan spray.

2. In a medium bowl, whisk together the flour, oats, ½ cup of the granulated sugar, ¼ cup of the brown sugar, the cinnamon, and the salt. Stir in the melted butter, vanilla, and egg until well combined. Scoop out 1 cup of the oatmeal mixture and set it aside. Transfer the remaining oatmeal mixture to the prepared pan. Use the bottom of a measuring cup or the back of a spoon to pack it smoothly into an even layer.

3. In a medium bowl, toss together the cranberries, remaining ¼ cup granulated sugar, and the cornstarch. Scatter the cranberries over the oatmeal base (not all the cornstarch and sugar will adhere to the berries; sprinkle anything that remains in the bowl evenly over the cranberries once they are in the pan).

4. Stir the remaining 1 tablespoon brown sugar into the reserved oatmeal mixture. Use your fingertips to break the mixture into crumbles. Scatter the crumbles over the cranberries in an even layer, pressing down gently to help them adhere.

5. Bake until the cranberries are soft and bubbling and the crumble is deeply golden brown, about 50 minutes. Let mixture rest in the pan for 20 minutes, then use the parchment to lift the bars out of the pan and transfer them to a wire rack to cool completely, 1 to 1½ hours. Slice into 9 bars and serve. Leftovers will keep, covered with plastic wrap, in the refrigerator for up to 5 days.

TAHINI AND APRICOT
OAT BARS

These chewy oat bars are ideal for tucking into lunchboxes or backpacks for a boost of energy while you're traveling. Instead of peanut or almond butter, this recipe is bound together with tahini, a paste made from sesame seeds. When she makes granola bars, Cydney from Season 5 says she likes to add different types of dried fruit for a pop of sweetness; here dried apricots pair especially well with the tahini, but you could easily swap in dried cherries, cranberries, apples, or raisins instead if that's what you're craving.

MAKES 10 BARS

Nonstick pan spray
2¼ cups rolled oats
7 tablespoons unsalted butter
¼ cup packed light brown sugar
½ cup sweetened condensed milk
⅓ cup tahini
2 tablespoons honey
½ cup chopped dried apricots
⅔ cup chopped pecans
3 tablespoons sesame seeds or flaxseeds

1. Preheat the oven to 350°F. Line an 8-inch square baking pan with parchment paper, leaving a few inches of paper overhanging on two sides. (This will help you lift the bars out of the pan after baking.) Coat the pan and the parchment with pan spray.

2. Place the oats in a large bowl and set aside. In a medium saucepan, combine the butter, brown sugar, and condensed milk and cook over medium heat, stirring, until the mixture is smooth and the sugar has dissolved, about 3 minutes. Remove the pan from the heat and stir in the tahini and honey. Pour the butter mixture over the oats and stir until very thick, sticky, and well combined. Stir in the dried apricots, pecans, and sesame seeds.

3. Spoon the mixture into the prepared pan and spread it into an even layer. Bake until just golden on top, 15 to 20 minutes. Let the bars rest in the pan for 30 minutes, then use the parchment to lift them out of the pan and transfer them to a wire rack to cool completely. (Warm bars will crumble when sliced.) Slice into 10 bars and serve. Leftovers will keep in an airtight container for up to 1 week.

SWEET YEAST DOUGH

This sweet dough is enriched with milk, eggs, and butter—and, though decadent, it's also super versatile and can work as the base of tender sticky buns (page 94), gooey monkey bread (page 96), sugar-dusted jelly doughnuts (page 100), and much more. Working with yeast might seem a little intimidating—all that kneading and rising and shaping!—but the truth is that the process is quite simple, and with a little practice, you'll quickly start to feel comfortable. Just be patient and remember that you're in charge. And trust us: The first time you bite into a fresh, warm doughnut that you've made from scratch, all your effort and time will seem worth it!

1¼ cups whole milk

¼ cup sugar

6 tablespoons (¾ stick) unsalted butter, plus more for greasing the bowl

1 teaspoon kosher salt

1 large egg

3½ cups all-purpose flour, plus more for shaping

1 (7 g) envelope instant (Rapid Rise) yeast (2¼ teaspoons)

TIP Most recipes call for 110°F milk or water to activate yeast. One way to tell if you're at the right spot is to dip your finger in the liquid: It should feel warm but not hot. If you have a thermometer, it's a good idea to double-check, because if your water is too cold, the yeast won't activate, and if it's too hot, it may kill the yeast—either way, it can result in a dough that doesn't rise.

1. In a small saucepan, combine the milk, sugar, butter, and salt. Warm over medium heat, stirring frequently, until the sugar has melted and the mixture comes to a low simmer. Remove the pan from the heat and transfer the mixture to a small bowl. Let cool until warm but not hot, about 110°F. Whisk in the egg until well combined.

2. In a stand mixer fitted with the dough hook (or in large bowl if you're kneading by hand, see page 234), whisk together the flour and yeast. Add the warm milk mixture and mix until just combined. Set the mixer to medium-low speed and knead the dough until smooth and elastic, about 6 minutes (or up to 15 minutes if you're kneading by hand). Grease a large bowl lightly with butter and place the dough in it. Cover the bowl with plastic wrap and set the dough aside in a warm, draft-free spot (if your kitchen is cold, the top of the refrigerator is usually a warm spot, or you can place the bowl in the oven—just be sure to not turn it on!) until the dough has doubled in size, 1½ to 2 hours.

3. Press down on the dough to deflate it and transfer it to a lightly floured work surface. At this point, it's ready to be shaped into sticky buns, monkey bread, or doughnuts.

CINNAMON-SUGAR
STICKY BUNS
WITH CREAM CHEESE ICING

With a gooey ribbon of brown sugar and cinnamon caramel running through the center, these sticky buns are the ultimate breakfast indulgence. When she bakes them, Cydney from Season 5 uses a secret weapon to get each slice just right: dental floss! Here's how it works: After you've rolled the dough into a log, slide a long strand of (unflavored!) floss underneath the log and at right angles to it. Position the strand wherever you'd like to make a cut, then pull it taut, cross the ends of the floss over each other, and pull. Presto: a perfectly neat slice!

MAKES 16 STICKY BUNS

STICKY BUNS

Sweet Yeast Dough (page 93)
1½ sticks (6 ounces) unsalted
    butter
1½ cups packed dark brown sugar
3 tablespoons light corn syrup
1½ teaspoons ground cinnamon
¼ teaspoon kosher salt
1 large egg, beaten
All-purpose flour, for shaping

CREAM CHEESE ICING

4 ounces cream cheese, at room
    temperature
1 cup confectioners' sugar
½ teaspoon ground cinnamon
1 tablespoon whole milk

TIP Freeze extra cinnamon buns by letting the second tray of buns cool, wrapping them tightly with foil and stashing them in the freezer for up to 2 months. Before serving, thaw them in the refrigerator overnight before warming them in a 350°F oven.

1. Prepare the sweet yeast dough as directed on page 93.

2. While the dough is rising, in a small saucepan, melt 1 stick (4 ounces) of the butter with 1 cup of the brown sugar and the corn syrup over low heat, stirring often, until smooth. Remove from the heat and divide the mixture evenly between two 8-inch round cake pans, spreading the syrup around so that the surfaces are evenly coated. Set the pans aside.

3. In a small saucepan or in the microwave, melt the remaining 4 tablespoons (½ stick) butter and set aside to cool. In a small bowl, combine the remaining ½ cup brown sugar, the cinnamon, and the salt.

4. Once the dough has doubled in size, gently punch it down and transfer it to a lightly floured work surface. Roll it into an 18 × 10-inch rectangle. Brush the melted butter evenly over the surface and sprinkle it evenly with cinnamon–brown sugar mixture, leaving a ½-inch border on all sides. Starting with a long side, roll the dough into a tight log and pinch the top seam to seal. With a serrated knife or a length of dental floss (see headnote), cut the log into 16 even slices. Arrange 1 piece cut-side up in the center of each of the prepared pans, then arrange 7 more pieces around each of the center rolls. Cover the pans

with plastic wrap and set aside in a warm, draft-free spot until the dough has nearly doubled in size again, the edges of the buns are touching, and the pans look full, about 1 hour. (This process is called proofing, and the speed at which it happens depends on the temperature of the room.)

5. Preheat the oven to 375°F.

6. Brush the surface of the buns with the beaten egg and bake until the buns are puffed and golden, the filling is bubbling, and the internal temperature reads 190°F on an instant-read thermometer, 25 to 30 minutes.

7. Make the cream cheese icing: In a medium bowl, using an electric mixer, beat the cream cheese, confectioners' sugar, and cinnamon on medium-high speed until smooth. Add the milk to thin the icing and beat until smooth.

8. Remove the buns from the oven and run a knife around the edges of the pans to loosen the sticky edges. Using oven mitts, carefully invert the pans and turn the buns onto two dishes or a parchment-lined baking sheet. (Be very careful, as the sugar syrup will be *extremely* hot: You may want to ask an adult for help.) Use a silicone spatula to scrape any glaze still in the pans onto the buns. Drizzle the buns lightly with the icing and serve warm or at room temperature. The buns will be best the day they are made, but leftovers can be wrapped tightly in plastic wrap and stored at room temperature for up to 2 days.

CHOCOLATE-CINNAMON
MONKEY BREAD

This festive treat is a longtime Christmas-morning tradition in Mikey's (Season 6) family. "Every year we pile in the car after opening gifts and head to my grandparents house for breakfast and everyone's favorite, sticky monkey bread," he says. "It's always a fight for the last piece!" A cinnamon-sugar coating is the classic way to finish monkey bread, but, like a holiday present, our version also has an extra surprise tucked into every bite: a warm, melty chocolate kiss!

SERVES 8 TO 10

Sweet Yeast Dough (page 93)

1 cup packed light brown sugar

1 tablespoon unsweetened Dutch-process cocoa powder

1 teaspoon plus 1 tablespoon ground cinnamon

Nonstick pan spray

1½ sticks (6 ounces) unsalted butter, melted

1 (12-ounce) bag chocolate kisses, unwrapped

3 tablespoons granulated sugar

1. Prepare the sweet yeast dough as directed on page 93.

2. In a shallow bowl, whisk together the brown sugar, cocoa powder, and 1 teaspoon of the cinnamon.

3. Coat a 10- to 12-cup Bundt pan lightly with pan spray. Pour ½ cup of the melted butter into a small bowl. After punching down the dough, divide it into about 50 small pieces, 1½ to 2 tablespoons each. Place 1 chocolate kiss in the center of each piece and roll the dough around it to form a ball with the kiss sealed inside. Lightly dip each ball in the melted butter, then roll in the brown sugar–cocoa mixture. Place the balls seam-side down in the prepared pan, stacking them until all the dough has been used. Cover the pan loosely with plastic wrap and set in a warm place until the dough is springy to the touch and nearly doubled in size again, 45 minutes to 1½ hours.

4. Preheat the oven to 350°F.

5. Uncover the pan (discard the plastic) and transfer it to the oven. Bake until the bread is golden brown, sounds hollow when tapped, and the internal temperature reads 190°F on an instant-read thermometer, 35 to 40 minutes. (Check the pan occasionally during baking: If the bread looks like it is browning quickly but is still not completely cooked through, tent the top with foil.)

6. Meanwhile, in a bowl, combine the granulated sugar and the remaining 1 tablespoon cinnamon. Set the cinnamon-sugar aside.

7. Remove the pan from oven and let the bread rest in the pan for 5 minutes. Then center a large plate or platter over the pan, and, using oven mitts, hold the two together and quickly flip them so that the pan is inverted and the bread releases onto the plate. (Be very careful, as the sugar syrup will be *extremely* hot: You may want to ask an adult for help!) Brush the monkey bread with the remaining melted butter and sprinkle generously with the cinnamon-sugar. Serve warm. Monkey bread is best the day it is made, but any leftovers can be wrapped tightly in plastic wrap and stored at room temperature for up to 2 days.

BAKED HONEY-VANILLA
DOUGHNUTS
WITH GREEN TEA AND CHOCOLATE ICINGS

These delectable doughnuts won raves from the judges—and helped
Remy clinch the victory in the Season 6 no-sugar challenge. Gordon
called her use of honey instead of refined sugar as a sweetener
"groundbreaking" and Christina said she was super impressed that
Remy had been able to make such delicious, decadent doughnuts
without going near a deep fryer. On the show, Remy used both a rich
chocolate and a sophisticated matcha (green tea) icing to decorate
her batch. Both options are included here; you can choose whichever
you like or mix-and-match. (Both icings should yield enough for all
the doughnuts.) Because the doughnuts are baked, to make the recipe
you will have to invest in doughnut pans (which are sort of like muffin
tins with doughnut-shaped cavities). But once you realize how easy it
is to whip up a dozen doughnuts whenever a craving strikes, chances
are you'll get plenty of use out of them!

MAKES 12 DOUGHNUTS

SEASON 6

REMY

DOUGHNUTS

Nonstick pan spray

2 cups all-purpose flour

2 teaspoons baking powder

1 teaspoon kosher salt

2 large eggs

¾ cup heavy cream

½ cup honey

1 tablespoon unsalted butter,
   melted

1 vanilla bean, split lengthwise

GREEN TEA ICING

4 ounces cream cheese, at room
   temperature

1 tablespoon honey

1 teaspoon matcha powder
   (green tea powder)

Freeze-dried strawberries,
   crumbled, for garnish

CHOCOLATE ICING

1 cup bittersweet chocolate chips

1 teaspoon honey

½ cup heavy cream

Toasted coconut flakes, for
   garnish

1. Make the doughnuts: Preheat the oven to 350°F. Spray two 6-cavity nonstick metal doughnut pans with pan spray.

2. In a medium bowl, whisk together the flour, baking powder, and salt.

3. In a large bowl, combine the eggs, cream, honey, and melted butter. With the tip of a paring knife, scrape the vanilla seeds out of the pod into the bowl. Using an electric mixer fitted with the whisk attachment, beat on medium speed until the mixture is pale, smooth, and slightly thickened, about 3 minutes. Reduce the speed to low and slowly add the flour mixture, beating until incorporated.

4. Spoon the batter into a pastry bag fitted with a small plain tip. (If you don't have a pastry bag, you can improvise one by snipping off a small corner of a large zip-top storage bag.) Pipe the batter into the prepared doughnut pans. Bake until the doughnuts are lightly golden and spring back when touched, about 14 minutes. Let the doughnuts rest in the pan for 5 minutes, then turn them out onto a wire rack to cool completely.

5. Make your choice of icing: For the green tea icing, in a medium bowl, using an electric mixer, beat the cream cheese, honey, matcha powder, and 6 tablespoons warm water until completely smooth, about 1 minute. For the chocolate icing, in a heatproof medium bowl, combine the chocolate chips and honey. In a small saucepan, bring the cream to a simmer over medium heat. Pour the hot cream over the chocolate chips and honey and let stand for 1 minute, then stir until smooth.

6. Dip the tops of the cooled doughnuts in the icing of your choice. Garnish the green tea doughnuts with freeze-dried raspberries and the chocolate doughnuts with toasted coconut flakes.

GLAZED AND SUGARED
JELLY DOUGHNUTS

Get the hang of this recipe and you'll be able to have doughnut shop-quality treats anytime you want! Donovan from Season 5 says he likes all kinds of doughnuts, but jelly is his all-time favorite. Of course, you can fill these dunkers with whatever you like—in addition to jelly, lemon curd, apple butter, or homemade Pastry Cream (page 211) would all be delicious options. Until you get comfortable with the process, you'll probably want to ask an adult to help you with frying—for crispy, golden doughnuts, the oil needs to be very hot!

MAKES 16 TO 18 DOUGHNUTS

Sweet Yeast Dough (page 93)

All-purpose flour, for shaping

Vegetable oil, for deep-frying

1¼ cups seedless jelly, apple butter, lemon curd, or pastry cream

1 cup confectioners' sugar, plus more for dusting

1. Prepare the sweet yeast dough as directed on page 93.

2. Line two baking sheets with parchment paper. After gently punching down the dough, transfer it to a floured work surface and roll it into a 12 × 17-inch rectangle about ⅓ inch thick. Using a 3-inch round cutter, cut out rounds and place them on the prepared baking sheets. Cover the baking sheets lightly with plastic wrap and let the dough rest in a warm, draft-free spot until the rounds are springy to the touch and nearly doubled in size again, 45 minutes to 1½ hours. (This process is called proofing and the speed at which it happens depends on the temperature of the room.)

3. Prepare to fry: Line a wire rack with paper towels. Pour at least 2 inches of vegetable oil into a large, deep, heavy-bottomed pot (the amount of oil you need depends on the size of your pot) and heat the oil over medium-high heat until a pinch of flour sizzles when you drop it into the oil or a candy thermometer reads 360°F.

4. Add the doughnuts to the oil two at a time. (If you add too many at once, they'll get crowded and the oil will drop sharply in temperature, meaning the doughnuts won't fry properly.) Fry the doughnuts, flipping them once, until puffed and golden brown, about 1½ minutes per side. Using a slotted spoon or a

Step 1: Fry the doughnuts, flipping once, until puffed and golden. Do not crowd the pot.

Step 2: When doughnuts are cool enough to handle, use a pastry bag to fill with the filling of your choice.

Step 3: Brush warm doughnuts with glaze before dusting with confectioners' sugar.

fine-mesh skimmer, lift the doughnuts out of the oil, letting the excess oil drain back into the pot, then transfer them to the lined wire rack to drain, and let rest until cool enough to handle. Check the oil's temperature—you want it at 360°F, so adjust the heat accordingly before frying the remaining dough.

5. To fill the doughnuts, place the jelly in a small bowl and whisk until smooth. Spoon it into a pastry bag fitted with a medium round tip. (If you don't have a pastry bag, you can improvise one by snipping off a small corner of a large zip-top storage bag.) Using a chopstick or a skinny round handle of a wooden spoon, poke a hole into one side of each doughnut, making sure not to punch through to the other side. Remove the chopstick, then insert the tip of the bag into each doughnut and squeeze until just filled.

6. In a small bowl, whisk together the confectioners' sugar and 3 tablespoons water until smooth. Using a pastry brush, brush the glaze over both sides of the warm, filled doughnuts until they are shiny. Let the glaze set for 10 minutes, then dust with additional confectioners' sugar. Serve immediately. The doughnuts will be best the day they are made, but if you have leftovers, they can be covered loosely in a paper bag or plastic wrap and stored at room temperature (for jelly fillings) or in the refrigerator (for cream fillings) for up to 2 days.

CUPCAKES

Orange Spice Doodle
Cupcakes with Cinnamon
Buttercream, page 104

ORANGE SPICE DOODLE CUPCAKES
WITH CINNAMON BUTTERCREAM

These whimsical, gently spiced cupcakes by Malia and Jaala wowed the judges during the Season 7 cupcake challenge with their unexpected and elegant good looks and perfectly balanced flavors. Christina was especially impressed by Malia's piping skills, which she called "visually A+!" To make playful orange zigzags to top the cupcakes, the girls use candy melts, which (as their name suggests) melt easily and smoothly and are useful when making decorative confections. Candy melts come in all sorts of colors and look sort of like big chocolate chips; you can find them online or in most baking or craft supply stores.

MAKES 12 CUPCAKES • **See photograph on page 103**

SEASON 7

CUPCAKES

2½ cups all-purpose flour

1 teaspoon baking powder

1 teaspoon kosher salt

2 sticks (8 ounces) unsalted butter, at room temperature

1½ cups granulated sugar

2 large eggs

3 large egg yolks

1 teaspoon pure vanilla extract

1 teaspoon orange extract

½ teaspoon fresh lemon juice

1½ teaspoons finely grated orange zest

1 cup whole milk

CINNAMON-VANILLA BUTTERCREAM

2 sticks (8 ounces) unsalted butter, at room temperature

1 teaspoon pure vanilla extract

4 cups confectioners' sugar

2 teaspoons ground cinnamon

DECORATIONS

¾ cup orange candy melts

6 chocolate cream–filled straw cookies (such as Pirouttes), halved

White chocolate curls (see Tip)

Dark chocolate curls (see Tip)

TIP You can buy chocolate curls at craft stores and cake decorating supply shops, but it's also fun (and easy!) to make your own. For small curls, like the ones used in this recipe, simply draw a vegetable peeler steadily and smoothly along the edge of a bar of chocolate so that the chocolate comes away in a curling ribbon. For the best results, before beginning, make sure the bar is slightly warm, but not melting. Once the curls are formed, spread them on a plate or a small tray and refrigerate until you need them.

1. Make the cupcakes: Preheat the oven to 350°F. Line a 12-cup muffin tin with paper liners.

2. In a medium bowl, whisk together the flour, baking powder, and salt.

3. In a large bowl, using an electric mixer with the paddle attachment, beat the butter and granulated sugar on medium-high speed until light and fluffy, about 5 minutes. Reduce the mixer speed to medium-low and add the whole eggs and egg yolks one at a time, pausing to scrape down the sides and bottom of the bowl as needed. Beat in the vanilla, orange extract, lemon juice, and orange zest. Reduce the mixer speed to low and add the flour mixture in three additions, alternating with the milk, beginning and ending with the flour. Beat until just combined.

4. Divide the batter evenly among the prepared muffin cups, filling each three-quarters full. Bake until the tops feel springy and a toothpick inserted into the largest cupcake comes out clean, 20 to 22 minutes. Let the cupcakes rest in the pans for 5 minutes, then transfer them to a wire rack to cool completely.

5. Make the cinnamon-vanilla buttercream: In a large bowl, using an electric mixer fitted with the paddle attachment, beat the butter and vanilla on medium-high speed until light and fluffy, about 2 minutes. Reduce the mixer speed to low and add the confectioners' sugar ½ cup at a time, beating well after each addition. Add the cinnamon and beat on high until the frosting is smooth, about 20 seconds. Cover and refrigerate the frosting until ready to use. (Buttercream will stiffen as it chills; to get it back to spreading consistency, give it time to come to cool room temperature before loosening it up with a whisk or an electric mixer.)

6. Make the decorations: Put the orange candy melts in a microwave-safe bowl and microwave on medium for 40 seconds. Stir the candy, then microwave until completely smooth, 15 to 20 seconds more. Spoon the mixture into a pastry bag fitted with a small plain tip. Pipe 12 small decorative zigzag or squiggle designs onto a sheet of parchment paper. Set aside until cooled and hardened.

7. When the cupcakes are completely cool, use a pastry bag fitted with a small plain tip or a small spoon or spatula to frost each cupcake with the buttercream. Garnish each one with a candy melt design, a chocolate straw cookie, and white and dark chocolate curls.

GERMAN CHOCOLATE
CUPCAKES
WITH GANACHE FILLING
AND PECAN-COCONUT FROSTING

Evan chose these sweet, nutty, and deeply fudgy cupcakes as his dish for the Season 6 chocolate ingredient challenge. When you bite into one, you get three layers of deliciousness: tender cake, a gooey chocolate ganache filling, and gobs of rich coconut-praline frosting. Traditionally, German chocolate cake batter is made with sweetened chocolate, but you can substitute an equal weight of bittersweet chocolate if that's what you have at home. But the best part of German chocolate cake may be that the batter is as simple to make as it is scrumptious!

MAKES 18 CUPCAKES

SEASON 6

EVAN

CHOCOLATE CUPCAKES

2 cups all-purpose flour

1 teaspoon baking soda

¼ teaspoon kosher salt

5 ounces sweet chocolate baking bar (such as Baker's German's), chopped

1½ sticks (6 ounces) unsalted butter

1⅓ cups granulated sugar

1 teaspoon pure vanilla extract

3 large eggs

1 cup buttermilk

GANACHE FILLING

1 cup bittersweet chocolate chips

½ cup heavy cream

1 tablespoon unsalted butter

⅛ teaspoon kosher salt

PECAN-COCONUT FROSTING

1 (14-ounce) can sweetened condensed milk

4 large egg yolks

1 cup packed dark brown sugar

1½ teaspoons pure vanilla extract

1 teaspoon kosher salt

1¾ cups chopped toasted pecans

2 cups sweetened coconut flakes, toasted

¼ cup sweetened coconut flakes, toasted, for garnish

36 whole pecan halves, toasted, for garnish

1. Make the chocolate cupcakes: Position racks in the upper and lower thirds of the oven and preheat the oven to 350°F. Line 18 cups of two standard muffin tins with paper liners.

2. In a medium bowl, combine the flour, baking soda, and salt.

3. Set a large heatproof bowl over a pan of simmering water (be sure the bottom of the bowl does not touch the water). Combine the chocolate and butter in the bowl and heat, stirring, until melted and completely smooth. Remove the bowl

from the heat. Add the granulated sugar and stir until smooth. Add the vanilla and eggs, one at a time, stirring after each addition. Using a rubber spatula, gently stir the flour mixture into the chocolate mixture in two batches, alternating with the buttermilk, and mix until just combined.

4. Divide the batter evenly among the prepared muffin cups, filling each three-quarters full. Bake, rotating the pans from the top to bottom rack and from front to back once halfway through, until the tops are springy to the touch and a toothpick inserted into the center of the largest cupcake comes out clean, about 20 minutes. Let the cupcakes rest in the pans for 5 minutes, then transfer them to a wire rack to cool completely.

5. Make the ganache filling: Place the chocolate chips in a heatproof medium bowl. In a small saucepan, bring the heavy cream and butter to a simmer over medium heat. Pour the hot cream mixture over the chocolate chips and let stand for 1 minute, then stir until smooth. Stir in the salt. Let cool at room temperature, then transfer to the refrigerator to chill until the ganache is the consistency of toothpaste, at least 30 minutes. (The ganache will stiffen more the longer it chills; if yours becomes too stiff handle, loosen it by microwaving it on high in 10-second bursts, stirring after each, until you reach the desired consistency.)

6. Make the pecan frosting: In a large saucepan, whisk together the condensed milk, egg yolks, brown sugar, vanilla, and salt until smooth. Cook the mixture over medium heat, stirring often, until small bubbles appear at the edges of the pan and the mixture comes to just shy of a boil, about 3 minutes. Reduce the heat and cook, stirring almost constantly, until the mixture is thick, sticky. and deeply golden, about 8 minutes more. Remove from the heat. Stir in the pecans and coconut. Let cool.

7. When the cupcakes are completely cool, cut a grape-size hole in the top of each one, removing a bit of the cupcake. Fill the holes with the ganache filling. Use a spoon or a small offset spatula to frost each cupcake with the pecan frosting. Sprinkle the cupcakes with the toasted coconut and garnish each one with 2 pecan halves.

HOW TO MAKE GANACHE

Ganache—a mixture of melted chocolate and cream—is a secret weapon of pastry chefs everywhere and a favorite of the contestants in the *MasterChef Junior* kitchen, too. It's easy to see why: The recipe is as easy as it is versatile!

There are probably 1,001 ways to use ganache, but some of the most common are as icing for cakes and cupcakes, a filling for tarts and pastries, and a base for homemade truffles. Though the basic ingredients in ganache are the same no matter how you use it, the proportions do vary depending on how thick or drizzly you want it to be. Here are three basic formulas—plus a few helpful tips—that are guaranteed to come in handy on your baking adventures.

Important note: The ratios that follow refer to *weight*, not volume—so if you have a kitchen scale, this is a great time to use it. But if you don't have one, just remember that 1 cup chopped chocolate/chocolate chips weighs roughly 6 ounces. Now you're good to go!

GANACHE GLAZE

Best for: pouring over cakes and drizzling on ice cream
Ratio: 1 part chocolate to 2 parts cream

Place 6 ounces (1 cup) chopped chocolate or chocolate chips in a heatproof medium bowl. In a small saucepan, bring 12 ounces (1½ cups) heavy cream to a simmer over medium heat. Pour the hot cream over the chocolate and let stand for 1 minute, then stir until smooth. Stir in ¼ teaspoon kosher salt.

GANACHE FILLING AND ICING

Best for: filling tart shells, sandwiching between cookies or cake layers, and piping into éclairs or cupcakes
Ratio: 1 part chocolate to 1 part cream

Place 6 ounces (1 cup) chopped chocolate or chocolate chips in a heatproof medium bowl. In a small saucepan, bring 6 ounces (¾ cup) heavy cream to a simmer over medium heat. Pour the hot cream over the chocolate and let stand for 1 minute, then stir until smooth. Stir in ¼ teaspoon kosher salt. Let cool at room temperature until spreadable.

GANACHE TRUFFLES

Best for: homemade candy
Ratio: 2 parts chocolate to 1 part cream

Place 12 ounces (2 cups) chopped chocolate or chocolate chips in a heatproof medium bowl. In a small saucepan, bring 6 ounces (¾ cup) heavy cream to a simmer over medium heat. Pour the hot cream over the chocolate chips and let stand for 1 minute, then stir until smooth. Stir in ¼ teaspoon kosher salt. Transfer the mixture to a shallow dish and cover. Refrigerate until very firm, then use a spoon to scoop the ganache into balls (about 2 tablespoon each). Use your hands to roll the balls smooth. Dust each one with cocoa powder or the coating of your choice.

1

2

A

B

C

Step 1: Pour the hot cream over the chopped chocolate.

Step 2: Stir until smooth.

A: Ganache glaze Drizzle over ice cream or cake (page 108 for A–C).

B: Ganache filling Perfect for filling tarts, making sandwich cookies, or frosting cake and cupcakes.

C: Thick, chilled ganache Roll into balls and coat in cocoa for truffles.

FLAVORING GANACHE

Infuse your ganache with flavor by steeping tea or citrus zest (or both) in the cream for 10 minutes, then strain the cream through a fine-mesh sieve into the chocolate. You can also stir a few drops of liqueur or extracts like vanilla, mint, or almond into the warm cream, too.

STORING GANACHE

Scrape any leftover ganache into an airtight container and refrigerate it for up to 3 days. To reheat it, return it to a bowl set over a pan of simmering water and stir it slowly until it reaches the desired consistency. Or microwave on high in 10-second bursts, stirring until smooth.

ORANGE BLOSSOM
CUPCAKES
WITH HONEY BUTTERCREAM AND CANDIED ORANGES

Our contestants do some crazy things in the name of food and fun! Having to work with one leg tied to her partner didn't stop Adaiah from wowing the judges with these delicate honey-frosted cupcakes during the Season 2 cupcake challenge. In this version, four layers of orange flavor in the batter—fresh juice, grated zest, extract, and orange blossom water—create a complex, fragrant citrus cake. The candied dried orange slices on top may look fancy (and they take 2½ hours to bake, so plan accordingly), but they're actually very simple to make—and can even be made up to 3 days ahead. They're versatile, too: You can use them to garnish other desserts, like the Chocolate-Citrus Olive Oil Cake with Orange Glaze and Whipped Ricotta (page 150), for a little extra flair and whimsy.

MAKES 18 CUPCAKES

CANDIED ORANGE SLICES

2 navel oranges, thinly sliced into rounds

¼ cup granulated sugar

ORANGE BLOSSOM CUPCAKES

2½ cups all-purpose flour

1⅓ cups granulated sugar

1½ teaspoons baking soda

1 teaspoon baking powder

½ teaspoon kosher salt

¾ cup canola oil

2 teaspoons finely grated orange zest

1 cup fresh orange juice

2 large eggs

1 cup sour cream

2 teaspoons orange blossom water

1½ teaspoons orange extract

HONEY BUTTERCREAM

2 sticks (8 ounces) unsalted butter, at room temperature

5 cups confectioners' sugar

⅓ cup honey

⅓ cup sour cream

¼ teaspoon kosher salt

TIP Orange blossom water (sometimes called orange flower water) is a flavor extract that comes from the blossoms of the bitter orange tree. It adds a lovely subtle floral flavor to baked goods and creams, but if you don't have any on hand, you can usually substitute an equal amount of fresh orange juice.

1. Make the candied orange slices: Preheat the oven to 200°F. Line a baking sheet with parchment paper and place the orange slices on the baking sheet in a single layer. Sprinkle them lightly with the granulated sugar. Bake until the peels are stiff and dry, about 2½ hours. (If you would like to make the orange slices ahead, they will keep in an airtight container for up to 3 days.)

2. Make the orange blossom cupcakes: Position racks in the upper and lower thirds of the oven and preheat the oven to 350°F. Line 18 cups of two standard muffin tins with paper liners.

3. In a medium bowl, whisk together the flour, granulated sugar, baking soda, baking powder, and salt.

4. In a large bowl, using an electric mixer fitted with the whisk attachment, beat the oil, orange zest, orange juice, eggs, and sour cream until smooth and glossy, about 2 minutes. Add the orange blossom water and orange extract and beat to combine. Reduce the mixer speed to low and add the flour mixture in two additions, beating until just combined, using a rubber spatula to scrape down the sides and bottom of the bowl. Divide the batter evenly among the prepared muffin cups, filling each three-quarters full.

5. Bake the cupcakes, rotating the pans from the top to bottom rack and from front to back once halfway through, until the tops feel springy and a toothpick inserted into the largest cupcake comes out clean, about 20 minutes. Remove the cupcakes from the oven and let them rest in the pans for 5 minutes, then transfer them to a wire rack to cool completely.

6. Make the honey buttercream: In a large bowl, using an electric mixer, beat the butter on medium-high speed until light and fluffy, about 2 minutes. Reduce the speed to low and add the confectioners' sugar ½ cup at a time, beating well after each addition. Add the honey, sour cream, and salt and beat on high until the frosting is smooth, about 30 seconds. Cover and refrigerate until you're ready to frost the cupcakes. (The buttercream will stiffen as it chills; to get it back to spreading consistency, give it time to come to cool room temperature before loosening it up with a whisk or an electric mixer.)

7. When the cupcakes are completely cool, use a small offset spatula, spoon, or pastry bag fitted with a small plain tip to frost them with the buttercream. Decorate the cupcakes with frosting swirls and then finish each one with a candied orange slice.

VANILLA BEAN CUPCAKES
WITH PINEAPPLE PUREE AND FRUIT COCKTAIL BUTTERCREAM

SEASON 6

When Quani presented these elegant cupcakes to the judges during the Season 6 canned food challenge, they could hardly believe that what had begun as such humble ingredients became such an adorable, showstopping dessert! The tender vanilla cake and the fruity buttercream are lovely on their own, but when you bite in you find another delicious surprise: a pocket of tropical pineapple, filling. All of it adds up to a dish that is, in the words of judge Gordon Ramsay, "fragrant, sweet, and absolutely spot on."

MAKES 18 CUPCAKES

CUPCAKES

2½ cups all-purpose flour

2 teaspoons baking powder

¼ teaspoon kosher salt

1½ sticks (6 ounces) unsalted butter, at room temperature

1¼ cups granulated sugar

2 large eggs

1 vanilla bean, split lengthwise

1¼ cups whole milk

PINEAPPLE PUREE

1 cup drained canned crushed pineapple

¼ cup granulated sugar

1 tablespoon cornstarch

1 tablespoon unsalted butter

¼ teaspoon ground ginger

FRUIT COCKTAIL BUTTERCREAM

1 (8.5-ounce) can fruit cocktail, undrained

2 sticks (8 ounces) unsalted butter, at room temperature

4 cups confectioners' sugar

1 teaspoon pure vanilla extract

⅛ teaspoon kosher salt

ASSEMBLY

18 dried pineapple slices

18 maraschino cherries with stems

1. Make the cupcakes: Position racks in the upper and lower thirds of the oven and preheat the oven to 375°F. Line 18 cups of two standard muffin tins with paper liners.

2. In a medium bowl, whisk together the flour, baking powder, and salt.

3. In a large bowl, using an electric mixer fitted with the paddle attachment, beat the butter and granulated sugar on medium-high speed until light and fluffy, about 5 minutes. Add the eggs, one at a time, beating well after each addition and scraping

down the bowl as needed. (Don't worry if the batter looks a bit curdled; it will come together when you add the flour.) With the tip of a paring knife, scrape the vanilla seeds out of the vanilla bean into the bowl. Add the milk and beat to combine. Reduce the speed to low and gradually beat in the flour mixture until just combined, scraping the bottom and sides of the bowl as needed. Divide the batter among the prepared muffin cups, filling each three-quarters full.

4. Bake the cupcakes, rotating the pans from the top to bottom rack and from front to back once halfway through, until golden and a toothpick inserted into the center of the largest cupcake comes out clean, 16 to 18 minutes. Let the cupcakes rest in the pans for 5 minutes, then transfer them to a wire rack to cool completely.

5. Meanwhile, make the pineapple puree: In a medium saucepan, combine the crushed pineapple, granulated sugar, cornstarch, and butter. Cook over medium heat, stirring frequently, until bubbling and thickened to the consistency of chunky applesauce, about 6 minutes. Remove from the heat, stir in the ginger, scrape the puree into a small bowl, and set aside to cool completely.

6. Make the fruit cocktail buttercream: In a blender or food processor, puree the fruit cocktail (with its juice) until smooth. In a large bowl, using an electric mixer fitted with the paddle attachment, beat the butter on high speed until light and creamy, about 2 minutes. Reduce the speed to medium-low and add the confectioners' sugar about ½ cup at a time, beating well after each addition.

Add ¼ cup of the fruit cocktail puree and the vanilla and beat on high speed for 10 seconds, until the frosting is smooth. Cover and refrigerate until ready to use. (The buttercream will stiffen as it chills; to get it back to spreading consistency, give it time to come to cool room temperature before loosening it up with a whisk or an electric mixer.)

7. Assemble the cupcakes: When the cupcakes are completely cool, cut a grape-size hole in the top of each one, removing a bit of the cupcake. Fill the holes with the pineapple puree. Use a small offset spatula, spoon, or pastry bag fitted with a small plain tip to frost each cupcake with the buttercream. Garnish each one with a slice of dried pineapple and a maraschino cherry.

MINI CHOCOLATE CHIP
CUPCAKES
WITH ESPRESSO BUTTERCREAM

The combination of vanilla-scented cake studded with tiny chocolate chips and topped with buzzy espresso buttercream is one of Avani's signature treats. Cake flour gives these mini cupcakes a delicate crumb, but if you don't have any on hand, just remember this clever trick: To substitute all-purpose flour for cake flour, subtract 2 tablespoons of flour from every cup, replace it with cornstarch, and sift until well blended.

MAKES 48 MINI CUPCAKES

CUPCAKES

2 cups cake flour

1 teaspoon baking powder

¼ teaspoon kosher salt

1½ sticks (6 ounces) unsalted butter, at room temperature

1 cup granulated sugar

2 teaspoons vanilla extract

3 large eggs, at room temperature

¾ cup buttermilk

⅔ cup mini chocolate chips

ESPRESSO BUTTERCREAM

1½ sticks (6 ounces) unsalted butter, at room temperature

1 teaspoon finely ground espresso powder

2½ cups confectioners' sugar

1 teaspoon pure vanilla extract

⅛ teaspoon kosher salt

1 tablespoon whole milk

Chocolate-covered espresso beans, for garnish

1. Make the cupcakes: Position racks in the upper and lower thirds of the oven and preheat the oven to 325°F. Line two 24-cup mini-muffin tins with paper liners.

2. In a medium bowl, whisk together the cake flour, baking powder, and salt.

3. In a large bowl, using an electric mixer fitted with the paddle attachment, beat the butter and granulated sugar on medium-high speed until pale and fluffy, about 5 minutes. Reduce the mixer speed to medium-low and add the vanilla and eggs, one at a time, beating well after each addition and scraping down the sides and bottom of the bowl as needed. Add the flour mixture in three additions, alternating with the buttermilk, beginning and ending with the flour. Beat until the batter is just combined. Use a rubber spatula to fold in the mini chocolate chips.

4. Spoon the batter into the prepared mini-muffin cups, filling each three-quarters full. Bake until the cupcakes are domed and golden and a toothpick inserted into the center comes out clean, 10 to 15 minutes. Let the cupcakes rest in the pans for 5 minutes, then transfer them to a wire rack to cool completely.

5. Make the espresso buttercream: In a large bowl, using an electric mixer fitted with the paddle attachment, beat the butter on medium-high speed until smooth and creamy, about 2 minutes. Reduce the speed to medium-low and beat in the espresso powder and confectioners' sugar, about ½ cup at a time, beating well after each addition. Add the vanilla, salt, and milk and beat until smooth, about 30 seconds. Cover the bowl with plastic wrap and refrigerate until ready to use. (The buttercream will stiffen as it chills; to get it back to spreading consistency, give it time to come to cool room temperature before loosening it up with a whisk or an electric mixer.)

6. When the cupcakes are completely cool, use a small offset spatula, spoon, or pastry bag fitted with a small plain tip to frost each cupcake with the buttercream. Garnish with chocolate-covered espresso beans.

DARK CHOCOLATE CUPCAKES
WITH SMOKY STRAWBERRY COMPOTE AND SPICED BUTTERCREAM

In the Season 5 cupcake challenge, Adam showed off his mad-scientist side and impressed judge Gordon Ramsay when he decided to set up an indoor smoker to infuse his baking spices. To simplify things a bit for the home kitchen without sacrificing the complex flavor, this version uses a bit of store-bought smoked paprika to give the fresh strawberry compote a smoky, sophisticated edge that pairs beautifully with the dark chocolate.

MAKES 18 CUPCAKES

SEASON 5

DARK CHOCOLATE CUPCAKES

1¾ cups all-purpose flour

¾ cup unsweetened Dutch-process cocoa powder

1 tablespoon espresso powder

1½ teaspoons baking powder

1 teaspoon kosher salt

1 stick (4 ounces) unsalted butter, at room temperature

2 cups granulated sugar

2 large eggs, at room temperature

1 cup buttermilk

1 teaspoon pure vanilla extract

SMOKY STRAWBERRY COMPOTE

2 cups fresh or frozen sliced strawberries (thawed if frozen)

3 tablespoons fresh lemon juice

1 tablespoon granulated sugar

1 teaspoon smoked paprika

SPICED BUTTERCREAM

4 cups confectioners' sugar

½ cup unsweetened Dutch-process cocoa powder

1½ teaspoons ground cinnamon

¼ teaspoon nutmeg, preferably freshly grated

⅛ teaspoon cayenne pepper

2 sticks (8 ounces) unsalted butter, at room temperature

¼ cup whole milk

Crushed freeze-dried strawberries, for garnish

1. Make the dark chocolate cupcakes: Position racks in the upper and lower thirds of the oven and preheat the oven to 375°F. Line 18 cups of two standard muffin tins with paper liners.

2. In a medium bowl, whisk together the flour, cocoa powder, espresso powder, baking powder, and salt.

3. In a large bowl, using an electric mixer with the paddle attachment, beat the butter and granulated sugar on medium-high speed until light and fluffy, about 5 minutes. Reduce the speed to medium-low and add the eggs one at a time, beating well after each addition. Beat in the buttermilk and vanilla. Reduce the speed to low and gradually beat in the flour mixture until just combined and no streaks of flour are visible.

4. Divide the batter among the prepared muffin cups, filling each three-quarters full. Bake, rotating the pans from the top to bottom rack and front to back once halfway through, until puffed and set and a toothpick inserted into the center of a cupcake comes out clean, 12 to 15 minutes. Let the cupcakes rest in the pans for 5 minutes, then transfer them to a wire rack to cool completely.

5. Make the strawberry compote: In a small saucepan, roughly mash the sliced strawberries with a fork or potato masher. Add the lemon juice, granulated sugar, and 3 tablespoons water. Bring the mixture to a simmer over medium heat and cook until thickened and reduced by half, about 15 minutes. Remove from the heat and stir in the smoked paprika. Set aside to cool.

6. Make the spiced buttercream: In a medium bowl, whisk together the confectioners' sugar, cocoa powder, cinnamon, nutmeg, and cayenne. In a large bowl, using an electric mixer fitted with the paddle attachment, beat the butter on medium-high speed until smooth and creamy, about 2 minutes. Reduce the speed to medium-low and gradually add the confectioners' sugar mixture, about ½ cup at a time, beating well after each addition. Add the milk and beat until smooth, about 30 seconds. Cover and refrigerate until ready to use. (The buttercream will stiffen as it chills; to get it back to spreading consistency, give it time to come to cool room temperature before loosening it up with a whisk or an electric mixer.)

7. Assemble the cupcakes: When the cupcakes are completely cool, cut a grape-size hole in the top of each one, removing a bit of the cupcake. Fill the holes with the strawberry compote. Use a small offset spatula, spoon, or pastry bag fitted with a plain tip to frost the cupcakes with the spiced buttercream. Garnish each one with a sprinkle of crushed freeze-dried strawberries.

RED VELVET CUPCAKES
WITH MARSHMALLOW BUTTERCREAM

These striking crimson cupcakes are always one of Quani's (from Season 6) first picks when it comes time to choose a birthday treat. Besides their cool color, he says he likes how the unsweetened cocoa powder in the batter gives the cupcakes a light chocolate flavor without being too rich. Using a few scoops of fluffy white marshmallow crème in the buttercream makes the frosting beautifully smooth and light and is the perfect sweet finishing touch.

MAKES 18 CUPCAKES

RED VELVET CUPCAKES

2½ cups self-rising cake flour (see Tip)

¼ cup unsweetened Dutch-process cocoa powder

1 cup plain whole-milk yogurt

1 tablespoon cider vinegar

1 stick (4 ounces) unsalted butter

1⅓ cups granulated sugar

3 large eggs

2 teaspoons pure vanilla extract

1½ tablespoons red gel food coloring

MARSHMALLOW BUTTERCREAM

2 sticks (8 ounces) unsalted butter, at room temperature

1 (7-ounce) jar marshmallow crème (such as Fluff)

1 cup confectioners' sugar

1 teaspoon pure vanilla extract

¼ teaspoon kosher salt

1. Make the red velvet cupcakes: Position racks in the upper and lower thirds of the oven and preheat the oven to 350°F. Line 18 cups of two standard muffin tins with paper liners.

2. In a medium bowl, whisk together the cake flour and cocoa powder. In a separate bowl, whisk together the yogurt and vinegar. Set both aside.

3. In a large bowl, using an electric mixer fitted with the paddle attachment, beat the butter and granulated sugar on medium-high speed until pale and light, about 5 minutes. Reduce the speed to medium-low and add the eggs one at a time, beating well after each addition and scraping down the bowl as needed. Add the vanilla and food coloring and beat until smooth.

4. Reduce the mixer speed to low and add the flour mixture in three batches, alternating with the yogurt mixture, beginning and ending with the flour mixture. Beat until just combined. Stir in 2 tablespoons water.

5. Divide the batter evenly among the prepared muffin cups, filling each three-quarters full. Bake, rotating the pans from the top to bottom rack and front to back once halfway through, until the tops of the cupcakes feel springy and a toothpick inserted into the largest one comes out clean, about 20 minutes. Let the cupcakes rest in the pans for 5 minutes, then transfer them to a wire rack to cool completely.

TIP Can't find self-rising cake flour? Try making your own. For each 1 cup of cake flour you're using, whisk in 1¼ teaspoons baking powder and ¼ teaspoon fine salt, then proceed with the recipe.

6. Make the marshmallow buttercream: In a large bowl, using an electric mixer fitted with the whisk attachment, beat the butter and marshmallow crème on medium-high speed until light and fluffy, about 2 minutes. Reduce the speed to medium-low and add the confectioners' sugar, about ½ cup at a time, beating well after each addition. Add the vanilla and salt and beat for 15 seconds, until the frosting is smooth. Cover and refrigerate until ready to use. (The buttercream will stiffen as it chills; to get it back to spreading consistency, give it time to come to cool room temperature before loosening it up with a whisk or an electric mixer.)

7. When the cupcakes are completely cool, use a small offset spatula, spoon, or a pastry bag fitted with a small plain tip to frost each cupcake with the buttercream swirls.

SALTED CARAMEL
CUPCAKES
WITH SUGAR SWIRLS

During the Season 2 cupcake challenge, judge Joe Bastianich told the contestants that the way a cupcake looks is incredibly important because it tempts the eyes as well as the taste buds. So, when he saw Sean and Logan's cupcakes topped with dramatic caramel swirls, he was really wowed. These cupcakes take the caramel theme and run with it, combining delicate brown sugar cakes with rich salted caramel frosting and an eye-catching spun sugar swirl to finish them off. Making sugar decorations is much easier than it seems (see the MasterChef Lesson, page 122); you can use them as a garnish to elevate all sorts of desserts.

MAKES 18 CUPCAKES

SEASON 2

CARAMEL CUPCAKES

2¼ cups all-purpose flour

2 teaspoons baking powder

½ teaspoon baking soda

½ teaspoon kosher salt

2 sticks (8 ounces) unsalted butter, at room temperature

¾ cup granulated sugar

½ cup packed dark brown sugar

3 large eggs

⅔ cup whole milk

2 teaspoons pure vanilla extract

SALTED CARAMEL FROSTING

2 sticks (8 ounces) unsalted butter, at room temperature

⅓ cup caramel sauce or dulce de leche

4 cups confectioners' sugar

2 tablespoons pure vanilla extract

2 tablespoons whole milk

½ teaspoon kosher salt

SUGAR SWIRLS

1 cup granulated sugar

1. Make the caramel cupcakes: Position racks in the upper and lower thirds of the oven and preheat the oven to 350°F. Line 18 cups of two standard muffin tins with paper liners.

2. In a medium bowl, whisk together the flour, baking powder, baking soda, and salt. Set aside.

3. In a large bowl, using an electric mixer fitted with the paddle attachment, beat the butter, granulated sugar, and brown sugar on medium-high speed until pale and fluffy, about 5 minutes. Reduce the mixer speed to medium-low and add the eggs one at a time, beating well after each addition and

scraping down the bowl as needed. Beat in the milk and vanilla. Reduce the speed to low and beat in the flour mixture until just combined and no streaks of flour are visible.

4. Divide the batter among the prepared muffin cups, filling each three-quarters full. Bake, rotating the pans from the top to bottom rack and front to back once halfway through, until the tops of the cupcakes feel springy and a toothpick inserted into the largest one comes out clean, about 18 minutes. Let the cupcakes rest in the pans for 5 minutes, then transfer them to a wire rack to cool completely.

5. Make the salted caramel frosting: In a large bowl, using an electric mixer fitted with the whisk attachment, beat the butter on medium-high speed until light and creamy, about 2 minutes. Reduce the speed to medium-low, add the caramel sauce, and beat until smooth. Add the confectioners' sugar, about ½ cup at a time, beating well after each addition. Add the vanilla, milk, and salt and beat until light and smooth, about

30 seconds. Cover and refrigerate until ready to use. (The frosting will stiffen as it chills; to get it back to spreading consistency, give it time to come to cool room temperature before loosening it up with a whisk or an electric mixer.)

6. Make the sugar swirls: Line a baking sheet with parchment paper. In a small saucepan, combine the sugar and ⅓ cup water. Cook over medium heat, stirring just until dissolved. Continue cooking, without stirring, until the sugar bubbles and caramelizes and turns a dark amber color, about 10 minutes. Remove from the heat. Carefully dip a spoon into the caramel and drizzle it onto the prepared baking sheet in 24 small swirls. Let the swirls cool until hardened, about 5 minutes, then peel them away from the parchment paper.

7. When the cupcakes are completely cool, use a small offset spatula, spoon, or a pastry bag fitted with a small plain tip to top the cupcakes with the salted caramel frosting. Garnish each one with a sugar swirl.

DECORATING WITH SUGAR

Creating golden brown and almost celestial spun sugar decorations is a super-pro way to add a "wow" restaurant-worthy finish to your desserts.

As fancy as they look, the secret to making sugar garnishes is that they are surprisingly easy to whip up! Once you learn the technique, you can play with all sorts of designs—spirals, stars, hearts, corkscrews, or whatever else strikes your fancy. They'll be beautiful crowning cupcakes, balanced on top of birthday cakes, or perched on top of puddings. And all the method requires is a cupful of sugar, a saucepan, a baking sheet, and a careful cook.

Some rules of thumb to remember:

- It's important to pay close attention throughout the entire process. When sugar melts, it cooks very quickly, and the amount of time it takes to go from perfectly golden to burnt is only moments.
- If you do burn your caramel, you'll know not just by the color (dark!) but also by the bitter smell. The only thing you can do at that point is start over. (Try, try again!)
- If you need to clean burnt or hardened caramel out of your saucepan, try this neat trick: Add more water to the pan and bring the mixture to a simmer. Then watch as the caramel releases from the sides and dissolves in the water— like magic!

Here's the basic method. It yields enough for about 24 small decorations.

1. Line a baking sheet with parchment paper.

2. In a small saucepan, combine 1 cup granulated sugar and ⅓ cup water. Cook the mixture over medium heat, stirring until the sugar dissolves, then stop stirring.

3. Let the sugar cook, undisturbed, until it is bubbling and dark amber in color, about 10 minutes.

4. Remove the pan from the stove. Dip a teaspoon into the caramel (whatever you do, *do not touch* the caramel or drip any on your skin—it is molten hot!). At this point it should be thick and syrupy and run off the spoon in a long strand. If it is too stiff, gently rewarm it over low heat.

5. Working quickly, drizzle the warm caramel onto the prepared baking sheet in the design of your choice. For large sugar "shards," spoon the caramel into large puddles, then let them cool and break them into pieces. To make little sugar domes or "cages," coat the outside of an upturned small bowl or teacup with nonstick pan spray, then drizzle the caramel back and forth in a crisscross pattern over it.

6. Let the designs cool completely, about 10 minutes, then peel them away from the parchment paper. Use immediately or store in an airtight container for up to 5 days.

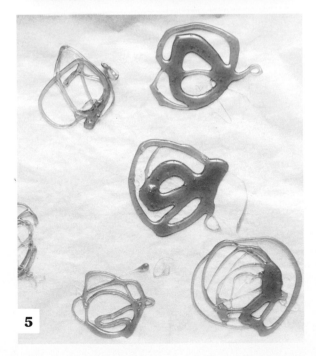

Step 1: Cook the sugar and water over medium heat, stirring until the sugar dissolves.

Step 2: Continue cooking. The caramel will begin to darken.

Step 3: After about 10 minutes, it will be thick, syrupy, and dark amber in color.

Step 4: Remove the pan from the stove. To make designs, dip a teaspoon into the pan and let the caramel run off it in a long strand.

Step 5: Drizzle caramel onto parchment paper and cool until firm.

BLOOD ORANGE
CUPCAKES
WITH BLOOD ORANGE BUTTERCREAM AND RASPBERRY DRIZZLE

Judge Christina Tosi told Peyton from Season 5 that her blood orange cupcakes were "bright, bold, and pretty darn delicious." Finished with a tall swirl of buttercream frosting and an unexpected fresh raspberry drizzle, they certainly are as pretty as a picture. The combo of olive oil and yogurt in the batter helps make the cake wonderfully moist. And though blood oranges bring an exotic edge and a pop of color to the recipe, if they're out of season or hard to find in your grocery store, you can use regular oranges in their place.

MAKES 18 CUPCAKES

SEASON 5

BLOOD ORANGE CUPCAKES

2½ cups all-purpose flour

1½ cups granulated sugar

1 teaspoon baking powder

1 teaspoon baking soda

½ teaspoon kosher salt

¾ cup extra-virgin olive oil

1 tablespoon finely grated blood orange zest (substitute regular orange zest if fresh blood oranges are hard to find)

1 cup blood orange juice, preferably fresh

2 large eggs

1¼ cups plain whole-milk yogurt

RASPBERRY DRIZZLE

½ cup fresh or frozen raspberries

2 tablespoons granulated sugar

⅓ cup seedless raspberry jam

BLOOD ORANGE BUTTERCREAM

8 ounces cream cheese, at room temperature

1 stick (4 ounces) unsalted butter, at room temperature

4 cups confectioners' sugar

1 tablespoon finely grated blood orange zest (substitute regular orange zest if fresh blood oranges are hard to find)

¼ cup blood orange juice, preferably fresh

¼ teaspoon kosher salt

Red and orange food coloring (optional)

1. Make the blood orange cupcakes: Position racks in the upper and lower thirds of the oven and preheat the oven to 350°F. Line 18 cups of two standard muffin tins with paper liners.

2. In a medium bowl, whisk together the flour, granulated sugar, baking powder, baking soda, and salt.

3. In a large bowl, using an electric mixer fitted with the whisk attachment, beat the olive oil, blood orange zest, blood orange juice, eggs, and yogurt on medium-high speed until smooth and slightly thickened, about 2 minutes. Reduce the mixer speed to low and add the dry ingredients in two batches, beating until just combined.

4. Divide the batter evenly among the prepared muffin cups, filling each three-quarters full. Bake, rotating the pans from the top to bottom rack and front to back once halfway through, until the tops of the cupcakes feel springy and a toothpick inserted into the largest one comes out clean, about 20 minutes. Let the cupcakes rest in the pans for 5 minutes, then transfer them to a wire rack to cool completely.

5. Make the raspberry drizzle: In a small saucepan, combine the raspberries, granulated sugar, and 1 tablespoon water. Bring to a simmer over medium-high heat and cook, stirring occasionally, until slightly thickened and jammy, about 5 minutes. Transfer to a blender and add the raspberry jam. Process until mostly smooth but with a few small pieces of raspberry still visible, about 30 seconds. Cover and refrigerate until completely cool, about 45 minutes. The drizzle will thicken as it cools.

6. Make the blood orange buttercream: In a large bowl, using an electric mixer fitted with the paddle attachment, beat the cream cheese and butter on medium-high speed until light and fluffy, about 2 minutes. Reduce the speed to medium-low and add the confectioners' sugar, about ½ cup at a time, beating well after each addition. Add the blood orange zest, blood orange juice, salt, and 2 drops each of red and orange food coloring (if using). Beat until the frosting is smooth, about 20 seconds. Cover and refrigerate until ready to use. (The buttercream will stiffen as it chills; to get it back to spreading consistency, give it time to come to cool room temperature before loosening it up with a whisk or an electric mixer.)

7. When the cupcakes are cool, use a small offset spatula, spoon, or pastry bag fitted with a plain tip to top each cupcake with the buttercream. Garnish each one with a small spoonful of the raspberry drizzle.

MILK CHOCOLATE
CUPCAKES
WITH PEANUT BUTTER–CREAM CHEESE FROSTING

If there was ever a doubt that milk chocolate and peanut butter are a marriage made in heaven, these delectable cupcakes, inspired by ones that Abby and Mitchell made in Season 2, would be all the proof needed. While natural peanut butter may be great for a lunchtime PB&J, to get this addictively sweet-and-tangy frosting perfectly smooth, it's better to stick to regular creamy peanut butter (the kind without oil at the top).

MAKES 18 CUPCAKES

SEASON 2

MILK CHOCOLATE CUPCAKES

2 cups all-purpose flour

½ cup unsweetened natural cocoa powder

½ teaspoon baking powder

½ teaspoon baking soda

1 teaspoon kosher salt

2 sticks (8 ounces) unsalted butter, at room temperature

1 cup granulated sugar

½ cup packed light brown sugar

3 large eggs

¾ cup sour cream

¼ cup whole milk

1 tablespoon pure vanilla extract

PEANUT BUTTER–CREAM CHEESE FROSTING

8 ounces cream cheese, at room temperature

1 cup creamy peanut butter (not "natural," which has oil at the top)

1 cup confectioners' sugar

1 teaspoon pure vanilla extract

¼ teaspoon kosher salt

½ cup heavy cream

18 mini peanut butter cups

1. Make the milk chocolate cupcakes: Position racks in the upper and lower thirds of the oven and preheat the oven to 350°F. Line 18 cups of two standard muffin tins with paper liners.

2. In a medium bowl, whisk together the flour, cocoa powder, baking powder, baking soda, and salt.

3. In a large bowl, using an electric mixer with the paddle attachment, beat the butter, granulated sugar, and brown sugar on medium-high speed until light and fluffy, about 5 minutes. Add the eggs one at a time, beating well after each addition and scraping down the sides of the bowl as needed. Beat in the sour cream, milk, and vanilla. Reduce the speed to low and beat in the flour mixture until just combined.

4. Divide the batter among the prepared muffin cups, filling each three-quarters full. Bake, rotating the pans from the top to bottom rack and front to back once halfway through, until the tops of the cupcakes feel springy and a toothpick inserted into the largest one comes out clean, 15 to 20 minutes. Let the cupcakes rest in the pans for 5 minutes, then transfer them to a wire rack to cool completely.

5. Make the peanut butter–cream cheese frosting: In a large bowl, using an electric mixer with the paddle attachment, beat the cream cheese, peanut butter, confectioners' sugar, vanilla, and salt on medium-high speed until smooth, about 2 minutes. Reduce the mixer speed to low and slowly drizzle the heavy cream into the bowl. Increase the speed to medium and beat until the frosting is thick, smooth, and spreadable, about 1 minute more. Cover the bowl and refrigerate until ready to use. (The frosting may stiffen as it chills; to get it back to spreading consistency, give it time to come to cool room temperature before loosening it up with a whisk or an electric mixer.)

6. When the cupcakes are completely cool, use a small offset spatula, spoon, or a pastry bag fitted with a plain tip to top each cupcake with swirls of the frosting. Garnish each one with a peanut butter cup.

CAKES

Confetti Party Cake
page 144

DULCE DE LECHE
LAVA CAKES
WITH WHIPPED CREAM AND COCOA

These decadent personal-size cakes filled with dulce de leche (see page 132) are Evan's fun twist on traditional chocolate lava cakes and a creative way to work the butterscotch-flavored spread into a classic dessert. Just remember to keep an eye on the clock—as judge Christina Tosi advised in Season 6, overbaking the cakes by even a minute can make them lose their signature gooeyness. This is one recipe where strategy and timing are key. Because these petite cakes are quite sweet, topping them with barely sweetened whipped cream provides a nice contrast. A final flurry of cocoa powder on top finishes the whole thing off.

MAKES 4 INDIVIDUAL CAKES

LAVA CAKES

2 tablespoons unsalted butter, plus more at room temperature for the ramekins

1 cup dulce de leche (see MasterChef Lesson, page 132)

¼ cup all-purpose flour

¼ teaspoon ground cinnamon

¼ teaspoon kosher salt

1 large egg

2 large egg yolks

2 tablespoons light brown sugar

1 teaspoon pure vanilla extract

WHIPPED CREAM

⅓ cup heavy cream

½ teaspoon confectioners' sugar

Sweetened cocoa powder, for garnish

1. Make the lava cakes: Preheat the oven to 425°F. Lightly butter four 6-ounce ramekins.

2. In a small saucepan, melt 2 tablespoons butter over low heat. Add the dulce de leche and stir until smooth. Remove from the heat.

3. In a small bowl, whisk together the flour, cinnamon, and salt.

4. In a large bowl, using an electric mixer fitted with the whisk attachment, whip the whole egg, egg yolks, brown sugar, and vanilla until the mixture is pale and thick and has doubled in volume, about 3 minutes. Spoon in the dulce de leche mixture and continue whipping until combined, about 1 minute. Use a rubber spatula to gently fold in the flour mixture until just combined and no streaks of flour are visible. Divide the batter evenly among the prepared ramekins. Place the ramekins on a baking sheet and bake until the cakes are golden brown but still wobbly in the center, about 12 minutes. Let the cakes rest for 1 minute before serving.

5. While the cakes are in the oven, make the whipped cream: In a bowl, using an electric mixer fitted with the whisk attachment, beat the cream and confectioners' sugar on medium-high speed until the cream forms soft peaks, 2 to 3 minutes. Set aside.

6. To serve, run a knife around the edge of each ramekin to loosen the cakes. Invert each ramekin onto a dessert plate. Spoon the whipped cream on each cake, dust with a pinch of cocoa powder, and serve immediately.

HOMEMADE DULCE DE LECHE

Dulce de leche is crazy delicious not only in cute little cakes but also swirled into brownies, as the filling for sandwich cookies, or even as a dip for apple slices.

Cans of this creamy caramel spread can be found in many grocery stores, usually in the baking aisle. But it's also super easy to DIY! Here's how:

Peel the label from a can of sweetened condensed milk and place the can (completely sealed/unopened) in a deep saucepan or pot of water, making sure that the can is covered by at least 2 inches of water. Bring the water to a boil over medium heat, then reduce the heat to low and simmer for about 3 hours, adding more water as needed as the water evaporates. (For safety reasons, you always want to make sure there is at least 1 inch of water covering the can.) After 3 hours, carefully remove the can from the water (it will be hot!) and let it cool completely, about 1 hour, before opening. You can also use an electric pressure cooker (like an Instant Pot) to make an even speedier version: Just place an unopened, label-free can of sweetened condensed milk on top of the rack insert, fill the cooker with enough water to cover the can by 1 inch, seal the lid, and cook on high pressure for 40 minutes. Do a quick pressure release, then let the can cool completely before opening.

Either way, the result is a batch of ooey-gooey, amazing dulce de leche. It's like magic! Once the dulce de leche is made, you can transfer it to a mason jar and keep it in the refrigerator for up to 1 month—though it's unlikely it will last that long before getting gobbled up!

APRICOT-ALMOND
SKILL CAKE

With a gentle almond flavor and a touch of cardamom spice, this simple, homey cake is super adaptable and just the sort of recipe every young chef should have in that back pocket whenever a sweet craving strikes or a flat of summer berries or stone fruit calls to you at the farmers' market. Because it is so forgiving, as long as you stick to the recipe's basic formula, you can easily swap out the apricots for other fruits such as sliced pears, plums, or even a generous scoopful of blueberries. Just don't skip the final sprinkling of coarse cardamom sugar—it creates a thin, caramelized crust on top that is guaranteed to have you reaching for another slice.

SERVES 8

Nonstick pan spray

1¼ cups all-purpose flour

1 teaspoon baking powder

¾ teaspoon ground cardamom

½ teaspoon kosher salt

1 stick (4 ounces) unsalted butter, at room temperature

¾ cup granulated sugar

2 large eggs

2 teaspoons pure almond extract

1½ pounds apricots (8 to 10), halved and pitted

1 tablespoon turbinado sugar (such as Sugar In the Raw)

TIP If you don't have a cast-iron skillet, you can use a 9-inch round cake pan or springform pan.

1. Preheat the oven to 350°F. Coat a 10-inch cast-iron skillet with pan spray.

2. In a medium bowl, whisk together the flour, baking powder, ½ teaspoon of the cardamom, and the salt.

3. In a large bowl, using an electric mixer with the paddle attachment, beat the butter and granulated sugar on medium-high speed until light and fluffy, about 5 minutes. Reduce the speed to medium-low and add the eggs one at a time, beating well after each addition and scraping down the sides and bottom of the bowl as needed. Add the almond extract and beat briefly. Reduce the mixer speed to low and add the flour mixture, beating until just combined.

4. Spoon the batter into the prepared skillet and smooth out the top. Arrange the halved apricots on top, skin-side up—they should nearly fill the surface. In a small bowl, stir together the remaining ¼ teaspoon cardamom and the turbinado sugar and sprinkle the mixture over the top of the cake.

5. Bake until the cake is golden, the apricots are soft, and a toothpick inserted into the center of the cake comes out clean, about 45 minutes. Transfer the skillet to a wire rack to cool. Slice the cake into wedges and serve slightly warm or at room temperature. Store, covered, in the refrigerator for up to 5 days.

FLOURLESS CHOCOLATE CAKE
WITH WHITE CHOCOLATE DRIZZLE AND ALMOND BRITTLE

Judge Gordon Ramsay called this fudgy flourless cake "perfection on a plate" when Quani presented it during the Season 6 chocolate challenge. Whipping whole eggs into the batter, rather than separating them, makes the cake intensely rich, smooth, and dense in the most delicious way. A drizzle of white chocolate over the top provides a nice contrast to the dark chocolate and gives the whole thing a fun "drip cake" look. While you could certainly leave the almond brittle garnish off, it's a cinch to make and so tasty. In fact, you might want to double the batch so you have extra to snack on!

MAKES ONE 8-INCH CAKE

FLOURLESS CHOCOLATE CAKE

Nonstick pan spray or butter

1½ cups chopped bittersweet chocolate (about 9 ounces)

1 stick (4 ounces) unsalted butter, cubed

4 large eggs

½ cup sugar

1 teaspoon pure vanilla extract

¼ teaspoon kosher salt

WHITE CHOCOLATE DRIZZLE

½ cup white candy melts

½ cup white chocolate chips

½ cup heavy cream

ALMOND BRITTLE

Nonstick pan spray

1 cup sliced almonds

¾ cup sugar

⅛ teaspoon cream of tartar

¼ teaspoon kosher salt

TIP To get perfect slices when serving the cake, dip a long serrated knife (like a bread knife) into warm water, wipe it clean, then slice. Repeat the dip-and-wipe before every slice.

1. Preheat the oven to 325°F. Lightly grease an 8-inch round cake pan with pan spray. Line the bottom of the pan with a round of parchment paper (see Tip, page 151) and grease the parchment as well.

2. Make the flourless chocolate cake: In a heatproof medium bowl set over a pan of simmering water (make sure the bottom of the bowl does not touch the water), combine the chocolate and butter and heat, stirring often, until melted and completely smooth, about 4 minutes. Use oven mitts to remove the bowl from the pan and set aside.

3. In a large bowl, using an electric mixer fitted with the whisk attachment, beat the eggs, sugar, vanilla, and salt on medium-high until the mixture is very pale and frothy and has doubled in volume, about 5 minutes. Gradually spoon the melted chocolate mixture into the egg mixture and use a rubber spatula to fold them together until just combined, taking care to deflate the batter as little as possible.

4. Pour the batter into the prepared pan. Bake until the surface of the cake has formed a thin crust and the edges look dry, 30 to 35 minutes. Let the cake rest in the pan for 5 minutes, then run a butter knife around the edges of the pan to loosen the cake. Using oven mitts, invert the cake onto a plate or serving platter. Transfer the cake to the refrigerator to cool completely.

5. Make the white chocolate drizzle: Place the candy melts and white chocolate chips in a heatproof medium bowl. In a small saucepan, bring the cream to a simmer over medium heat. Pour the hot cream over the candy melts and chocolate and set aside for 1 minute, then stir until smooth.

6. Starting at the center, slowly spoon the white chocolate drizzle over the cooled cake, letting some drip over the sides. Return the cake to the refrigerator to chill until set, about 30 minutes or up to overnight.

7. Meanwhile, make the almond brittle: Line a baking sheet with parchment paper and coat the parchment with pan spray.

8. In a medium skillet, toast the almonds over medium-high heat, stirring often, until golden and fragrant, 3 to 5 minutes. Turn off the heat, remove the almonds from the pan, and set aside.

9. In a medium saucepan, whisk together the sugar, cream of tartar, and ¼ cup water. Bring to a simmer over medium heat, stirring, just until the sugar dissolves, then cook, without stirring, until the mixture turns a deep amber and a thermometer inserted into the caramel reads around 310°F, about 10 minutes. Remove the pan from the heat and stir in the toasted almonds and the salt. Working quickly and carefully, pour the caramel mixture onto the prepared baking sheet and use a silicone spatula to spread it into a thin layer. (The caramel will be very hot; be very careful not to touch it or splatter it—you might want to ask an adult for help.) Set the baking sheet aside until the caramel hardens, about 30 minutes. Break the brittle into small shards. Arrange the almond brittle on top of the chilled cake and serve.

CHOCOLATE-HAZELNUT
CHEESECAKE

Judge Christina Tosi called Mikey's cheesecake "just divine" and said it was easily one of the best desserts she'd tasted on the show, ever! Crunchy, creamy, fudgy, and amped up with a generous helping of rich hazelnut spread, this decadent take on chocolate cheesecake won him the coveted golden apron and secured his place in the Season 6 semifinals. Adding ground hazelnut flour to the cookie crust adds another layer of flavor and ties together with the hazelnut elements in the filling and the toasted hazelnuts on top. Just remember: Because cheesecakes need hours to chill before serving, you'll need to plan accordingly.

SERVES 10 TO 12

SEASON 6

CHOCOLATE-HAZELNUT CRUST

Nonstick pan spray or butter

28 chocolate sandwich cookies (such as Oreos), crushed

1 cup hazelnut flour, store-bought or homemade (see Tip)

½ teaspoon kosher salt

6 tablespoons (¾ stick) unsalted butter, melted

CHOCOLATE-HAZELNUT CHEESECAKE FILLING

8 ounces bittersweet chocolate, finely chopped

½ cup hazelnut spread (such as Nutella), at room temperature

3 (8-ounce) bricks cream cheese, at room temperature

1 cup sour cream

1 cup sugar

⅓ cup unsweetened Dutch-process cocoa powder

½ teaspoon kosher salt

1 tablespoon pure vanilla extract

4 large eggs

HAZELNUT GANACHE

½ cup bittersweet chocolate chips

¼ cup heavy cream

1 tablespoon chocolate-hazelnut spread

¼ teaspoon kosher salt

½ cup chopped hazelnuts, for garnish

TIP This recipe uses hazelnut flour, which is made by grinding whole hazelnuts until they are fine and powdery. Many grocery stores carry hazelnut flour in the alternative flour section of the baking aisle—but if you have a high-powered blender, you can also make your own!

1. Make the chocolate-hazelnut crust: Preheat the oven to 325°F. Grease a 9-inch springform pan with pan spray and wrap the bottom tightly with two layers of foil.

2. In a food processor, pulse the cookies until finely ground. Add the hazelnut flour, salt, and melted butter and pulse until it is evenly combined and has the texture of damp sand, about three 5-second pulses. Pour the crumb mixture into the prepared pan and use the bottom of a spoon or measuring cup

to press it evenly over the bottom and about ½ inch up the sides of the pan. Bake until firm, about 12 minutes, then transfer to a wire rack to cool. Keep the oven at 325°F.

3. Make the chocolate-hazelnut cheesecake filling: In a heatproof medium bowl set over a pan of simmering water (make sure the bottom of the bowl doesn't touch the water), melt the chocolate, stirring until completely smooth. Add the hazelnut spread and stir until smooth. Using oven mitts, remove the bowl from the pan and set aside to cool to room temperature.

4. In a large bowl, using an electric mixer with the whisk attachment, beat the cream cheese and sour cream on medium-low speed until smooth, about 2 minutes. Beat in the sugar, cocoa powder, salt, and vanilla. Add the eggs one at a time, beating well after each addition and scraping down the sides and bottom of the bowl as needed. Beat in the melted chocolate mixture.

5. Bring a teakettle of water almost to a boil. Pour the batter into the prepared pan and tap gently against the counter to release any air bubbles. Place the pan inside a 9 × 13-inch baking dish. Open the oven and, wearing oven mitts, pull the center rack so it extends out of the oven. Set the baking dish on the oven rack. Pour enough hot water from the teakettle into the baking dish to come halfway up the sides of the springform pan. Bake until the center of the cheesecake is set and the top is no longer shiny, about 1 hour

15 minutes. Turn off the oven and let the cake rest inside for 30 minutes more.

6. Ask an adult to help you remove the baking dish from the oven. Carefully transfer the springform pan to a flat surface and discard the foil. Run a butter knife around the inside of the pan to loosen the edges of the cheesecake. Transfer the pan to a wire rack to cool for 30 minutes, then cover and refrigerate for at least 5 hours or up to 3 days.

7. At least 1 hour before serving, make the hazelnut ganache: Place the chocolate in a heatproof medium bowl. In a small saucepan, bring the cream to a simmer over medium heat. Pour the hot cream over the chocolate and let stand for 1 minute, then stir until smooth. Whisk in the chocolate-hazelnut spread and salt. Set aside to cool for 15 minutes.

8. Release the chilled cheesecake from the springform pan and, with the cake still resting on the metal base, transfer it to a serving dish. Spread the hazelnut ganache over the cake, pushing it to the edges and letting some drizzle down the sides. Return the plated cake to the refrigerator to chill until the ganache has set, 20 to 30 minutes.

9. Meanwhile, in a medium skillet, toast the chopped hazelnuts over medium-high heat, stirring often, until golden and fragrant, about 5 minutes. Turn off the heat and transfer the hazelnuts to a plate to cool.

10. Scatter the toasted hazelnuts over the top of the cake and serve.

DOUBLE-VANILLA
POUND CAKE

Moist, tender pound cake is one of the first treats many *MasterChef Junior* contestants learn to bake. This classic version includes a splash of buttermilk and a double dose of vanilla for big flavor. Serve it thickly sliced and pair it with whipped cream and fresh fruit—or take a page out of Cydney's playbook and make it the centerpiece of a fondue dessert buffet.

MAKES ONE 8½ × 4½-INCH LOAF

1½ sticks (6 ounces) unsalted butter at cool room temperature (see MasterChef Lesson, page 54), plus 1 tablespoon softened butter for the pan

2 cups all-purpose flour

1½ teaspoons baking powder

½ teaspoon kosher salt

1 cup sugar

2 teaspoons pure vanilla extract

1 vanilla bean, split lengthwise

3 large eggs, at room temperature

¾ cup buttermilk

1. Preheat the oven to 325°F. Grease an 8½ × 4½-inch loaf pan with the softened butter and line it with parchment paper, leaving a few inches of overhang on both of the long sides. (This will help you lift the loaf out of the pan after baking.)

2. In a medium bowl, whisk together the flour, baking powder, and salt.

3. In a large bowl, using an electric mixer with the paddle attachment, beat 1½ sticks of the cold butter and the sugar on medium-high speed until light and fluffy, about 5 minutes. Add the vanilla extract and use the tip of a paring knife to scrape the vanilla seeds out of the vanilla pod into the bowl. Beat on medium-low speed to combine. Add the eggs one at a time, beating well after each addition and scraping down the sides and bottom of the bowl as needed. Remove the bowl from the mixer and use a rubber spatula to add the flour mixture in three additions, alternating with the buttermilk, beginning and ending with the flour. Scrape down the sides of the bowl and stir until just combined; do not overmix. (It is okay if the batter still looks lumpy.)

4. Scrape the batter into the prepared pan. Bake until the cake is tall, domed, and golden and a toothpick inserted into the tallest part of the cake comes out clean, about 1 hour 15 minutes. Let the cake rest in the pan for 20 minutes, then use the parchment to lift it out onto a wire rack to cool completely. Store at room temperature, tightly wrapped in plastic wrap, for up to 1 week.

PINEAPPLE-LYCHEE
UPSIDE-DOWN CAKE

An exotic twist on traditional pineapple upside-down cake, this recipe inspired lots of applause in the Season 6 canned food challenge, especially from judge Christina Tosi, who called the coconut milk sponge cake "to die for!" Avery's choice to add chopped lychees to the batter helps make the dish extra moist and sweet, but if you have trouble tracking down a can, you can substitute an equal amount of crushed pineapple (about ½ cup) and leave them off the top.

SERVES 8

Nonstick pan spray

1⅓ cups all-purpose flour

2 teaspoons baking powder

½ teaspoon kosher salt

½ cup full-fat canned coconut milk

2 teaspoons pure vanilla extract

1 (20-ounce) can juice-packed pineapple rings, drained, ¼ cup juice reserved

1 (20-ounce) can pitted lychees, drained

1½ cups granulated sugar

½ cup vegetable oil

1 large egg

4 tablespoons (½ stick) unsalted butter

⅓ cup packed light brown sugar

½ teaspoon ground ginger

⅛ teaspoon ground allspice

1. Preheat the oven to 375°F. Lightly grease a 9-inch round cake pan with pan spray.

2. In a small bowl, whisk together the flour, baking powder, and salt. In another small bowl, combine the coconut milk, vanilla, and reserved pineapple juice. Set aside 8 whole lychees, then coarsely chop the remainder and transfer to a small bowl.

3. In a large bowl, using an electric mixer fitted with the whisk attachment, beat ½ cup of the granulated sugar and the oil on medium-high speed until smooth and slightly thickened, about 2 minutes. Beat in the egg and the coconut milk mixture. Reduce the mixer speed to low and gradually add the flour mixture, until just combined. Fold in the lychees and set aside.

4. In a small skillet, melt the butter over medium heat. Stir in the brown sugar, ginger, and allspice until incorporated. Transfer the mixture to the prepared cake pan (don't worry if the mixture clumps or separates—it will loosen during baking). Place one pineapple ring in the center of the pan, then add the others in a circle around it. Place a whole lychee in the center of each ring.

5. Spread the batter over the fruit to the edges of the pan. Bake until the cake is set and a toothpick inserted into the center comes out clean, 30 to 35 minutes. Let the cake rest in the pan for 3 minutes, then carefully invert it onto a serving plate. Wait 1 minute, then lift the pan away, taking care to avoid any steam that escapes. Serve warm or at room temperature. Refrigerate leftovers for up to 3 days.

QUADRUPLE-GINGER
SNACK CAKE

This dark, sticky cake, inspired by cupcakes that Samuel made in Season 2, may look unassuming, but thanks to a four-part dose of ginger—in the form of ground ginger, fresh ginger, candied ginger, and even ginger beer—it's absolutely bursting with complex, spicy flavor. A final flurry of confectioners' sugar sprinkled on before serving makes the cake look like something right out of a winter wonderland!

SERVES 8

SEASON 2

SAMUEL

Nonstick pan spray

1½ cups all-purpose flour

½ teaspoon baking powder

2 tablespoons ground ginger

½ teaspoon freshly ground black pepper

¼ teaspoon kosher salt

¾ cup spicy ginger beer

½ teaspoon baking soda

⅔ cup packed light brown sugar

½ cup plus 1 tablespoon robust molasses

¼ cup granulated sugar

2 large eggs

⅓ cup vegetable oil

1 tablespoon plus 1 teaspoon grated fresh ginger

¼ cup chopped candied ginger

Confectioners' sugar, for dusting

TIPS Allowing the cake to bake a bit before sprinkling the candied ginger on top helps prevent the pieces from settling to the bottom of the pan.

Remember to pop a knob of ginger in the freezer for an hour before grating it to make the process a whole lot easier.

1. Preheat the oven to 350°F. Coat a 9-inch round baking pan with pan spray and line it with a round of parchment paper (see Tip, page 151).

2. In a large bowl, whisk together the flour, baking powder, ground ginger, pepper, and salt.

3. In a medium saucepan, bring the ginger beer to a low simmer over medium heat. Remove from the heat and stir in the baking soda, stirring constantly as it foams. Add the brown sugar, molasses, and granulated sugar and stir until well combined. Whisk in the eggs, oil, and fresh ginger.

4. Using a rubber spatula, scrape half the ginger beer mixture into the flour mixture and stir until mostly combined. Add the remaining ginger beer mixture and stir until just smooth. Transfer the batter to the prepared pan and smooth out the top.

5. Bake for 10 minutes, then quickly remove the pan from the oven and sprinkle the surface with the candied ginger. Return the pan to the oven and bake until the cake is set, springy to the touch, and golden on top, 20 to 25 minutes more. Let the cake rest in the pan for 5 minutes, then invert it onto a wire rack to cool completely.

6. To serve, dust the cake with confectioners' sugar and slice it into wedges. The cake will keep, covered, at room temperature for up to 5 days.

MEXICAN HOT CHOCOLATE
TRES LECHES CAKE
WITH CARAMEL AND KETTLE CORN

Tres leches cake is a classic Latin American dessert made by soaking sponge cake with three kinds of milk—condensed, evaporated, and cream—until it is sweet and tender! When Avery brought her imaginative twist on tres leches cake to the judges' table during the Season 6 finale, judge Christina Tosi congratulated her on its perfectly rich, luscious texture. This version gets a kick from cayenne pepper, which is nice with the cocoa, but you can omit it if you prefer.

SERVES 12

SEASON 6

AVERY

HOT CHOCOLATE TRES LECHES CAKE

Nonstick pan spray

1¼ cups all-purpose flour

½ cup plus 2 tablespoons unsweetened Dutch-process cocoa powder

1 tablespoon espresso powder

1½ teaspoons ground cinnamon

½ to ¾ teaspoon cayenne pepper, to taste

1½ teaspoons baking powder

¼ teaspoon kosher salt

6 large eggs, at room temperature

1¼ cups granulated sugar

⅓ cup whole milk

1 teaspoon pure vanilla extract

TRES LECHES CREAM

1 (14-ounce) can sweetened condensed milk

1 (12-ounce) can evaporated milk

½ cup heavy cream

2 tablespoons chocolate syrup

½ teaspoon kosher salt

CINNAMON WHIPPED CREAM

2½ cups heavy cream

2 tablespoons confectioners' sugar

1 teaspoon pure vanilla extract

½ teaspoon ground cinnamon

OPTIONAL GARNISHES

Store-bought caramel sauce, warmed

Store-bought kettle corn

1. Make the hot chocolate tres leches cake: Preheat the oven to 350°F. Generously grease a 9 × 13-inch baking dish with pan spray.

2. In a medium bowl, whisk together the flour, cocoa powder, espresso powder, cinnamon, cayenne, baking powder, and salt. Set aside.

3. Separate the eggs, placing the whites in one large bowl and the yolks in another large bowl. To the eggs yolks, add 1 cup of the granulated sugar and use an electric mixer fitted with the whisk attachment to beat the mixture until creamy and thick, about 3 minutes. With the mixer running, drizzle in the milk and vanilla and beat until combined, about 30 seconds. Set the bowl aside and carefully wash and dry the whisk attachment.

4. Using the mixer fitted with the clean, dry whisk attachment, beat the egg whites on high speed until light and frothy, 2 to 3 minutes. Add the remaining ¼ cup granulated sugar and beat until the mixture forms stiff, glossy peaks, about 2 minutes more.

5. Lightly whisk half the flour mixture into the egg yolk mixture, then gently fold in half the egg whites. Repeat with the remaining flour and egg whites, using a gentle touch, until everything is combined.

6. Scrape the batter into the prepared baking dish and smooth the surface. Bake until a toothpick inserted into the center of the cake comes out clean, about 22 minutes. Transfer the baking dish to a wire rack and let cool completely.

7. Make the tres leches cream: In a large saucepan, whisk together the condensed milk, evaporated milk, heavy cream, chocolate syrup, and salt until smooth. Cook over medium heat, stirring often, until the mixture is bubbling at the edges and just shy of a boil, about 5 minutes (don't walk away—cream has a tendency to boil over if not watched!). Remove from the heat.

8. Pierce the cooled cake all over with a very thin, sharp knife or a skewer, spacing the holes 1 inch apart and making sure they pierce to the bottom of the pan. Starting at the edges of the cake and circling your way toward the center, pour the warm tres leches cream over the cake, pausing to allow any cream that pools up to be absorbed. Continue until you have used all the cream and the cake is fully and evenly saturated. Cover the baking dish with plastic wrap and refrigerate until thoroughly chilled, at least 4 hours or up to 24 hours.

9. Before serving, make the cinnamon whipped cream: In a large bowl, using an electric mixer fitted with the whisk attachment, beat the heavy cream on high speed until it begins to thicken, about 1 minute. Slowly sprinkle in the confectioners' sugar, vanilla, and cinnamon and beat until the cream thickens and holds peaks, 1 to 2 minutes more.

10. To serve, cut the cake into 12 squares. Top each square with a generous dollop of whipped cream. If desired, drizzle the plate with caramel sauce and garnish with kettle corn.

CONFETTI PARTY CAKE

If there's one thing the *MasterChef Junior* kids agree on, it's that nothing screams "Happy Birthday!" like a colorful confetti cake. And when the homemade version is this fun and simple to make, you'll definitely want to ditch the boxed mix! A double dose of sprinkles—stirred into the fluffy yellow batter and strewn all over the vanilla buttercream frosting—are the secret to giving the cake its party-perfect look. Rainbow sprinkles are traditional, but if you'd like your cake to be even more personalized, try making your own sprinkle blend!

SERVES 12

CONFETTI CAKE

Nonstick pan spray

3 cups cake flour

2½ teaspoons baking powder

¾ teaspoon kosher salt

2 sticks (8 ounces) unsalted butter, at room temperature

1½ cups granulated sugar

4 large eggs, at room temperature

1 cup whole milk

1 tablespoon pure vanilla extract

1 cup multicolored sprinkles

VANILLA BUTTERCREAM

2 sticks (8 ounces) unsalted butter, at room temperature

5 cups confectioners' sugar

2 teaspoons pure vanilla extract

¼ cup heavy cream

¼ teaspoon kosher salt

2 cups multicolored sprinkles, for garnish

TIP For more on assembling and frosting layer cakes, see the MasterChef Lesson on page 146.

1. Make the confetti cake: Preheat the oven to 350°F. Grease three 8-inch round cake pans with pan spray and line the bottoms with rounds of parchment paper (see Tip, page 151).

2. In a medium bowl, whisk together the cake flour, baking powder, and salt.

3. In a large bowl, using an electric mixer with the paddle attachment, beat the butter and granulated sugar on medium-high speed until light and fluffy, about 5 minutes. Add the eggs one at a time, beating well after each addition and scraping the bowl as needed. Reduce the mixer speed to low and add the flour mixture in two additions, alternating with the milk. Add the vanilla and beat until just combined. Fold in the sprinkles. Divide the batter evenly among the prepared pans.

4. Bake until the cakes are golden, the center resists light pressure, and a toothpick inserted into the center comes out clean, 25 to 30 minutes. Let the cakes rest in the pans for 10 minutes, then unmold the cakes onto wire racks to cool completely.

5. Make the vanilla buttercream: Use an electric mixer with the paddle attachment. Beat the butter on medium-high speed until light and fluffy, about 2 minutes. Reduce the speed to medium-low and add the confectioners' sugar, about ½ cup at a time, beating well after each addition and scraping the bowl as needed. Add the vanilla, cream, and salt and beat on high speed until the frosting is light and fluffy, about 3 minutes. Cover and refrigerate the frosting until ready to use. (The buttercream will stiffen as it chills; to get it back to spreading consistency, let it sit at room temperature before whisking.)

6. To assemble the cake, place one layer, flat-side up, on a platter or cake stand. Using an offset spatula, spoon about ¾ cup of the buttercream onto the cake and spread it into an even layer. Top with a second layer of cake, flat-side up, and another ½ to ¾ cup of buttercream. Top with the third cake layer, flat-side up, and use the remaining buttercream to frost the top and sides. Decorate with sprinkles, moving around the cake until the surface is evenly covered. Refrigerate until ready to serve or for up to 24 hours. Let the cake come to room temperature before serving. Leftovers can be stored, covered, in the refrigerator for up to 5 days.

BUILDING A
BETTER LAYER CAKE

Do you dream of baking tall, graceful cakes dressed up with buttercream and perfect frosting rosettes and swirls—but always seem to wind up with something that looks more like the leaning tower of Pisa?

Learning how to assemble and decorate layer cakes like a pro takes patience. But knowing a few simple tricks can make the process a whole lot less painful.

USE THE RIGHT TOOLS

First, start with a long, serrated knife to trim uneven tops and slice layers horizontally into two or three thinner ones (this is also known as "torting"). A cake stand is great, too, not only for showing off your cake but also for supporting the layers and making it easier to get up close to the bottom and sides while you're frosting. If you don't have a cake stand, you can improvise one by setting a plate on a stack of books or an overturned bowl. Place strips of parchment paper on the cake stand before setting the cake layer on top to protect the stand from drips and spills (and the strips are easy to remove and toss away before serving). A small offset spatula helps you frost even the littlest crevices cleanly and smoothly. Finally, make sure to plan ahead and clear some space in your refrigerator: You're going to want plenty of room to let the cake chill without fear of it being smushed by a teetering ketchup bottle!

COOL CAKES COMPLETELY

Because cakes are fragile when they're warm, always let them cool in the pans on a wire rack for 10 to 15 minutes before trying to unmold them. After the layers are out of the pans, let them cool to room temperature, then wrap them tightly in plastic wrap and chill them in the refrigerator for at least 1 hour before continuing. Pro tip: Chilled cake layers are much easier to cut and trim.

TRIM THE LAYERS

When you're ready to begin assembly, clear your work area and make sure your frosting and utensils are nearby. Inspect the chilled layers for any cracks or other issues. If the layers have little domes on top, use your serrated knife to even them off (and, of course, help yourself to the scraps!). For safety's sake, when trimming the layers horizontally, always steady the cake by placing your hand on top of it, not on the side. This will spare your fingers in case the knife slips. To slice the layers horizontally into two thinner layers, hold a ruler perpendicular to the cake and measure upward from the bottom. Use four toothpicks to mark the midpoint, inserting one pick each at the twelve o'clock, three o'clock, six o'clock, and nine o'clock positions. Using the toothpicks as a guide, use a long serrated knife to gently slice the cake into two even sections.

Step 1: When slicing or trimming layers, steady the cake by placing your hand on top of it, not on the side.

Step 2: Use an offset spatula to smooth a thin layer of icing all over the cake. This is called the crumb coat.

Step 3: To smooth the surface, rotate the plate or cake stand as you work your spatula over the top of the cake in a large, even swirl.

BUILD FROM THE BOTTOM UP!

Invert the first layer of cake onto the stand so that the flat bottom faces up and the trimmed side faces down—this gives you a perfectly flat surface to frost. Use an offset spatula to put a large dollop of frosting (about ¾ cup) on the center of the layer, then work it around until it is smooth and covers all the way to the edges. Place the next layer on top of the frosting, flat-side up, and repeat. Inspect your architecture: Is the frosting between layers even? Does the cake seem to be leaning? Get in there and make any adjustments before proceeding. Sometimes cakes start leaning when the frosting gets too soft, allowing the structure to shift. If you notice that happening, pause and chill the cake for a few minutes to allow the frosting to firm up again, and ease it into proper position before placing the last layer of cake on top with its flat side facing up.

FROST LIKE A PRO

Now it's time to tackle the rest of the frosting. Use an offset spatula to smooth a thin layer of icing all over the cake, starting with the top, and then frosting the sides. Don't worry about looks yet: This is just the "crumb coat"—the underlayer that helps seal in the crumbs and keeps them from marking the finished cake. (Cakes that have been crumb-coated always look 100 percent neater than ones that haven't—so trust us, you don't want to skip this step!) Place the cake in the refrigerator for about 15 minutes to let the crumb coat harden, then finish it with a final layer of frosting. Start by dolloping a large scoop of frosting on the top of the cake and rotate the cake stand as you work the spatula over the top, smoothing the surface in a large, even swirl. Dab a scoop of frosting onto the side of the cake and, holding an offset spatula (or butter knife) perpendicular to the stand, work it into a smooth layer. Add frosting and repeat until the sides are completely covered. Give the top one more look and make any touch-ups. Add any last-minute garnishes or sprinkles—and then stand back and admire your handiwork!

APPLE BUTTER
BUNDT CAKE
WITH CINNAMON-SUGAR

Beautiful domed Bundt cakes are a classic homestyle American dessert and one of Shayne's favorite baking projects. A generous helping of apple butter in the batter and a sparkling coating of cinnamon-sugar makes this version taste just like a giant apple cider doughnut!

SERVES 10 TO 12

Nonstick pan spray

2½ cups all-purpose flour

2 teaspoons baking powder

½ teaspoon baking soda

1 tablespoon plus 2 teaspoons ground cinnamon

1½ teaspoons nutmeg, preferably freshly grated

½ teaspoon kosher salt

1¼ cups apple butter

1 tablespoon pure vanilla extract

1 stick (4 ounces) unsalted butter, at room temperature

1 cup sour cream

¼ cup packed light brown sugar

1 cup plus 3 tablespoons granulated sugar

4 large eggs

⅔ cup confectioners' sugar

1. Preheat the oven to 350°F. Generously coat a 12-cup Bundt pan with pan spray.

2. In a medium bowl, whisk together the flour, baking powder, baking soda, 1 tablespoon of the cinnamon, the nutmeg, and the salt. In a small bowl, stir together the apple butter and the vanilla. Set both aside.

3. In a large bowl, using an electric mixer with the paddle attachment, beat the butter, sour cream, brown sugar, and 1 cup of the granulated sugar on medium-high speed until very light and smooth, about 6 minutes. Reduce the mixer speed to medium-low and add the eggs one at a time, scraping down the sides and bottom of the bowl as needed, about 2 minutes.

4. Reduce the mixer speed to low and add the flour in two additions, alternating with the apple butter mixture. Beat just until combined. Scrape the batter into the prepared pan and smooth the surface with a rubber spatula.

5. Bake until a toothpick inserted into the center of the cake comes out clean, about 55 minutes. Let the cake rest in the pan for 10 minutes, then turn it out onto a wire rack to cool completely.

6. In a small bowl, combine the remaining granulated sugar and cinnamon. In another small bowl, combine the confectioners' sugar and 2 tablespoons water and stir until smooth. Brush the cake with the confectioners' sugar mixture, then immediately sprinkle the cinnamon-sugar over the cake, turning it so that all sides get coated. Serve warm or at room temperature.

CHOCOLATE-CITRUS
OLIVE OIL CAKE
WITH ORANGE GLAZE AND WHIPPED RICOTTA

This heady, citrus-scented cake—inspired by the one Che made for the big Season 7 finale—looks and tastes so sophisticated, it's hard to believe it requires just two bowls and can be mixed by hand in a matter of minutes. A touch of almond flour in the batter lends it a subtle crumbly texture and a faint nuttiness that pairs beautifully with the bitter chocolate, fruity olive oil, and rich ricotta cream.

SERVES 10

SEASON 7

CHE

CHOCOLATE-CITRUS OLIVE OIL CAKE

Butter or nonstick pan spray

1½ cups all-purpose flour

½ cup almond flour

¼ cup unsweetened Dutch-process cocoa powder

1¾ cups granulated sugar

¾ teaspoon kosher salt

1 teaspoon baking powder

½ teaspoon baking soda

1⅓ cups extra-virgin olive oil

3 large eggs

1¼ cups whole milk

2 tablespoons grated orange zest

½ cup fresh orange juice

2 teaspoons orange extract

ORANGE GLAZE

1½ cups confectioners' sugar

1 tablespoon grated orange zest

2 tablespoons fresh orange juice

WHIPPED RICOTTA

1 cup whole-milk ricotta cheese

1 teaspoon extra-virgin olive oil

1 teaspoon grated orange zest

1 teaspoon fresh orange juice

½ cup confectioners' sugar

Chopped candied orange peel, for garnish (optional)

1. Make the chocolate-citrus olive oil cake: Preheat the oven to 350°F. Grease the bottom and sides of a 9-inch springform pan with butter or pan spray and line the bottom with a round of parchment paper (see Tip, opposite).

2. In a medium bowl, whisk together the all-purpose flour, almond flour, cocoa powder, granulated sugar, salt, baking powder, and baking soda. In a large bowl, whisk together the olive oil, eggs, milk, orange zest, orange juice, and orange extract until smooth and glossy. Gently stir the flour mixture into the oil mixture until just combined.

3. Pour the batter into the prepared pan and bake until the cake is domed and springy and a toothpick inserted into the center comes out clean, about 1 hour 10 minutes. Let the cake rest in the pan for 10 minutes, then run a butter knife around the edges, release the springform ring, and transfer the cake (still on the metal base) to a wire rack to cool completely, about 1 hour.

4. Make the orange glaze: In a medium bowl, whisk together the confectioners' sugar, orange zest, and orange juice until smooth and opaque.

5. Transfer the cooled cake to a serving platter or cake stand. Spoon the glaze over the top of the cake and let it drip over the sides. Let rest until the glaze has set, about 20 minutes. (If your kitchen is especially warm or humid, transfer the cake to the refrigerator to allow the glaze to firm up.)

6. Make the whipped ricotta: In a food processor, combine the ricotta, olive oil, orange zest, orange juice, and confectioners' sugar. Process until smooth, about 1 minute.

7. Spoon the whipped ricotta onto the center of the cake. Garnish with candied orange peel (if using, or the candied dried orange slices from the Orange Blossom Cupcakes on page 110) and serve immediately.

TIP It's easy to make a perfectly round parchment liner to fit your pan. Here's how: Tear off a piece of parchment that is slightly larger than your pan. Fold it in half from top to bottom, then in half again from left to right. You will have a squat rectangle. Fold one side of the rectangle over, corner to corner, to form a triangle (sort of like if you were making a paper airplane). Fold the triangle over again, corner to corner, so you have what looks like a long, skinny funnel with a pointed tip. Place the parchment against the bottom of the pan with the pointed tip touching the center. Mark the parchment where it meets the edge of the pan, then cut the parchment just inside that line. Unfold and voilà: a perfect round!

THE EASIEST
CHOCOLATE CAKE

This ridiculously easy, seriously sinful chocolate cake should come with a warning—because once you realize how dangerously simple it is to make, you may find yourself inventing a new cake-worthy occasion every day. (Callbacks for the school play? Deserves a slice! Made the semifinals in soccer? Cupcake time!) Unsweetened Dutch-process cocoa gives the batter a deep dark bite that's balanced by the caramel sweetness of brown sugar. Adding a spoonful of espresso powder boosts the chocolate flavor without overpowering it—but if you'd rather leave it out, it's not essential. All in all, the process may take a minute more work than a store-bought mix—but the results are more than worth it! This cake can also be used to make the Chocolate Layer Cake with Spiced Ganache and Raspberry-Chocolate Drizzle (page 154).

**MAKES ONE 9 × 13-INCH SHEET CAKE,
TWO 9-INCH ROUND CAKE LAYERS, OR 24 CUPCAKES**

Butter or nonstick pan spray

2 cups all-purpose flour

1 cup unsweetened Dutch-process cocoa powder

1⅓ cups granulated sugar

⅔ cup packed light brown sugar

1 tablespoon espresso powder (optional)

1½ teaspoons baking powder

1½ teaspoons baking soda

1 teaspoon kosher salt

2 large eggs

1 cup buttermilk

½ cup vegetable oil

2 teaspoons pure vanilla extract

1 cup boiling water

1. Preheat the oven to 350°F. Use butter or pan spray to grease one 9 × 13-inch baking pan, two 9-inch round cake pans, or two 12-cup muffin tins.

2. In a large bowl, whisk together the flour, cocoa powder, granulated sugar, brown sugar, espresso powder (if using), baking powder, baking soda, and salt. In a 4-cup measuring cup, whisk together the eggs, buttermilk, oil, and vanilla. Pour the egg mixture into the flour mixture and use an electric mixer fitted with the whisk attachment, to beat on medium-high speed until well combined, about 1 minute. Add the boiling water and beat briefly on medium-low speed to combine. (Don't be concerned if the batter seems very loose; that's the way it is supposed to be.)

3. Pour the batter into the prepared pan(s). Bake until set and springy and a toothpick inserted into the center comes out clean: about 35 minutes for sheet cakes or layer cakes or 25 minutes for cupcakes. Let the cakes rest in the pan(s) for 10 minutes, then remove from the pan (if making layers or cupcakes) and transfer to a wire rack to cool completely.

4. Top with the frosting of your choice. Maybe marshmallow buttercream (page 118) or salted caramel frosting (page 120)? Decorate as desired.

CHOCOLATE LAYER CAKE

WITH SPICED GANACHE AND RASPBERRY-CHOCOLATE DRIZZLE

This towering chocolate cake, inspired by the one Dara presented to the judges in Season 1, is made up of three complementary parts: moist, tender chocolate cake layers; a light yet rich whipped chocolate ganache infused with a kick of cinnamon and cayenne; and a tangy raspberry ganache drizzle. Judge Graham Elliot told Dara she "really hit it out of the park" and complimented her balanced use of spices and how the raspberry brings out the floral, fruity flavors in the chocolate. To get a tall, four-layer look that's packed with fudgy frosting, we baked two cake rounds and split each one in half horizontally—but if you'd like to leave them whole for a two-layer cake, it will still be an impressive sight!

SERVES 12

SEASON
1

The Easiest Chocolate Cake (page 152), baked as two 9-inch layers and cooled

SPICED GANACHE

4 cups bittersweet chocolate chips

2½ cups heavy cream

1 teaspoon ground cinnamon

½ teaspoon cayenne pepper

1 teaspoon kosher salt

RASPBERRY-CHOCOLATE DRIZZLE

½ cup bittersweet chocolate chips

2 tablespoons seedless raspberry jam

¼ cup heavy cream

1 cup fresh raspberries, for garnish

TIP For more advice on assembling and frosting layer cakes see the MasterChef Lesson on page 146.

1. Bake and cool the cake layers as directed on page 152.

2. Make the spiced ganache: Place the chocolate chips in a heatproof medium bowl. In a small saucepan, bring the cream to a simmer over medium heat. Pour the hot cream over the chocolate chips and let stand for 1 minute, then sprinkle in the cinnamon, cayenne, and salt and stir until smooth. Set the ganache aside until cool (the consistency should be similar to toothpaste), about 1½ hours. Once cooled, beat the ganache

with an electric mixer fitted with the whisk attachment until light, fluffy, and nearly doubled in volume, about 4 to 6 minutes.

3. To assemble the cake, use a long serrated knife to slice each layer in half horizontally so that you are left with 4 thinner layers (see page 146 for more on this technique; you can also leave the layers whole for a two-layer cake). Place one layer on a serving platter or cake stand, flat-side up. Using an offset spatula, spoon about ¾ cup of the ganache onto the center of the cake and spread it into an even layer. Top with a second layer of cake, flat-side up, and another ½ to ¾ cup of the ganache. Repeat with a third layer of cake and another ½ to ¾ cup of the ganache, then top with the final cake layer, flat-side up. If desired, make a "crumb coat" (see page 147) by smoothing a thin layer of the ganache all over the cake, starting with the top, and then chill the cake until firm. After the crumb coat has firmed up, frost the top and sides of the cake. (If not making a crumb coat, simply use the remaining ganache to frost the top and sides of the cake.) Transfer the cake to the refrigerator to allow the ganache to set.

4. Meanwhile, make the raspberry-chocolate drizzle: Place the chocolate chips in a heatproof medium bowl. In a small saucepan, bring the raspberry jam and cream to a simmer over medium heat, whisking until the jam is melted and smooth. While still hot, pour the cream mixture over the chocolate chips. Let stand for 1 minute, then stir until smooth. Set aside for 20 minutes to cool.

5. Remove the frosted cake from the refrigerator. Slowly spoon the raspberry-chocolate drizzle around the top edge of the cake, letting it drip down over the sides. Garnish the top of the cake with the fresh raspberries. Store leftovers in the refrigerator, loosely wrapped in plastic wrap, for up to 5 days.

PIES AND TARTS!

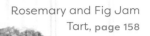

Rosemary and Fig Jam
Tart, page 158

ROSEMARY AND
FIG JAM TART

Herbs may not be an ingredient you associate with baking, but professional pastry chefs often play with ways to meld sweet and savory flavors—and herbs are a great way to do it! Here a spoonful of rosemary adds a gentle piney edge to the crumbly shortbread crust that's the perfect contrast to the sweet fig jam filling. Think of it as a super-sophisticated Fig Newton!

SERVES 8 • **See photograph on page 157**

1 stick (4 ounces) unsalted butter, at room temperature, plus more for greasing

½ cup granulated sugar

1 large egg

1 large egg yolk

1¼ cups all-purpose flour

½ cup finely ground cornmeal

2 teaspoons finely chopped fresh rosemary

1½ teaspoons baking powder

½ teaspoon kosher salt

Nonstick pan spray

1½ cups fig preserves (about one 13-ounce jar)

1 tablespoon turbinado sugar (such as Sugar In the Raw)

TIP This tart can be made in a snap with whatever jam you have in your fridge or pantry. For a basic recipe that works with just about any store-bought preserves, omit the rosemary and cornmeal, and increase the all-purpose flour to 1¾ cups.

1. In a large bowl, using an electric mixer with the whisk attachment, beat the butter and granulated sugar on medium-high speed until light and fluffy, about 3 minutes. Beat in the whole egg and egg yolk one at a time, beating well after each addition and scraping the bowl as needed.

2. In a medium bowl, whisk together the flour, cornmeal, rosemary, baking powder, and salt. Gradually add the flour mixture to the butter mixture and beat on low until just combined.

3. Spray a 9-inch tart pan with a removeable bottom with pan spray. Transfer the dough to a work surface. Pull off one-third of the dough, roll it into an 8-inch log, and wrap it tightly with plastic wrap. With greased fingertips, gently press the remaining dough over the bottom and up the sides of the prepared pan in an even layer. Lightly cover the tart pan with plastic wrap and transfer both the log of dough and the pan to the refrigerator to chill for at least 1 hour.

4. Preheat the oven to 375°F. Spoon the fig jam into the chilled tart shell, spreading it evenly over the pastry. Remove the log of dough from the refrigerator and slice it into thin rounds. Arrange the rounds on top of the jam with their edges touching (they will not cover the whole surface of the tart; feel free to experiment with your own designs). Sprinkle with the turbinado sugar.

5. Bake until the crust is golden, 30 to 35 minutes. Transfer the tart to a wire rack to cool completely, then remove from the pan, slice into wedges, and serve.

PUFF PASTRY PLUM TART
WITH ALLSPICE AND HONEY

Using ripe, seasonal fruit is a simple way to bring sweetness to your baked treats without adding a ton of sugar. That's why Maria chose to make a plum tart just like this one in Season 6 when judge Christina Tosi challenged the cooks to make a dessert without relying on refined sugar. Frozen puff pastry is a great tool to always keep in your baking arsenal. With a package in your freezer and some fresh fruit on hand, an impressive (and easy!) dessert is never more than an hour away.

SERVES 8

½ teaspoon ground allspice

¼ teaspoon freshly ground black pepper

⅛ teaspoon kosher salt

All-purpose flour, for rolling

1¼ pounds black plums (6 or 7 medium), halved, pitted, and cut into ½-inch-thick slices

1 10 inch sheet frozen all-butter puff pastry (from a 14-ounce package), thawed

2 tablespoons honey, for serving

1. Preheat the oven to 425°F. Line a baking sheet with parchment paper.

2. In a small bowl, combine the allspice, pepper, and salt. Set aside.

3. On a lightly floured surface, use a rolling pin to lightly roll the puff pastry into a 10 × 12-inch rectangle. Transfer the pastry to the prepared baking sheet. Leaving a ¾-inch border untouched around the edges, prick the pastry here and there with the tines of a fork (this is called "docking," which prevents the pastry from puffing up too much during baking). Arrange the plum slices in overlapping rows inside the border until the surface is filled. Sprinkle the fruit evenly with the allspice mixture.

4. Bake the tart until the pastry is puffed and golden brown and the plums are juicy and tender, about 25 minutes. Let the tart cool on the pan for at least 15 minutes before transferring it to a cutting board and slicing into 8 rectangles. Drizzle with honey before serving.

~ MASTER THIS ~

ALL-BUTTER PIE DOUGH
(PÂTE BRISÉE)

Whether you're prepping a pumpkin pie for Thanksgiving, a cheesy quiche for Sunday brunch, or just about any other sweet or savory recipe that involves a flaky pastry crust, you're going to want to begin with a batch of pâte brisée, also known as pie dough! Despite its fancy French name, pâte brisée is basically just a combination of flour, salt, and butter with a little water drizzled in to bind it all together. We like to add a whole egg because it makes the dough richer and a little easier to roll out. If you want to take the dough in a sweeter direction, a spoonful of sugar will do the trick.

Just like when you're making biscuits or scones, the keys to getting perfectly flaky pâte brisée are the temperature of the butter (ice cold!) and the way you combine it with the flour in large, pebbly pieces. (This technique is called "cutting in" butter; for more on the method, see MasterChef Lesson, page 32.)

Using a food processor makes the task unbelievably fast and easy, but you do have to be careful not to overprocess the dough, because that will make it tough; you'll know the texture is right if the dough just comes together but is still quite chunky and shaggy. If you don't have a food processor, it's no big deal—the recipe is easy to make by hand.

Once you've made the dough, shape it into a 1-inch-thick disc and wrap it tightly in plastic wrap. It then needs to be chilled to relax the gluten in the flour so the dough is easy to roll and stays nice and tender. Pâte brisée is so handy to have around that once you get the hang of it, you might want to make a habit of always having a batch or two stashed away! It keeps beautifully in the refrigerator for up to 4 days, or you can freeze the discs of dough for up to 2 months.

**MAKES ENOUGH DOUGH FOR 1 DOUBLE-CRUST PIE,
2 SINGLE-CRUST PIES, 2 GALETTES, OR 6 MINI GALETTES**

3 cups all-purpose flour
1 tablespoon sugar (optional)
½ teaspoon kosher salt
2 sticks (8 ounces) unsalted butter,
    cubed and frozen
1 large egg
¼ cup ice water

1. In a food processor, pulse together the flour, sugar (if using), and salt to combine. Add the butter and pulse until the mixture looks sandy, with a few pea-size pieces of butter still visible, about 1 minute.

2. In a small glass, whisk together the egg and ice water. Add the egg mixture to the food processor and pulse in 5-second increments until the dough is moistened and starting to pull away from the sides of the bowl, about 30 seconds. (If the dough still seems dry, add ice water 1 teaspoon at a time; do not overprocess, or your dough will be tough.)

3. Transfer the shaggy dough to a clean work surface and divide it in half. Shape each half into a 1-inch-thick disc and wrap each tightly in plastic wrap. Refrigerate for at least 30 minutes or up to 3 days before using.

OLD-FASHIONED
BLUEBERRY PIE

It may look simple, but mastering the perfect summer pie is no easy feat. That's why budding chefs should always have a few tricks up their sleeves. To make sure you'll get thick, jammy slices, use a deep-dish pie pan and don't skimp on the berries, and if you want to keep practicing your fruit pie skills, you can try swapping out the blueberries for an equal amount of sliced peaches or plums. The flavors are so bright and tasty you don't need anything to dress it up—though if you serve it à la mode with *Easy Vanilla Ice Cream* (page 220), it's doubtful anyone will object!

SERVES 8

All-Butter Pie Dough (page 160)

7 cups blueberries

1 cup granulated sugar

3 tablespoons small tapioca pearls (such as Kraft Minute brand)

Grated zest and juice of 1 lemon

¼ teaspoon nutmeg, preferably freshly grated

¼ teaspoon kosher salt

All-purpose flour, for rolling

1 large egg

1 tablespoon turbinado sugar (such as Sugar In the Raw)

1. Prepare and chill the pie dough as directed on page 160.

2. In a large bowl, combine the blueberries, granulated sugar, tapioca, lemon zest, lemon juice, nutmeg, and salt. Stir the mixture gently until the fruit is coated with the sugar and the tapioca is evenly distributed. Set aside at room temperature for 15 minutes to let the fruit macerate and the tapioca soften.

3. Remove one disc of dough from the refrigerator. Unwrap the dough and, on a lightly floured surface, roll it into a 12-inch round about ⅛ inch thick, dusting the top and underside with more flour as needed to keep the dough from sticking. Drape the dough into a 9½-inch deep-dish pan so that it lies across the bottom and over the edges of the pan without needing to be pulled or stretched. Return the pan to the refrigerator to keep the pastry cool while you roll out the remaining dough.

4. Preheat the oven to 425°F.

5. Remove the second disc of dough from the refrigerator. On a lightly floured surface, roll it into a 12-inch round about ⅛ inch thick.

6. Remove the pie shell from the refrigerator. Fill it with the blueberry mixture, piling the berries in the center of the pie shell in a small mound. Place the second round of dough over the fruit to cover it. Trim away any dough that is hanging over

the edges of the pie pan (for pie tips and techniques, see MasterChef Lesson, page 164). Using your fingers, press the edges of the dough together to seal and create a fluted edge. With a sharp knife, slice three small vents in the middle of the top crust (this allows steam to escape during baking and helps prevent the crust from splitting).

7. In a small bowl, whisk together the egg and 1 tablespoon water. Brush the mixture onto the top and edges of the pie in a thin layer so the egg wash doesn't pool around the edges. Sprinkle the surface of the pie with the turbinado sugar.

8. Place the pie pan on a rimmed baking sheet and bake until the crust looks pale and dry, about 25 minutes. Reduce the oven temperature to 375°F and bake until the crust is a deep golden brown and the fruit is bubbling, about 35 minutes more. Transfer the pie to a wire rack. Because the tapioca and the fruit need to cool in order to set, let the pie rest for at least 3 hours before slicing and serving.

PREPARING PIE CRUST

Making pies from scratch can intimidate even experienced bakers, but one of the nicest things about pies is that they look pretty even when they're not perfect. Filling leaking a little? Crust a bit cracked? Don't fret—just call it "rustic!" And once you've learned a reliable dough recipe (like the recipe on page 160) and a couple of simple techniques, the task of rolling and shaping the crust really does get a whole lot easier. For painless pie making, just remember these rules of thumb:

- Always chill your dough for at least 30 minutes before rolling it out. Not only does this make it easier to handle, it gives the gluten proteins inside the dough a chance to relax, which helps keep the crust tender.
- When you're ready to roll the dough, work quickly and confidently. To get nice flakes, it's important that the flecks of butter in the dough stay firm and cold, not melty. If the dough starts to seem warm or saggy while you're working, pause and pop it back in the fridge (you can transfer it to a parchment-lined baking sheet so it chills in a flat layer) for a few minutes.
- Dust your work surface generously with flour. And if your dough still starts to stick during rolling, work it up with a spatula or a bench scraper and sprinkle a bit more flour underneath and on top of the dough. You can always use a pastry brush to wipe the excess flour off before baking.
- All pies look lovelier when they're finished with an egg wash and a sprinkling of sugar. To make the egg wash, just beat a large egg with a couple of spoonfuls of water and use a pastry brush to paint it on the dough just before you put the pie in the oven. Just make sure to use a light touch: If you put the egg wash on too thick, it will drip and collect in dark pools at the edges of the pie. Then sprinkle it all over with a few pinches of coarse turbinado sugar. After baking, the crust will emerge beautifully golden, shiny, and sparkling. Granulated sugar on top can be pretty, too, for more of a glistening sparkle.

ROLLING OUT DOUGH: A STEP-BY-STEP

1. Set a chilled disc of dough on a well-floured work surface. Sprinkle a little flour on top of the dough. Place your rolling pin crosswise on the disc of dough, with the end of the pin at the nine o'clock and three o'clock positions. Place your hands in the middle of the rolling pin and, applying steady downward pressure, make two or three strokes with the rolling pin, pushing it out and away from your body.

2. Lightly lift the dough with your fingertips or a spatula, sprinkle a little more flour underneath the dough if needed, and rotate it 90 degrees. Place the rolling pin over the dough again at the nine o'clock and three o'clock positions and repeat making two or three strokes, pushing the rolling pin out and away from your body.

3. Continue lifting the dough, sprinkling flour, rotating, and rolling until the dough forms a thin, even round. As your rolled piece of dough gets larger, continue to move your hands out to the ends of the rolling pin so you have an even thickness. For a 9- or 9½-inch deep-dish pie pan, you'll want a round that is about 12 inches in diameter.

Step 1: On a well-floured surface, use steady downward strokes with a rolling pin to roll the dough out and away from your body.

Step 2: To transfer rolled dough to the pie pan, roll it around the pin, move it, and then gently unroll it over the dish.

Step 3: Use a sharp knife or a pair of scissors to trim the edges of the dough, leaving about 1-inch of overhang on all sides.

Step 4: Use your thumb and index fingers to seal the edges of the pie with a decorative scalloped edge.

4. To transfer the dough to your pie pan, lightly roll it around the rolling pin, then slowly unroll it over the dish, make sure the dough is centered. Use your fingertips to lightly settle the dough into the pan, taking care not to stretch it to make it fit. (Stretching the dough can cause it to shrink during baking.)

5. Use a sharp knife or a pair of scissors to trim the dough, leaving about 1 inch hanging over the edge of the pan on all sides. Patch any cracks or holes in the dough with the scraps. Fill the pie. If making a double-crust pie, roll out and trim the remaining dough in the same fashion and use it to cover the filling.

FINISHING TOUCHES

Once your dough is snuggled into the pan, filled, and topped, it's time to seal (or "crimp") the edges of the dough and add any decorative finishing touches. One eye-catching option is to roll your dough scraps, cut them into shapes with cookie cutters, and arrange them on top of the pie (use egg wash to glue the shapes to the crust). Or, instead of slicing simple vents in the top of your pie, use small star- or heart-shaped cookie cutters (or any design you like!) to cut small decorative shapes out of the top crust. There are also all kinds of ways you can dress up your crust using little more than your fingertips, a knife, and a fork. Here are a few you might want to try:

Scalloped edge: This wavy edge is one of the most traditional finishes. To make it, hold the thumb and index of your left hand about 1 inch apart on the rim of the pie shell, resting on the outside edge of the pie pan. With the index finger of your other hand, press the dough outward toward them. Repeat to form an undulating scalloped design.
Herringbone edge: Trim the dough to the outside edge of the pan. Dip a fork in flour and press the tines down onto the rim of dough (but take care not to slice through it). Turn the fork 45 degrees and press next to the first set of marks, creating a herringbone pattern. Continue around the rim.
Checkerboard edge: Trim the dough even with the outside edge of the pan. Using scissors, make slices at ½- to 1-inch intervals all around the edge to create a series of tabs. (Make sure that you have an even number of tabs when you finish.) Fill the pie, then fold every other tab up over the filling, until the whole edge is finished. This design works best for single-crust fruit pies or custard pies, like pumpkin.

BLOOD ORANGE AND
LEMON CREAM PIE
WITH FRESH RASPBERRIES AND CREAM

Because she comes from a long line of Southern bakers, Adaiah felt confident going into the Season 2 cream pie challenge—and that confidence paid off when she presented this gorgeous citrus and raspberry pie to the judges. Judge Gordon Ramsay told the kids that the most important qualities to look for in a cream pie are a crispy, cracking crust and a custardy filling that's perfectly balanced between sweet and tart. Luckily for Adaiah, this one nails it on both counts!

SERVES 8

SEASON 2

ADAIAH

All-Butter Pie Dough (page 160)
All-purpose flour, for rolling

BLOOD ORANGE AND
LEMON CREAM FILLING

1 teaspoon unflavored powdered gelatin
3 cups plus 2 tablespoons whole milk
4 large egg yolks
½ cup plus 2 tablespoons granulated sugar

⅓ cup cornstarch
1 tablespoon pure vanilla extract
2 tablespoons unsalted butter
2 tablespoons finely grated blood orange zest, plus more for garnish
2 tablespoons blood orange juice
2 tablespoons finely grated lemon zest
2 tablespoons fresh lemon juice

WHIPPED CREAM

2 cups heavy cream
2 tablespoons confectioners' sugar
1 teaspoon pure vanilla extract

ASSEMBLY

1 pint fresh raspberries
Grated blood orange zest

1. Prepare and chill the pie dough as directed on page 160. You will only use one of the dough discs—save the other for another time.

2. Dust a work surface lightly with flour. Remove the chilled dough from the refrigerator and, using a rolling pin, roll it into a 12-inch round about ⅛ inch thick. (For pie dough rolling and trimming tips, see page 164.) Drape the dough into a 9½-inch deep-dish pie pan so that it lies across the bottom and up the sides

without stretching. When the dough is in place, trim away the excess, leaving a 1-inch overhang of dough around the edges. Fold the overhang under and use a fork to crimp the edge. Pierce the bottom of the dough all over with the tines of a fork (this is called "docking") and place the pan in the freezer to chill for 15 minutes.

3. Preheat the oven to 400°F.

4. Remove the pie shell from the freezer. Line the pie shell with parchment paper and fill with enough dried beans or pie weights to cover the surface. Bake until the crust is pale golden around the edges, about 20 minutes. Carefully remove the parchment and the pie weights and return the pie crust to the oven. Bake until the bottom of the crust is dry and the edges are beginning to brown, about 8 minutes more. Transfer to a wire rack to cool completely.

5. Meanwhile, make the blood orange and lemon cream filling: In a small bowl, whisk the gelatin with 2 tablespoons of the milk until smooth. Set aside for 5 minutes. In a medium bowl, whisk the egg yolks, ½ cup of the milk, the graulated sugar, cornstarch, and vanilla until smooth.

6. In a large saucepan, bring the remaining 2½ cups milk to a low simmer over medium heat. Slowly drizzle ¼ cup of the hot milk into the egg yolk mixture, stirring constantly. (This is called "tempering" and helps prevent the eggs from curdling. See the MasterChef Lesson on page 210.) Beat the warm milk mixture into the eggs, ¼ cup at a time, until fully combined. Return the mixture to the saucepan and cook, whisking constantly, until thickened, 2 to 3 minutes. Add the butter, gelatin mixture, blood orange zest, blood orange juice, lemon zest, and lemon juice and whisk until smooth. Transfer the custard to a bowl, press a piece of plastic wrap against the surface to prevent a skin from forming, and refrigerate until cold, about 2 hours.

7. Make the whipped cream: In a large bowl, using an electric mixer fitted with the whisk attachment, beat the cream, confectioners' sugar, and vanilla on medium-high speed until the cream holds stiff peaks, 2 to 2½ minutes.

8. Assemble the pie: Spoon half the chilled custard into the cooled pie shell in an even layer. Scatter a single layer of raspberries over the top. Top with the remaining custard. Spoon whipped cream on top of the pie to cover. Garnish with the remaining raspberries and a flurry of blood orange zest. Serve chilled.

SWEET CHERRY
HAND PIES

What's better than a cherry pie? How about one that fits in your lunchbox? These adorable hand pies are golden, flaky, and filled with a fresh cherry filling that's jazzed up with brown sugar, lime zest, cinnamon, and allspice. Evan from Season 6 says the hardest part about making cherry pie is getting the pits out—without a cherry pitter, it can *literally* be the pits! Happily, you can order the tool online for just a couple of dollars. It's definitely a worthwhile investment! Make sure you buy the kind with a cherry juice guard—so you don't end up getting splattered!

MAKES 8

All-Butter Pie Dough (page 160)

1 pound sweet cherries, pitted and halved (see Tip)

1 teaspoon finely grated lime zest

1 tablespoon fresh lime juice

¼ cup packed light brown sugar

1 tablespoon cornstarch

½ teaspoon ground allspice

½ teaspoon ground cinnamon

¼ teaspoon kosher salt

1 teaspoon cider vinegar

1 large egg, lightly beaten

1 tablespoon turbinado sugar (such as Sugar In the Raw)

TIP If you don't have a cherry pitter, you can use a chopstick to remove the pits. Just place the point of the chopstick at the stem end of the cherry, give it a push, and pop the pit out the other side.

1. Prepare and chill the pie dough as directed on page 160. You will only use one of the dough discs—save the other for another time.

2. Meanwhile, in a medium saucepan, combine the cherries, lime zest, and lime juice and cook, stirring frequently, until the cherries begin to release their juices, about 3 minutes. In a small bowl, whisk together the brown sugar, cornstarch, allspice, cinnamon, and salt. Whisk the sugar mixture into the warm cherry mixture. Reduce the heat to low and simmer, stirring frequently, until the mixture is smooth, jammy, and thickened, about 3 minutes. Remove from the heat and whisk in the vinegar. Transfer to a bowl, cover with plastic wrap, and refrigerate until cool.

3. Remove the dough from the refrigerator and let it rest at room temperature until slightly pliable, 3 to 5 minutes. Divide the dough into 8 equal pieces and gently press each piece into a small disc. On a lightly floured work surface, use a rolling pin to roll each disc into a 6-inch round about ⅛ inch thick.

4. Line a baking sheet with parchment paper. Dip your finger in cold water and lightly moisten the edges of the rounds. Place one heaping spoonful (about 2 tablespoons) of the cherry filling in the center of each round, then fold the dough over to make a

half-moon. Use your fingers to press the edges together, then use a fork to crimp the edges to seal. Arrange the pies on the prepared baking sheet, spacing them at least 1 inch apart. Transfer to the refrigerator to chill for 1 hour or up to 2 days.

5. Preheat the oven to 400°F.

6. Before baking, brush the pies lightly with the beaten egg thinned with 1 tablespoon water. Using a sharp knife, cut two small slits in the top of each pie and sprinkle with the turbinado sugar. Bake until deeply golden, about 30 minutes (don't worry if they leak a little—they'll still be delicious!). Let the pies rest on the baking sheet for 10 minutes, then transfer to a wire rack to cool. Serve slightly warm or at room temperature. Store leftover pies in an airtight container in the refrigerator for up to 4 days.

LEMON MERINGUE PIE
WITH VANILLA COOKIE CRUST

This lovely lemon meringue pie has a buttery vanilla cookie crust that comes together in a snap, making it a surprisingly quick project. Because it's easiest to separate eggs when they are cold (and even the tiniest trace of yolk in the whites will make the meringue hard to whip), separate the eggs for this recipe as soon as you take them out of the refrigerator. Then put the egg whites in a bowl on the counter and let them come to room temperature while you're preparing the filling. When your pie comes out perfectly, you may not get to throw it in Gordon Ramsay's face like the Season 3 contestants did after their lemon meringue pie challenge—but you *will* get the pleasure of eating it!

SERVES 8

VANILLA COOKIE CRUST

40 vanilla wafer cookies (such as Nilla wafers)

6 tablespoons (¾ stick) unsalted butter, melted

¼ cup sugar

½ teaspoon kosher salt

LEMON FILLING

⅓ cup cornstarch

1 cup sugar

6 large egg yolks

½ cup plus 2 tablespoons fresh lemon juice (from 3 or 4 lemons)

¼ teaspoon kosher salt

2 tablespoons finely grated lemon zest

2 tablespoons cold unsalted butter, thinly sliced

MERINGUE

6 large egg whites, at room temperature

½ teaspoon cream of tartar

⅛ teaspoon kosher salt

½ cup sugar

1. Make the vanilla cookie crust: Preheat the oven to 375°F. In a food processor, process the vanilla wafer cookies until finely crushed, about 1 minute. In a medium bowl, combine 2 cups of the crushed cookies, the melted butter, sugar, and salt. Mix well until the crumbs are saturated. Using the back of a spoon or the bottom of a measuring cup, press the mixture evenly over the bottom of a 9-inch pie pan.

2. Bake until lightly golden, about 10 minutes. Transfer the pie pan to a wire rack to cool completely. Keep the oven on.

3. Make the lemon filling: In a medium saucepan, whisk together the cornstarch, sugar, egg yolks, and lemon juice. Add 1¼ cups water and whisk until smooth. Bring to a boil over medium heat, whisking constantly, until the mixture is thick and bubbling, about 6 minutes. Cook, whisking and scraping the sides of the pan, for 1 minute more, then remove from the heat and stir in the lemon zest and butter until completely combined. Immediately spread the warm filling evenly into the prepared crust.

4. Make the meringue: In a large, clean, dry bowl, using an electric mixer fitted with the whisk attachment, beat the egg whites and cream of tartar on medium-high speed until soft peaks form, about 4 minutes. With the mixer running, add the salt and then sprinkle in the sugar, a tablespoon at a time, until the meringue forms stiff, glossy peaks, 2 to 3 minutes more.

5. Spoon the meringue over the warm lemon filling, spreading and piling it in peaks so that it covers the surface and touches the crust all the way around. (Making sure that the meringue touches and covers the edges of the crust helps prevent the meringue from shrinking and exposing the filling.) Bake until the meringue is golden, about 15 minutes. Transfer to a wire rack to cool to room temperature before slicing and serving.

APPLE-PERSIMMON
CROSTATAS
WITH WALNUT CRUMBLE AND CRÈME ANGLAISE

The terms *crostata* and *galette* are just alternate names for a rustic freeform pie. To make a crostata, instead of shaping the pastry inside a pie pan, roll the dough flat and lay the filling inside before folding the edges of the dough up and over it. When Beni presented her fragrant and nutty apple crostatas to the judges in Season 6, Christina Tosi said there "wasn't one element done with anything less than perfection." And Gordon Ramsay liked them so much, he actually licked his plate clean! If you can't find persimmons, replace them with three more apples.

SERVES 6

SEASON 6

All-Butter Pie Dough (page 160)

WALNUT CRUMBLE

¼ cup all-purpose flour

¼ cup packed dark brown sugar

¼ cup finely chopped walnuts

2 tablespoons rolled oats

¼ teaspoon kosher salt

3 tablespoons unsalted butter, cubed

APPLE-PERSIMMON FILLING

2 tablespoons all-purpose flour

¼ cup granulated sugar

1 teaspoon pure vanilla extract

1 teaspoon ground cinnamon

1 teaspoon nutmeg, preferably freshly grated

½ teaspoon ground cardamom

3 Granny Smith apples, peeled, quartered, cored, and thinly sliced

3 Fuyu persimmons, seeded and thinly sliced (see Tips)

CRÈME ANGLAISE

1 cup whole milk

1 tablespoon pure vanilla extract

⅓ cup granulated sugar

¼ teaspoon kosher salt

3 large egg yolks

CROSTATAS

⅓ cup walnut pieces

All-purpose flour, for rolling

1 large egg, beaten

2 tablespoons turbinado sugar (such as Sugar In the Raw)

1. Prepare and chill the pie dough as directed on page 160.

2. Make the walnut crumble: Preheat the oven to 400°F. Line a baking sheet with parchment paper.

3. In a small bowl, whisk together the flour, brown sugar, walnuts, oats, and salt. Add the butter and rub the mixture between your fingers until crumbly, with a few pea-size pieces of butter still visible. Spread the crumble evenly over the prepared pan and

bake until crisp and golden, about 10 minutes. Set aside to cool, then use your fingers to break the crumble into small pieces. Leave the oven on for the crostatas.

4. Meanwhile, make the apple-persimmon filling: In a large bowl, whisk together the flour, granulated sugar, vanilla, cinnamon, nutmeg, and cardamom. Add the apples and persimmons and gently toss to combine. Set aside.

5. Make the crème anglaise: Set up an ice bath by filling a medium bowl with ice cubes and placing another small bowl inside it; set aside. In a medium saucepan, whisk together ⅔ cup of the milk, the vanilla, granulated sugar, and salt. Bring to a simmer over medium heat, stirring to dissolve the sugar. In a small heatproof bowl, whisk together the remaining ⅓ cup milk and the egg yolks. Ladle ⅓ cup of the hot milk into the yolk mixture, while whisking constantly, then return the yolk mixture to the pan. Bring the sauce almost to a simmer over medium heat, stirring often, but do not let it boil (boiling will curdle the eggs and make the sauce lumpy). Test for doneness by dipping a spoon into the sauce and running your finger over the back of the spoon: If it leaves a clean trail in the sauce, it is done. Remove the pan from the heat and immediately pour the custard through a fine-mesh sieve held over the bowl sitting in the ice bath. Stir until smooth, then cover with plastic wrap and refrigerate until ready to serve.

6. Make the crostatas: Line two baking sheets with parchment paper. Remove the chilled dough from the refrigerator and let it rest at room temperature for 10 minutes.

7. Using a food processor and the small bowl insert, pulse the walnuts until finely ground, about 30 to 45 seconds.

8. Dust a work surface lightly with flour. Divide each disc of dough evenly into 3 pieces and gently press each piece into a 1-inch-thick disc. One at a time, roll the discs into rounds ⅛ inch thick. Transfer the rounds to the prepared baking sheets. Sprinkle the ground walnuts into the center of each round. Top each with the apple-persimmon mixture, arranging the slices of fruit in tightly packed swirls and leaving 1 inch of dough bare around the edges. Fold the edges of the dough up and over the fruit to form a packet, with some fruit still peeking out in the center. Brush the tops and edges of the crostatas with the beaten egg and sprinkle with the turbinado sugar.

9. Bake until the fruit is soft and the pastry is deeply golden, about 30 minutes. Let the crostatas rest on the baking sheets for 5 minutes, then transfer them to a wire rack to cool. Serve warm or at room temperature, garnished with the walnut crumble and drizzled with the crème anglaise.

TIPS

Most persimmons that you find in markets in fall are one of two varieties: Hachiya or Fuyu. Though both are orange-skinned, Fuyus are squatter and Hachiyas have more of an acorn shape. They also ripen differently. Hachiyas are ready to eat when they feel soft to the touch and the interior is soft and custardy; Fuyus, on the other hand, are eaten firm, like an apple.

To get the flavor of crème anglaise without all the work, buy a pint of high-quality all-natural vanilla ice cream (which is essentially *frozen* crème anglaise) and let it melt in your refrigerator. Before serving, transfer the melted ice cream to a bowl and whip it briefly with a whisk or an electric mixer. No one will know your secret!

MINI SALTED CHOCOLATE CARAMEL
TARTS

Like ganache and pâte brisée, homemade caramel is one of the basic elements in the pastry chef's toolbox and a staple in the *MasterChef Junior* kitchen. Because it involves melting sugar until it is extremely hot, learning to make caramel can seem scary at first, but if you work carefully (and have an adult on hand to help you out), you might be surprised at how quickly you get comfortable with the process. Once you do, these miniature salted caramel tartlets are a delicious way to get in some practice! Using confectioners' sugar in the chocolate pastry shell gives it a tender, cookie-like crumb, and adding a pinch of flaky sea salt on top of the ganache is a sparkling finishing touch.

MAKES 8

CHOCOLATE TART SHELLS

1 large egg, at room temperature

2 tablespoons ice water

½ teaspoon pure vanilla extract

1 cup all-purpose flour

½ cup plus 2 tablespoons almond flour

¼ cup unsweetened Dutch-process cocoa powder, plus more for rolling

½ cup confectioners' sugar

¼ teaspoon kosher salt

10 tablespoons (5 ounces) cold unsalted butter, cubed

Nonstick pan spray

CARAMEL

1½ cups granulated sugar

3 tablespoons light corn syrup

½ teaspoon kosher salt

6 tablespoons (¾ stick) unsalted butter

7 tablespoons heavy cream

GANACHE

1 cup bittersweet chocolate chips or chopped bittersweet chocolate (about 6 ounces)

½ cup heavy cream

1½ teaspoons flaky sea salt (such as Maldon), for garnish

1. Make the chocolate tart shells: In a small bowl, whisk together the egg, ice water, and vanilla. Set aside.

2. In a food processor, pulse together the all-purpose flour, almond flour, cocoa powder, confectioners' sugar, and kosher salt to combine. Add the butter and pulse until the mixture is sandy, with a few pea-size pieces of butter still visible, about 45 seconds to 1 minute. Add the egg mixture and pulse until the dough is moistened and starting to pull away from the sides of

recipe continues

the bowl, about 30 seconds. (If the dough is still dry, add ice water 1 teaspoon at a time; do not overprocess.) Transfer the dough to a clean work surface and shape it into a 2-inch-wide log. Slice the log crosswise into 8 equal pieces and gently flatten each one into a small disc. Wrap the discs in plastic wrap and refrigerate for at least 2 hours or up to 3 days.

3. Lightly coat eight 4-inch tart pans with removable bottoms with pan spray. Dust a clean work surface with a sprinkling of cocoa powder. Working with one piece at a time, roll each chilled disc of dough into a 6-inch round. Gently transfer the rounds to the prepared tart pans, pressing the pastry over the bottom and up the sides of the fluted pans. Once the dough is in place, roll a rolling pin over the top of the pans to trim any excess dough hanging over the sides. If there are tears or holes in the crusts, use the scraps to patch them. Pierce the bottom of the dough all over with the tines of a fork (this is called "docking"). Place the pans on a baking sheet and transfer to the freezer to chill for 10 minutes.

4. Preheat the oven to 350°F.

5. Remove the baking sheet from the freezer, line each tart pan with a small square of parchment paper, and fill with pie weights or dried beans. Bake until the shells are firm and dry, about 20 minutes. Transfer the tart pans to a wire rack to cool.

6. Meanwhile, make the caramel: In a medium saucepan, whisk together the granulated sugar, corn syrup, kosher salt, and 6 tablespoons water. Cook over medium heat, stirring, until the sugar has dissolved. Bring to a boil and cook, without stirring but swirling the pan occasionally, until the syrup turns a deep golden amber and a candy thermometer inserted into the mixture reads 350°F, 6 to 8 minutes. Remove the pan from the heat and whisk in the butter and cream (be very careful—the mixture will be very hot and bubble up a lot). Whisk until smooth, about 1 minute. Set the mixture aside to cool for 2 minutes, then divide the caramel among the cooled tart shells. Return the tart pans to the baking sheet and chill in the refrigerator until the caramel has set up, about 1 hour or for up to 3 days.

7. Make the ganache: Place the chocolate chips in a heatproof medium bowl. In a small saucepan, bring the cream to a simmer over medium heat. Pour the hot cream over the chocolate chips and let stand for 1 minute, then stir until smooth. Divide the ganache evenly among the cooled tarts and use a teaspoon or a small offset spatula to spread it over the caramel in an even layer.

8. Sprinkle each tart with a pinch of flaky sea salt. Return the tart pans to the baking sheet and place in the refrigerator until the ganache is set and the caramel is cool, at least 1 hour or for up to 3 days. Serve chilled.

PUMPKIN TART
WITH CRANBERRY COMPOTE

Beni's dish from the Season 6 canned food challenge was an elegant update on a traditional holiday favorite: pumpkin pie. She combined two of Thanksgiving's most iconic flavors—creamy pumpkin and bright, tart cranberries—and adds a blend of cinnamon, nutmeg, and coriander (for a citrusy kick) that dresses up the creamy pumpkin filling. Here the cranberry compote is really just a sweet-and-spicy cranberry sauce—so if your family already has a favorite recipe, feel free to use that one instead.

SERVES 8

SEASON
6

TART SHELL

1¼ cups all-purpose flour, plus more for rolling

½ cup confectioners' sugar

1 stick (4 ounces) unsalted butter, cubed and frozen

¼ teaspoon kosher salt

1 large egg

Nonstick pan spray

1 large egg white, beaten

PUMPKIN FILLING

½ cup granulated sugar

¼ cup cornstarch

½ teaspoon ground cinnamon

¼ teaspoon ground coriander

¼ teaspoon nutmeg, preferably freshly grated

⅛ teaspoon kosher salt

2 cups whole milk

2 large egg yolks

1 tablespoon pure vanilla extract

1 cup canned unsweetened pumpkin puree

CRANBERRY COMPOTE

1¼ cups fresh or frozen cranberries

⅓ cup packed dark brown sugar

¼ cup apple cider

1 tablespoon grated orange zest

¼ teaspoon ground cinnamon

⅛ teaspoon ground allspice

½ teaspoon grated orange zest, for garnish

1. Make the tart shell: In a food processor, pulse together the flour, confectioners' sugar, butter, and salt until the mixture is sandy, with a few pea-size pieces of butter still visible, about 1 minute. Add the egg and pulse until the dough is moistened and starting to pull away from the sides of the bowl, about 30 seconds. (If the dough is still dry, add ice water 1 teaspoon at a time; do not overprocess.) Shape the dough into a 1-inch-thick disc and wrap it tightly with plastic wrap. Transfer to the refrigerator to chill for at least 30 minutes or up to 3 days.

recipe continues

2. Coat an 11 × 7-inch tart pan with a removable bottom with pan spray. (You may also use a standard round tart pan if you prefer.) Dust a work surface lightly with flour. Remove the chilled dough from the refrigerator and, using a rolling pin, roll it into a 13 × 9-inch rectangle about ⅛ inch thick. Gently transfer the dough to the tart pan and press it over the bottom and up the sides. Once the dough is in place, roll the rolling pin over the top of the pan to trim off any excess dough that is hanging over the sides. (If there are any tears or holes in the crust, you can use the scraps to patch them.) Pierce the bottom of the pastry all over with the tines of a fork (this is called "docking"). Place the tart pan on a baking sheet and transfer to the freezer to chill for 15 minutes.

3. Preheat the oven to 375°F.

4. Remove the pan from the freezer and line the pastry with parchment paper, then fill with dried beans or pie weights. Bake until pale golden around the edges, 20 to 25 minutes. Remove the parchment and the pie weights and return the pan to the oven. Bake until the pastry is dry and the edges are just beginning to brown, 4 to 5 minutes more. Brush the inside of the crust with the beaten egg white (see Tip) and bake until dry, about 1 minute. Transfer the pan to a wire rack to cool completely.

5. Meanwhile, make the pumpkin filling: Set up an ice bath by filling a large bowl with ice cubes and 1 cup water. In a medium saucepan, whisk together the granulated sugar, cornstarch, cinnamon, coriander, nutmeg, and salt. Whisk in the milk, then the egg yolks, whisking until smooth. Bring the mixture to a simmer over medium heat, stirring constantly, and cook until thick, 6 to 7 minutes. Whisk in the vanilla and the pumpkin puree and cook, stirring, until smooth, about 1 minute more. Submerge the bottom of the saucepan in the prepared ice bath (be careful not to get water in the pan) and whisk occasionally until the filling is cool, about 15 minutes. Transfer the filling to a bowl and press a piece of plastic wrap against the surface to prevent a skin from forming. Chill for at least 3 hours or up to 3 days.

6. Make the cranberry compote: In a medium saucepan, combine the cranberries, brown sugar, cider, orange zest, cinnamon, and allspice. Bring to a boil over medium heat, then reduce the heat and simmer, stirring occasionally, until the cranberries are soft and the sauce is thick, about 15 minutes. Remove from the heat, transfer to a bowl, and refrigerate until cool, at least 1 hour or for up to 3 days.

7. To assemble the tart: Spoon the pumpkin filling into the cooled tart shell and spread it in an even layer. Spoon the cooled cranberry compote onto the center of the tart in a pretty mound and garnish with the orange zest.

TIP Brushing egg white over the inside of the tart shell during baking forms a moisture barrier over the crust and provides protection against sogginess.

CITRUS-MASCARPONE
TART
WITH SUMMER BERRIES

When judge Christina Tosi introduced the fruit tart challenge in Season 6, she reminded the young bakers that the way a fruit tart looks is just as important as the flavor. The secret to nailing that straight-from-the-pâtisserie look? A thin, firm, flaky shell and a balanced ratio of creamy filling to fruit topping. Olivia learned how to make tarts like this one with her great-grandmother and was excited to show the judges her skills. Her tangy, no-cook lemon curd filling is a great and easy alternative to pastry cream. When it's time to arrange the fresh fruit topping, choose a combination of whatever berries look best at the market, and remember judge Tosi's advice: "This shouldn't just be a work of art—it should be a masterpiece!"

MAKES ONE 9-INCH TART (SERVES 6 TO 8)

SEASON 6

OLIVIA

TART SHELL

1¼ cups all-purpose flour, plus more for rolling

½ cup confectioners' sugar

1 stick (4 ounces) unsalted butter, cubed and frozen

¼ teaspoon kosher salt

1 large egg

Nonstick pan spray

1 large egg white, lightly beaten

CITRUS-MASCARPONE FILLING

1 cup mascarpone cheese

½ cup cream cheese, at room temperature

½ cup store-bought lemon curd (see Tips)

2 tablespoons finely grated lemon zest

⅓ cup confectioners' sugar

ASSEMBLY

2 pints mixed fresh berries, such as blueberries, blackberries, raspberries, golden raspberries, or red currants

TIPS For a glossy, bakery-perfect look, after you've finished the berry topping, brush the fruit lightly with a little warmed strawberry jelly thinned with a teaspoon of warm water.

Lemon curd is widely available in grocery stores: Look for a jar alongside the jams and jellies or in the British section of the international food aisle.

1. Make the tart shell: In a food processor, pulse together the flour, confectioners' sugar, butter, and salt until the mixture is sandy, with a few pea-size pieces of butter still visible, about 1 minute. Add the egg and pulse until the dough is moistened and starting to pull away from the sides of the bowl, about 30 seconds. (If the dough is still dry, add ice water 1 teaspoon at a time; do not overprocess.) Shape the dough into a 1-inch-thick disc and wrap it tightly with plastic wrap. Transfer to the refrigerator to chill for at least 30 minutes or up to 3 days.

2. Coat a 9-inch tart pan with a removable bottom with pan spray. Dust a work surface lightly with flour. Remove the chilled dough from the refrigerator and, using a rolling pin, roll it into a 12-inch round about ⅛ inch thick. Gently transfer the dough to the tart pan and press it over the bottom and up the sides of the pan. Once the dough is in place, roll the rolling pin over the top of the pan to trim off any excess dough that is hanging over the sides. (If there are any tears or holes in the crust, you can use the scraps to patch them.) Pierce the bottom of the dough all over with the tines of a fork (this is called "docking"). Place the tart pan in the freezer to chill for 15 minutes.

3. Preheat the oven to 375°F.

4. Remove the tart shell from the freezer. Line the crust with parchment paper, then fill it with dried beans or pie weights. Bake until the crust is pale golden around the edges, 20 to 25 minutes. Carefully remove the parchment and the pie weights and return the tart shell to the oven. Bake until the crust is dry and the edges are just beginning to brown, 4 to 5 minutes more. Brush the inside of the crust with the beaten egg white and bake until dry, about 1 minute more. Transfer the pan to a wire rack to cool completely.

5. Make the citrus-mascarpone filling: In a large bowl, using an electric mixer with the paddle attachment, beat the mascarpone, cream cheese, lemon curd, lemon zest, and confectioners' sugar on medium-high speed until light and smooth, 1 to 2 minutes.

6. Assemble the tart: Spoon the filling into the cooled tart shell and spread it into an even layer. Arrange the berries on top. Chill until ready to serve.

PASTRIES AND FANCY DESSERTS

Caramelized Banana Cannoli with
Ricotta and Dark Chocolate
page 184

CARAMELIZED
BANANA CANNOLI
WITH RICOTTA AND DARK CHOCOLATE

SEASON 6

This is a very involved recipe, but if you're looking for an impressive special-occasion dessert, these little cannoli won't disappoint. Mikey was inspired by his Italian heritage when he made crunchy banana cream-filled pastries like these in Season 6—and the results were so amazing they even wowed self-described cannoli expert Joe Bastianich! Caramelizing the sliced bananas in a hot pan before incorporating them into the rich ricotta and cream cheese filling really brings out their butterscotch-y natural sweetness.

MAKES 16 TO 18 CANNOLI • See photograph on page 183

CANNOLI SHELLS

2 cups all-purpose flour

2 tablespoons granulated sugar

¼ teaspoon kosher salt

4 tablespoons (½ stick) cold unsalted butter, finely cubed

2 large eggs, beaten

2 tablespoons white wine vinegar

CARAMELIZED BANANA FILLING

8 ounces whole-milk ricotta cheese

1 tablespoon unsalted butter

2 tablespoons dark brown sugar

2 large ripe bananas, peeled and sliced into ¾-inch rounds.

8 ounces cream cheese, at room temperature

¼ cup whole milk

¼ cup honey

¼ teaspoon ground cinnamon

¼ teaspoon kosher salt

All-purpose flour, for rolling

Vegetable oil, for deep-frying

3 ounces bittersweet chocolate, very finely chopped, for garnish

¼ cup confectioners' sugar, for dusting (optional)

TIP To make DIY cannoli molds, fold a 12-inch square of foil in half and wrap it three times around a broom handle or 1-inch wooden dowel. Slide it off, set aside, and repeat until you've made 18 molds.

1. Make the cannoli shells: In a medium bowl, whisk together the flour, granulated sugar, and salt. Add the butter and, using your fingertips, cut it into the flour until the mixture is sandy, with some pea-size pieces of butter still visible. Using a fork, stir in the eggs and vinegar and mix until the dough just comes together. Turn the dough onto the counter and knead it three or four times until smooth. Press it into a large disc about 1 inch thick and wrap in plastic wrap. Transfer the disc to the refrigerator to rest for at least 20 minutes.

2. Meanwhile, make the caramelized banana filling: Scoop the ricotta into a fine-mesh sieve set over a medium bowl and set aside to drain for 30 minutes.

3. Meanwhile, in a large skillet, melt the butter over medium heat. Add the brown sugar and cook, stirring often, until the mixture is golden and thick, about 2 minutes. Arrange the banana slices cut-side down in the pan on top of the sugar mixture. Cook, undisturbed, until the banana slices are golden brown and caramelized on one side, about 3 minutes, then flip and repeat on the second side, about 3 minutes. Transfer the bananas to a large bowl and let cool to room temperature, about 15 minutes.

4. When the bananas have cooled, roughly mash them with a fork. Add the drained ricotta, cream cheese, milk, honey, cinnamon, and salt and beat, using an electric mixer with the whisk attachment on medium speed, until thick and well combined, about 1 minute. (Don't worry if there are still a few chunks of banana visible; a little bit of texture is good.) Cover and refrigerate the filling for at least 1 hour, while you fry the cannoli shells.

5. Remove the chilled cannoli dough from the refrigerator. Lightly dust a work surface with flour. Using a rolling pin, roll the dough as thin as possible, but no thicker than ⅛ inch. Using a 4-inch round cookie cutter or a similar-size glass, cut the dough into rounds, collecting the scraps and re-rolling them once. Wrap a round of dough around a cannoli mold, pulling one edge over the other so it overlaps, moisten the underside with a drop of water, and press firmly to seal. Repeat with 5 more

pieces of dough and cannoli molds. (You will need 6 cannoli molds to fry them in batches.) Transfer the unshaped rounds to a parchment-lined baking sheet and keep them cool in the refrigerator until ready to use.

6. To fry the shells, pour at least 2 inches vegetable oil into a large, deep, heavy-bottomed pot and heat the oil over medium-high heat until a pinch of flour sizzles when you drop it into the oil or a candy thermometer reads about 360°F. Line a wire rack with paper towels and have it nearby. Using tongs, carefully lower 3 cannoli molds into the oil. Fry, turning the shells slowly in the oil, until they are golden and crisp on all sides, 2 to 3 minutes. Use a frying spider to carefully remove the molds from the oil and transfer them to the paper towel–lined rack. Using an oven mitt to carefully hold the mold, grasp each cannoli shell lightly with a clean kitchen towel and very gently slide it off the mold. Let the cannoli mold rest until cool to the touch. Check that the oil temperature remains at 360°F or adjust the heat accordingly before frying the remaining dough. Let the shells cool to room temperature before filling.

7. To fill the shells, spoon the caramelized banana filling into a pastry bag fitted with a large plain tip. (If you don't have a pastry bag, you can improvise one by snipping off a small corner of a large zip-top storage bag.) Insert the tip of the bag into each shell and squeeze until filled. Dip both ends of the cannoli into the chopped chocolate so the chocolate sticks to the banana filling. If desired, dust the cannoli shells with the confectioners' sugar before serving.

CHURROS
WITH **MANGO-CHILE SAUCE**

There's nothing more delicious than a piping-hot churro dusted with cinnamon-sugar . . . except maybe one that's paired with a tangy mango sauce! Churros are usually served with thick, molten chocolate, but in Season 6, Zia had the brilliant idea to give the dish this fresh, tropical update. A pinch of chile powder and a squeeze of lime juice help give the sauce a little extra zip without making it too spicy.

SERVES 12

SEASON **6**

MANGO-CHILE SAUCE

3 large mangoes, pitted, peeled, chopped, and pureed (about 3 cups)

2 tablespoons sugar

1 teaspoon finely grated lime zest

2 tablespoons fresh lime juice

¼ teaspoon red chile powder (such as ancho)

CHURROS

1¼ cups sugar

3 tablespoons unsalted butter

1 teaspoon pure vanilla extract

½ teaspoon kosher salt

2 cups all-purpose flour

2 large eggs

1 tablespoon ground cinnamon

Vegetable oil, for deep-frying

1. Make the mango-chile sauce: In a medium saucepan, stir together the mango puree, sugar, lime zest, and lime juice. Bring to a simmer over medium heat, then partially cover and cook, stirring occasionally, until reduced to about 1 cup, about 30 minutes. Stir in the chile powder. Transfer the sauce to a bowl and let cool to room temperature. Cover with plastic wrap and refrigerate until chilled, at least 1 hour or for up to 3 days.

2. Make the churros: In a medium saucepan, combine ¼ cup of the sugar, the butter, vanilla, salt, and 2 cups water and bring to a simmer over medium heat, stirring until the butter melts. Add the flour and stir vigorously with a wooden spoon. Cook the mixture, stirring constantly, until the dough forms into a sticky ball and pulls away from the sides of the pan, 30 seconds to 1 minute. Remove the pan from the heat and transfer the dough to a large bowl. Let cool for 5 minutes. Using an electric mixer, add the eggs one at a time and beat on medium speed until the dough is smooth after each addition. Spoon the dough into a pastry bag fitted with a large star tip.

3. Preheat the oven to 200°F.

4. In a large bowl, whisk together the remaining 1 cup sugar and the cinnamon and set aside. Line a wire rack with paper towels and have it nearby.

5. Pour at least 2 inches of vegetable oil into a large, deep, heavy-bottomed pot and heat the oil over medium-high heat until a pinch of flour sizzles when you drop it into the oil or a candy thermometer reads around 360°F. Holding the pastry bag over the hot oil, squeeze about 3 inches of dough from the pastry bag, slicing it off at the tip end with a paring knife, and carefully let the dough fall into the hot oil. Repeat to make 5 churros. Fry the churros, using a fork or frying spider to turn them often, until they are evenly golden brown and cooked through, about 5 minutes.

Using a fork or a frying spider, transfer the churros to the paper towels to drain, then transfer them to a baking sheet and place in the oven to keep warm while you fry the remaining dough.

6. While the churros are still warm, toss them in the cinnamon-sugar mixture until well coated, shaking off any excess. Stir the chilled mango sauce to loosen. Serve the churros immediately, with the mango-chile sauce alongside for dipping.

~ MASTER THIS ~

SWEET OR SAVORY
PÂTE À CHOUX

Remember in Season 4 when the junior chefs were challenged to build a towering Croquembouche (page 190)—a stunning pyramid of cream puffs bound together with caramel and decorated with spun sugar—completely from scratch? Success or failure all came down to nailing their pâte à choux—and now you can master this pastry classic, too. This surprisingly simple, eggy dough is one of the most important recipes for pastry chefs to know and is the basis of all sorts of impressive treats. The sweet version is perfect for profiteroles, éclairs (page 194), and cream puffs (page 192). Or you can make the dough without sugar and bake small puffs to be filled with chicken salad, spinach artichoke dip, or any of your other favorite cheese spreads for an elegant party snack.

MAKES ENOUGH DOUGH FOR ABOUT 12 ÉCLAIRS, 24 LARGE CREAM PUFFS, OR 50 MINI PUFFS

1 stick (4 ounces) unsalted butter, cubed

2 tablespoons granulated sugar (optional, for the sweet version)

½ to 1 teaspoon kosher salt (½ teaspoon for sweet version; 1 teaspoon for savory version)

1¼ cups all-purpose flour

4 large eggs

1. In a medium saucepan, combine the butter, sugar (if using), salt, and 1 cup water. Bring to a simmer over medium heat, stirring until the butter melts. Add the flour all at once and stir vigorously with a wooden spoon. Cook, stirring constantly, until there is a thin film of dough on the bottom of the pan and the dough forms a sticky ball and pulls away from the sides of the pan, 30 seconds to 1 minute. Remove the pan from the heat and let the dough cool for 5 minutes.

2. Transfer the dough to a large bowl. Add the eggs one at a time and beat using an electric mixer with the whisk attachment on medium speed after each addition until the dough is smooth. Immediately transfer the dough to a pastry bag fitted with a large plain tip, or cover with plastic wrap and refrigerate for up to 2 days.

3. Preheat the oven to 425°F. Line two baking sheets with parchment paper.

4. Pipe the dough onto the parchment in the shape of your choice, leaving 1½ inches between them. Bake for 15 minutes,

Croquembouche, **page 190**

then reduce the oven temperature to 375°F and bake until the pastries are golden and puffed and sound hollow when you tap on them, about 25 minutes more. Immediately pierce the shells with a small, sharp knife to release steam (this helps them stay crispy) and transfer them to a wire rack to cool. Fill as directed or store unfilled shells in an airtight container for up to 2 days. Before serving, stuff with the filling of your choice.

— HOME CHALLENGE —

CROQUEMBOUCHE

Sam did so well on the croquembouche challenge in Season 4 that judge Christina Tosi offered him a job at her bakery on the spot! She was especially impressed by how neatly his puffs were filled and how the crispy shells made a nice hollow sound when she tapped on them. Why? Remember: It's important to use all of your senses when baking, and that sound—which indicated that the shells are crisp on the outside and airy inside—is one of the best ways to tell if the pâte à choux has been cooked correctly. A simple dusting of confectioners' sugar on top will make the croquembouche look extra impressive—but if you really want to pull out all the stops, ask a grown-up to help you warm any remaining caramel in the pan just until it is loose enough to drizzle. Then very carefully (remember, hot caramel is dangerous stuff!) dip a fork into the caramel and swirl it around the tower to make a web of spun sugar all around!

SERVES 12 OR MORE

SEASON 4

Sweet Pâte à Choux (page 188)
Pastry Cream (page 211)
1½ cups granulated sugar
½ cup light corn syrup
½ cup confectioners' sugar

1. Preheat the oven to 425°F. Line two baking sheets with parchment paper.

2. Prepare the sweet pâte à choux as directed through step 3. Pipe the batter onto the baking sheets into 1-inch rounds and bake for 15 minutes, then reduce the oven temperature to 375°F. Bake until the pastries are golden and puffed and sound hollow when you tap on them, about 25 minutes more. Pierce one side of each puff with a small, sharp knife to release steam (this helps the cream puffs stay crispy) and transfer to a wire rack to cool. (After they have cooled, the puffs can be stored in an airtight container for up to 2 days.)

3. Prepare and chill the pastry cream as directed on page 211.

4. Just before you're ready to assemble the croquembouche, spoon the chilled pastry cream into a pastry bag fitted with a small plain tip. Holding a cream puff in your palm, poke the tip of the pastry bag into the side where you made the steam vent and squeeze until filled. Repeat with the remaining cream puffs. (Refrigerate filled cream puffs until you begin assembly.)

5. In a medium saucepan, whisk together the sugar, corn syrup, and ½ cup water, stirring until the sugar has dissolved. Bring the mixture to a boil over medium heat and cook, without stirring, until the syrup turns a deep golden amber color and a candy thermometer inserted into the mixture reads 340°F, 6 to 8 minutes. Immediately get ready to assemble the croquembouche.

6. Set a cake stand or round serving platter on your work surface. Hold the cream puffs at the rounded tip and very, very carefully dip the flat end of one cream puff into the warm caramel until just lightly coated (the caramel is very hot—take care not to accidently dip your fingertips in the hot caramel—be sure a grown-up is nearby in case you need help). Place the cream puff, caramel-side down, at the edge of the cake stand. Continue dipping and placing cream puffs until you have formed a roughly 8-inch circle of cream puffs around the perimeter of the cake stand. (You'll need about 12 cream puffs for the first layer.) Next make a smaller layer on top of the first, dipping and placing the cream puffs so that they are staggered with the layer below. Continue dipping and placing cream puffs, building circles on top of each other, until you have formed a pyramid-shaped tower that narrows at the top. Finish with a single cream puff at the top. Dust with the confectioners' sugar and serve.

NOTE The assembled croquembouche can hold at room temperature for a couple of hours, but because its structure is delicate and it is filled with pastry cream (which needs to be refrigerated), it is best to assemble it as close as possible to serving. If you'd like to break up the work, prepare the cream puffs and the pastry cream filling a day or two ahead. Then, an hour or two before the party, fill the puffs, make the caramel, and assemble the tower.

CHOCOLATE
CREAM PUFFS
WITH DARK CHOCOLATE GLAZE

This pâtisserie classic is so much simpler than it seems. In Season 6, Anthony had some issues when his filling got a bit too stiff and heavy, but this one—basically a cocoa-infused whipped cream—is as light and airy as a dream. If you're feeling ambitious, or want to make the puffs even richer, you could fill them with Chocolate Pastry Cream (page 211). Adding a spoonful of corn syrup to the ganache glaze helps keep it beautifully shiny.

MAKES ABOUT 24 (3-INCH) CREAM PUFFS

Sweet Pâte à Choux (page 188)

COCOA-CREAM FILLING

⅔ cup confectioners' sugar

⅓ cup unsweetened Dutch-process cocoa powder

2 cups heavy cream

1 tablespoon pure vanilla extract

DARK CHOCOLATE GLAZE

½ cup bittersweet chocolate chips

¼ cup heavy cream

1 tablespoon light corn syrup

⅓ cup confectioners' sugar, for dusting

1. Preheat the oven to 425°F. Line two baking sheets with parchment paper.

2. Prepare the sweet pâte à choux as directed through step 3. Pipe the batter onto the baking sheets into 2-inch rounds. Bake for 15 minutes, then reduce the oven temperature to 375°F and bake until the pastries are golden and puffed and sound hollow when you tap on them, about 25 minutes more. Pierce one side of each puff with a small, sharp knife to release steam (this helps the cream puffs stay crispy) and transfer them to a wire rack to cool. (After they have cooled, the puffs can be stored in an airtight container for up to 2 days.)

3. Make the cocoa-cream filling: In a small bowl, whisk together the confectioners' sugar and cocoa powder until combined. In a large bowl, using an electric mixer fitted with the whisk attachment, beat the cream on medium-high speed until frothy, about 1 minute. With the mixer running, reduce the speed to medium-low, slowly sprinkle in the vanilla and the sugar-cocoa mixture, and beat until the cream holds stiff, smooth peaks, 1 to 1½ minutes more.

4. Make the dark chocolate glaze: Place the chocolate chips in a heatproof medium bowl. In a small saucepan, bring the cream and corn syrup to a simmer over medium heat, whisking to combine. Pour the hot cream mixture over the chocolate chips. Let stand for 1 minute, then stir until smooth. Set aside while you assemble the cream puffs.

5. To assemble the puffs, halve the cream puffs horizontally. Using a small spoon, fill the bottom halves with the cocoa-cream, then cover with the tops and drizzle each one with chocolate glaze. Chill until the glaze sets, about 30 minutes. Just before serving, dust the puffs with the confectioners' sugar.

MEYER LEMON ÉCLAIRS

This sunny, sweet lemon cream is one of Justise's favorite pastry fillings and is sure to brighten any day. Meyer lemons are a cross between conventional lemons and mandarin oranges and have juice that's slightly sweeter and deeper in color than that of their ordinary lemon cousins. Look for them in the market from November to February, when they're in season, but if you have trouble tracking them down, it's fine to use regular lemons in their place.

SERVES 12

Pastry Cream (page 211)

¼ cup Meyer lemon juice (from about 2 Meyer lemons)

Sweet Pâte à Choux (page 188)

MEYER LEMON GLAZE

2 cups confectioners' sugar

1 tablespoon finely grated Meyer lemon zest

2 to 3 tablespoons Meyer lemon juice

1 or 2 drops yellow gel food coloring (optional)

2 teaspoons finely grated Meyer lemon zest, for garnish

1. Prepare and chill the pastry cream as directed on page 211, slowly stirring in the Meyer lemon juice with the butter in step 2.

2. Preheat the oven to 425°F. Line two baking sheets with parchment paper.

3. Make the sweet pâte à choux as directed through step 3. Pipe the batter onto the prepared baking sheets in strips that are 5 inches long and 1 inch wide. Run a moistened fingertip along the surface of the strips, smoothing out any peaks or rough edges. Bake for 15 minutes, then reduce the oven temperature to 375°F and bake until the pastries are golden and puffed and sound hollow when you tap on them, about 25 minutes more. Pierce the pastries at one end with a thin, sharp knife to release steam (this helps them stay crispy), and transfer to a wire rack to cool completely. (After they've cooled, they can be stored in an airtight container for up to 2 days.)

4. Make the glaze: In a medium bowl, whisk together the confectioners' sugar, lemon zest, 2 tablespoons of the lemon juice, and the food coloring (if using) until smooth. The glaze should be very shiny, thick, and almost pasty; if needed, add a bit more juice or confectioners' sugar until it reaches the right consistency.

5. Assemble the éclairs: Split the pastries in half horizontally. Fill the bottom half with chilled pastry cream and replace the top. Carefully spoon the glaze over the tops. Garnish with zest. Chill for 30 minutes to set, then serve.

PEACH MELBA PAVLOVA
WITH YOGURT WHIPPED CREAM

This stunning layered dessert of vanilla-scented meringue, sliced peaches, raspberry sauce, and airy whipped cream is like summertime on plate. Though it certainly looks impressive, once you've mastered making meringue (see MasterChef Lesson, page 72), it actually comes together in a snap. Adding a scoopful of yogurt to the whipped cream lightens it and lends it a subtle tang that's a perfect complement to the sweetness of the meringue and the fresh fruit. While peaches are lovely in this version, if they're out of season (or just not what you're craving), feel free to swap in another stone fruit or a pile of mixed berries in their place.

SERVES 8 TO 10

MERINGUES

6 large egg whites, at room temperature

⅛ teaspoon kosher salt

1 teaspoon cream of tartar

1½ cups superfine sugar

2 tablespoons cornstarch

1 teaspoon pure vanilla extract

RASPBERRY SAUCE

1 cup fresh or frozen raspberries

¼ cup granulated sugar

¾ cup seedless raspberry jam

PEACHES

4 large peaches, pitted and thinly sliced (about 3 cups)

2 tablespoons granulated sugar

½ teaspoon ground ginger

YOGURT WHIPPED CREAM

2 cups heavy cream

1 cup plain whole-milk yogurt

2 teaspoons pure vanilla extract

2 tablespoons confectioners' sugar

⅛ teaspoon kosher salt

Fresh mint, for garnish

1. Make the meringues: Position racks in the center and lower third of the oven and preheat the oven to 250°F. Line two baking sheets with parchment paper. In the center of each sheet of parchment, use a pencil to draw a 9-inch-diameter circle (the easiest way to do this is to trace a 9-inch cake pan). Flip the parchment pencil-side down.

2. In a large bowl, using an electric mixer fitted with the whisk attachment, beat the egg whites and salt on medium-high speed until foamy, about 1 minute. Add the cream of tartar and

recipe continues

beat until soft peaks form, about 2 minutes. In a medium bowl, whisk together the superfine sugar and cornstarch. With the mixer running, slowly sprinkle the sugar mixture into the egg whites and beat until stiff, shiny peaks form, about 3 minutes more. Using a rubber spatula, gently fold in the vanilla.

3. Divide the meringue between the 2 circles on the parchment paper. Use a spoon or an offset spatula to spread the meringue to the edges of the circles and smooth it out. Transfer the pans to the oven and bake for 1 hour, switching the pans from the center to bottom rack once halfway through. Turn off the oven and let the meringues cool and dry completely in the oven until they are no longer tacky to the touch, about 1½ hours. When they are done, they will be stiff and crisp on the outside and tender and chewy inside. (The meringue layers can be prepared up to 3 days ahead and stored lightly wrapped in parchment paper at room temperature until you're ready to assemble the Pavlova. Do not refrigerate.)

4. Make the raspberry sauce: In a small saucepan, combine the raspberries, granulated sugar, and 2 tablespoons water. Bring to a simmer and cook, stirring occasionally, until soft and jammy, about 5 minutes. Transfer the raspberry mixture to a blender, add the raspberry jam, and puree until mostly smooth but with a few small pieces of raspberry still visible, about 30 seconds. Transfer the sauce to a small measuring cup and refrigerate until cool, about 1 hour. (The sauce can be prepared up to 3 days ahead and stored, covered, in the refrigerator.)

5. Prepare the peaches: In a medium bowl, gently toss together the peaches, granulated sugar, and ginger. Cover and refrigerate until ready to use.

6. Just before assembling, make the yogurt whipped cream: In a large bowl, using an electric mixer fitted with the whisk attachment, beat the cream, yogurt, vanilla, confectioners' sugar, and salt on medium-high speed until it holds soft peaks, 2 to 3 minutes.

7. Assemble the Pavlova: Place one of the meringue rounds on a large platter. Spoon half the yogurt whipped cream into the center of the round and smooth it slightly with the back of a spoon. Scoop up half the sliced peaches with a slotted spoon and arrange them on top. Drizzle with 2 tablespoons of the raspberry sauce and top with the second meringue round. Spoon the remaining yogurt whipped cream on top and arrange the remaining sliced peaches in the center. Drizzle with 2 more tablespoons of the raspberry sauce and garnish with mint. Pour the remaining raspberry sauce into a small pitcher. Serve the Pavlova immediately, with the extra sauce on the side.

— HOME CHALLENGE —

CHOCOLATE SOUFFLÉ

When judge Christina Tosi introduced the Season 4 semifinalists to the soufflé challenge, she reminded them that soufflés are "one of the hardest desserts to master in the entire world" and that sometimes even professional pastry chefs get nervous about them! Her advice: For light, airy, delicious results every time, it's incredibly important to concentrate on technique. That means making sure to carefully separate your egg whites and yolks, get your chocolate base thick and smooth, and beat your egg whites until they are shiny and firm but not overwhipped. And once you fill your ramekins and pop them in the oven, resist the urge to take a peek! Opening the oven door makes the temperature inside dip, which can cause the delicate batter to sink and fall. With attention to detail and patience, you and your soufflés will both rise to the challenge!

MAKES 8 INDIVIDUAL SOUFFLÉS

3 tablespoons unsalted butter, at room temperature

¾ cup granulated sugar, divided

4 large egg yolks

1¼ cups whole milk

2 tablespoons cornstarch

1 tablespoon unsweetened Dutch-process cocoa powder

¼ teaspoon kosher salt

4 ounces bittersweet chocolate, finely chopped (about ⅔ cup)

1 teaspoon pure vanilla extract

8 large egg whites, at room temperature

½ teaspoon cream of tartar

¼ cup confectioners' sugar, plus more for dusting

1. Position a rack in the lower third of the oven and preheat the oven to 375°F. Use 2 tablespoons of the butter to lightly grease eight 6-ounce straight-sided ramekins. Use ¼ cup of the granulated sugar to coat the insides of the ramekins, turning them to coat the sides and bottom evenly, then tap out any excess.

2. Make an ice bath by filling a large bowl with ice cubes and 1 cup water. Set aside. In a medium saucepan, whisk together the egg yolks, milk, remaining ½ cup granulated sugar, the cornstarch, cocoa powder, and salt. Cook over medium heat, whisking often, as the mixture comes to a low simmer and thickens, about 4 minutes (be sure to get the whisk—or a wooden spoon—into the corners of the pan so the mixture doesn't cook on the bottom!). Cook, whisking, until the mixture is smooth and thick, 1 to 2 minutes more. Remove from the heat and whisk in the chocolate, the remaining 1 tablespoon butter, and the vanilla until the mixture looks smooth and shiny. Scrape the chocolate mixture into a medium bowl. Set the bottom of

recipe continues

the bowl in the prepared ice bath, taking care not to let any water spill into the bowl. Let the mixture cool, whisking occasionally, until the chocolate base is smooth and cooled to room temperature, 10 to 12 minutes.

3. In a large, clean, dry bowl, using an electric mixer fitted with the whisk attachment, beat the egg whites and cream of tartar on medium-high speed until they form soft peaks, about 1½ to 2 minutes. Slowly sprinkle in the confectioners' sugar, a tablespoon or two at a time, and beat until the egg whites are glossy and form stiff peaks, about 1 minute more.

4. Using a rubber spatula, very gently fold half the egg whites into the cooled chocolate base. Repeat with the remaining egg whites, folding just enough to combine.

5. Divide the mixture evenly among the prepared ramekins and very carefully place them on a baking sheet. Lightly set the baking sheet on the oven rack and gently close the oven door. Bake until the soufflés rise and crack on top but are still slightly wobbly in the center, 15 to 20 minutes. Take care not to jump around or open the oven door before the soufflés are ready—any big movements or sudden changes in temperature can make them deflate!

6. Remove the baking sheet from the oven and carefully set it on a heatproof surface. Set each soufflé on a plate and dust the tops with confectioners' sugar. Serve immediately.

Step 1: Whisk the chocolate base until completely smooth and use an ice bath to chill to room temperature.

Step 2: Gently fold the egg whites into the chocolate base.

Step 3: Divide the mixture evenly among the prepared ramekins.

Step 4: Bake until the soufflés are tall and beginning to set on top but still wobbly at the center. Dust with confectioners' sugar and serve immediately.

CUSTARDS, PUDDINGS,

AND ICE CREAMS

Saffron Rice Pudding with Pistachios, Coconut, and Rose Petals
page 208

BUTTERMILK
PANNA COTTA
WITH BLACK PEPPER–BALSAMIC STRAWBERRIES

A bit sweet and a bit savory, syrupy balsamic vinegar is a surprisingly delicious pairing for fresh strawberries, which become even jammier and juicier when tossed with sugar and a pinch of black pepper. Season 5 winner Justise served the *MasterChef Junior* judges panna cottas like these as the big finish to her impressive finale menu. Tangy buttermilk cuts through the richness of the cream and gives the custards a subtle citrusy note.

SERVES 6

SEASON
5

BUTTERMILK PANNA COTTA

2 cups heavy cream

½ cup plus 1 tablespoon sugar

2 packets unflavored powdered gelatin

1 vanilla bean, split lengthwise

2 cups buttermilk

BLACK PEPPER–BALSAMIC STRAWBERRIES

2 pints strawberries, hulled and thinly sliced

3 tablespoons balsamic vinegar

1 tablespoon plus 1 teaspoon sugar

½ teaspoon freshly ground black pepper

Fresh mint, for garnish

1. Make the buttermilk panna cotta: In a saucepan, bring the cream and ½ cup of the sugar to a low simmer over medium heat, stirring to dissolve the sugar. Remove the pan from the heat and set aside. Pour ⅓ cup cool water into a small bowl and sprinkle the gelatin over the top. Set aside until the gelatin softens, about 5 minutes, then whisk the gelatin mixture into the cream. Use the tip of a small paring knife to scrape the vanilla seeds out of the vanilla pod into the pan. Add the buttermilk and stir to combine. Divide the mixture among six 6-ounce ramekins, cover with plastic wrap, and refrigerate until set, at least 4 hours or for up to 3 days.

2. Meanwhile, make the black pepper–balsamic strawberries: In a large bowl, combine the strawberries, vinegar, sugar, and pepper. Let stand at room temperature until the strawberries release some of their juices and the mixture is saucy, at least 30 minutes or for up to 24 hours.

3. To serve, unmold the panna cottas onto individual small plates. (To ease the panna cottas from the ramekins, dip the bottom of each ramekin into a bowl of hot water for 5 seconds before inverting it onto a plate.) Spoon the balsamic strawberries around the base of each panna cotta and drizzle with the juices. Garnish with fresh mint.

TIRAMISU TRIFLES

Trifle is a traditional British dessert that combines layers of cake or cookie crumbs, custard, and whipped cream. It's also one of judge Gordon Ramsay's favorite family desserts—which is why he picked it as the subject of one of the most epic challenges in Season 7! One of the best things about trifles is how adaptable they are. That's a lesson that Evan, from Season 6, says he learned when a cake he was making for his mother's birthday fell apart coming out of the pan. His brilliant solution: using the broken pieces to make mini trifles instead! This version riffs off the flavors of tiramisu, with sweetened espresso, mascarpone cream, and cocoa powder on top.

SERVES 6

1 cup mascarpone cheese, at room temperature

1¼ cups heavy cream, divided

1 teaspoon pure vanilla extract

¼ cup plus 1 tablespoon confectioners' sugar

⅓ cup brewed espresso or strong black coffee, hot

2 teaspoons granulated sugar

1½ cups crumbled ladyfingers or vanilla cake crumbs

1½ tablespoons unsweetened Dutch-process cocoa powder

1½ teaspoons ground cinnamon

1. In a medium bowl, combine the mascarpone, ¾ cup of the heavy cream, the vanilla, and ¼ cup of the confectioners' sugar. Using an electric mixer fitted with the whisk attachment, beat until soft peaks form, about 2 minutes. Set aside. In a small bowl, combine the hot espresso and granulated sugar and stir to dissolve the sugar.

2. Spoon about 2 tablespoons of the cookie crumbs into the bottom of six 8-ounce jars or glasses. Drizzle with a spoonful of the espresso mixture, then top with a layer of the mascarpone cream. Repeat layering the crumbs, espresso, and mascarpone cream until each glass contains two layers of each. Cover with plastic wrap and refrigerate until ready to serve, at least 2 hours or for up to 2 days.

3. Before serving, in a medium bowl, using an electric mixer fitted with the whisk, beat the remaining ½ cup heavy cream and 1 tablespoon confectioners' sugar on medium-high speed until soft peaks form, about 2 minutes. In a small bowl, whisk together the cocoa powder and cinnamon.

4. Remove the chilled jars from the refrigerator. Top each with a spoonful of the whipped cream and sprinkle with the cocoa-cinnamon mixture.

BASIL PANNA COTTA
WITH HONEY MASCARPONE AND BASIL DUST

Panna cotta literally means "cooked cream" in Italian, and one of the greatest things about this simple dish is how easy it is to switch up the flavor by steeping different spices, herbs, or even teas in the cream base. Basil may not be an ingredient you associate with desserts, but the herb's gentle licorice flavor is bright and refreshing—a quality that Logan took advantage of in Season 2, when he used it in the batter and frosting for his challenge-winning cupcakes. (It also helped Luca clinch the win in Season 4 of the adult *MasterChef*!) Here, a pretty garnish of finely ground basil leaves and granulated sugar provides another layer of zesty flavor.

MAKES 8 INDIVIDUAL PANNA COTTAS

BASIL PANNA COTTA

4 cups half-and-half

½ cup sugar

1 tablespoon finely grated
   lemon zest

12 large basil leaves

1½ packets unflavored powdered
   gelatin

HONEY MASCARPONE

1 cup mascarpone cheese, at
   room temperature

2 tablespoons honey

1 to 2 tablespoons half-and-half,
   if needed

BASIL DUST

½ cup sugar

6 large basil leaves

Small basil leaves, for garnish

1. Make the basil panna cotta: In a saucepan, combine the half-and-half, sugar, lemon zest, and basil leaves and bring to a low simmer over medium heat, stirring to dissolve the sugar. Remove from the heat, cover, and let steep for 30 minutes, then discard the basil.

2. Pour ⅓ cup cool water into a bowl and sprinkle the gelatin over the top. Set aside until the gelatin softens, about 5 minutes, then whisk the gelatin mixture into the basil-infused cream. Divide the mixture evenly among eight 6-ounce glasses or ramekins, cover with plastic wrap, and refrigerate for least 4 hours or up to 3 days.

3. Make the honey mascarpone: In a medium bowl, whisk together the mascarpone and honey until smooth and creamy, about 1 minute. If the mixture begins to separate, add a tablespoon or two of half-and-half and whisk until smooth.

4. Make the basil dust: In a food processor, pulse together the sugar and basil leaves until crumbly.

5. To serve, dollop a spoonful of the honey mascarpone on top of each panna cotta, sprinkle with basil sugar, and serve garnished with basil leaves.

SAFFRON RICE PUDDING
WITH PISTACHIOS, COCONUT, AND ROSE PETALS

Creamy rice pudding may be a comfort food classic, but adding coconut milk and a few fragrant spices transforms it into an exotic modern treat. This delicate saffron-and-cardamom-infused version is made in the style of an Indian pudding known as *kheer*, and was inspired by one that Avani from Season 5 learned to make from her grandfather. When shopping for saffron, always look for deep-red whole threads, which impart a purer flavor and more concentrated color.

SERVES 8 TO 10 • See photograph on page 203

1 cup white basmati rice

2 (13.5-ounce) cans full-fat coconut milk

½ cup packed light brown sugar

1 teaspoon orange blossom water

1 teaspoon ground cardamom

12 saffron threads, crushed until powdery

¼ teaspoon kosher salt

TOPPING

⅔ cup chopped pistachios

⅔ cup unsweetened coconut flakes

¼ teaspoon ground cardamom

¾ cup canned full-fat coconut milk, stirred until smooth

1½ tablespoons crumbled dried food-grade rose petals, for garnish (optional)

TIP This recipe uses coconut milk as its primary liquid, which gives the pudding a subtly sweet and tropical flavor. But you can substitute whole milk or almond milk for all or half the coconut milk, and it will still work.

1. Preheat the oven to 300°F.

2. In a deep 2-quart round casserole dish, whisk together the basmati rice, coconut milk, brown sugar, orange blossom water, cardamom, saffron, and salt until combined. Place the casserole dish on a baking sheet.

3. Bake the pudding, uncovered, for 30 minutes, then stir and bake for 25 minutes more. Stir the pudding again to dissolve any skin that has formed on top. Bake until the rice is tender and the coconut milk has reduced but the surface of the pudding still looks moist, 10 to 15 minutes more. Remove the pudding from the oven and let it cool until warm but not hot, about 10 minutes. (The pudding will continue to thicken as it cools.)

4. Meanwhile, make the topping: In a medium skillet, toast the pistachios and coconut flakes over medium-high heat, stirring often, until the mixture is golden and fragrant, about 6 minutes. Transfer to a bowl and stir in the cardamom until combined.

5. To serve, stir the pudding to loosen it, then spoon into small bowls. Drizzle each serving with coconut milk, top with a pinch of the topping, and garnish with dried rose petals (if using). Leftovers can be refrigerated, covered, for up to 5 days and eaten chilled or reheated.

DARK
CHOCOLATE PUDDING
WITH VANILLA WHIPPED CREAM

Chocolate pudding may seem simple, but this decadent version is anything but basic. How do you get such a luxuriously silky texture and deep, rich chocolate flavor? Adam from Season 5 says his secrets are using melted bittersweet chocolate and always adding some heavy cream to the milk. Here, dark brown sugar also gives the pudding a molasses note that is a great complement for the vanilla whipped cream.

SERVES 6

DARK CHOCOLATE PUDDING

¼ cup granulated sugar

2 tablespoons dark brown sugar

2 tablespoons cornstarch

1 tablespoon unsweetened Dutch-process cocoa powder

1½ cups whole milk

½ cup heavy cream

1 cup bittersweet chocolate chips

1 teaspoon pure vanilla extract

1 tablespoon unsalted butter

WHIPPED CREAM

½ cup heavy cream

1 tablespoon confectioners' sugar

1½ teaspoons pure vanilla extract

1. Make the dark chocolate pudding: In a medium saucepan, whisk together the granulated sugar, brown sugar, cornstarch, and cocoa powder. Set the pan over low heat, drizzle in the milk and cream, and whisk until smooth. Increase the heat to medium and cook, whisking constantly, until the mixture bubbles and thickens, 4 to 5 minutes. Remove the pan from the heat and whisk in the chocolate chips, vanilla, and butter until smooth.

2. Divide the pudding evenly among six 4-ounce ramekins. Cover each ramekin with plastic wrap, pressing it against the surface of the pudding to prevent a skin from forming. Chill until cold, about 1½ hours or for up to 3 days.

3. Make the whipped cream: In a medium bowl, using an electric mixer fitted with the whisk attachment, beat the cream, confectioners' sugar, and vanilla on medium-high speed until the cream holds soft peaks, about 2 minutes.

4. Serve the chilled puddings topped with a dollop of the whipped cream.

TEMPERING CUSTARDS

Custards are a diverse category of desserts and sauce ranging from crème anglaise to crème brûlée. While each one is prepared slightly differently, the one thread that runs through many custard recipes—at least the ones that contain eggs—is a technique known as "tempering."

Eggs thicken custards and add a silky texture and rich taste. They need to be cooked to 160°F to activate their thickening powers, but if you increase the temperature of the eggs too quickly, you could end up with a lumpy scrambled-egg custard! The solution is tempering: Add a small amount of warm liquid into the eggs to gently warm them, then add the rest of the warm liquid. This prevents the eggs from curdling.

Since tempering is a technique that comes up again and again, it's worth getting familiar with the basic method. Here's how it works:

1. Place the liquid (usually milk or cream) in a saucepan and bring it to a simmer.

2. In a separate bowl, whisk the eggs (sometimes sugar is whisked into the eggs, too).

3. Once the liquid has come to a simmer, turn off the heat. Very gradually drizzle ½ cup of the warm liquid into the beaten egg mixture in a slow, even stream while whisking constantly.

4. The eggs are now tempered, but you're not finished quite yet. Pour the mixture back into the saucepan with the remaining warm liquid and bring it to a simmer again, stirring constantly as the custard thickens. The eggs can still overcook if the mixture gets too close to the boiling point or sits on the bottom of the pan without being stirred. So, while tempering helps you start off on the right foot, you still need to pay close attention and cook the custard gently as it thickens. If you do notice a few lumps, don't worry—simply strain the custard through a fine-mesh sieve. No one will ever know the difference!

Step 1: Slowly drizzle warm liquid into the beaten egg mixture, whisking constantly.

Step 2: Cook the custard gently over low heat, stirring occasionally, until thickened.

PASTRY CREAM
(CRÈME PÂTISSIÈRE)

Pastry cream—or *crème pâtissière*—is a luxurious custard made from milk, sugar, and eggs, often thickened with a little cornstarch. It is one of the pastry chef's basic building blocks, and is used to fill all sorts of delights like doughnuts, éclairs, flaky Napoleons, and cream pies. The vanilla version is classic—but if you'd like, you can take yours in another direction by adding chocolate, caramel, or another flavor (see the Variations below).

MAKES ABOUT 3 CUPS

2 cups whole milk
⅔ cup granulated sugar, divided
3 tablespoons cornstarch
6 large egg yolks
1 tablespoon unsalted butter
1 tablespoon pure vanilla extract

VARIATIONS

Caramel Pastry Cream: Stir ½ cup chopped caramel candies into the hot pastry cream before chilling.

Chocolate Pastry Cream: Stir 1 cup finely chopped bittersweet chocolate into the hot pastry cream before chilling.

Orange Pastry Cream: Whisk 1½ teaspoons orange extract into the hot pastry cream before chilling.

1. Set up an ice bath by filling a medium bowl with ice cubes and about 2 cups of cold water. In a medium saucepan, bring the milk and ⅓ cup of the sugar to a low simmer over medium heat, whisking to dissolve the sugar.

2. In a large bowl, whisk together the remaining ⅓ cup sugar and the cornstarch. Add the egg yolks. Using an electric mixer fitted with the whisk attachment, beat on medium-high speed until smooth and pale, about 2 minutes.

3. With the mixer on low, very slowly drizzle ¼ cup of the warm milk mixture into the egg mixture. (This process is called "tempering"; see MasterChef Lesson opposite.) Beat in the milk mixture ¼ cup at a time until combined. Pour the mixture back into the saucepan and return it to the stove. Bring to a low simmer over medium heat and cook, whisking constantly, until the cream thickens and fully coats the back of a spoon, and when you run your finger over the surface of the spoon it leaves a thick trail that doesn't fill in immediately, 3 to 5 minutes. Immediately remove from the heat. Stir in the butter and vanilla until smooth. Submerge the bottom of the saucepan in the prepared ice bath and whisk the custard until it is smooth and cool.

4. Transfer the custard to a bowl and press plastic wrap directly against the surface of the custard to prevent a skin from forming. Refrigerate until chilled, at least 3 hours or for up to 3 days.

MALTED MILK
CRÈME BRÛLÉE
WITH CITRUS MARMALADE

In Season 3, Chef Ramsay told the junior chefs that the secret to getting that perfectly crackle-y, caramelized top on a crème brûlée is to use quick, even movements with a kitchen torch. The kind of sugar you use also makes a big difference: The bigger the sugar crystals are, the longer they take to caramelize and the chunkier they remain, which is why superfine sugar will produce the smoothest results. In this version of the classic French dessert, malted milk powder lends a warm, nutty flavor to the cream, and a thin layer of citrus marmalade at the bottom of the ramekins provides a wonderful tart surprise with every spoonful.

SERVES 6

4 large egg yolks

⅓ cup granulated sugar

2½ cups heavy cream

3 tablespoons malted milk powder

1 vanilla bean, split lengthwise

½ cup citrus marmalade, such as orange or grapefruit

6 tablespoons superfine sugar

1. Preheat the oven to 300°F.

2. In a large bowl, using an electric mixer fitted with the whisk attachment, beat the egg yolks and granulated sugar until pale and thick, about 2 minutes.

3. In a small saucepan, bring the cream to a simmer over medium heat. Add the malted milk powder and, using the tip of a small paring knife, scrape the vanilla seeds out of the vanilla bean into the pan; add the vanilla pod to the pan as well. Reduce the heat and cook, whisking occasionally, until the powder has dissolved, about 5 minutes. Discard the vanilla pod.

4. With the mixer running on low speed, very slowly beat ¼ cup of the warm cream mixture into the egg mixture. (This is called "tempering"; see MasterChef Lesson, page 210.) Beat in the cream mixture ¼ cup at a time until it is fully combined.

5. Spoon the marmalade evenly over the bottoms of six 6-ounce ramekins (about 1 heaping tablespoon for each ramekin). Top with the custard mixture, filling the ramekins to the top.

6. Bring a teakettle of water almost to a boil. Fold a kitchen towel so that it fits neatly inside a 9 × 13-inch baking dish and place the filled ramekins on top of it. (The towel will keep the ramekins from sliding as you move the pan.) Transfer the pan to a pulled-out rack in the oven. Pour enough hot water from the teakettle into the baking dish to come halfway up the sides of the ramekins.

7. Bake until the custards are just set (they should wobble just slightly when the pan is nudged), 50 to 55 minutes. Remove the baking dish from the oven. Carefully transfer the ramekins out of the water bath and onto a wire rack to rest for 15 minutes, then cover the ramekins with plastic wrap and carefully transfer them to the refrigerator. Chill for at least 2 hours or up to 2 days.

8. Uncover the chilled ramekins and use a paper towel to gently dab away any condensation on the surface of the custard. Sprinkle the top of each custard evenly with 1 tablespoon of the superfine sugar in a thin layer. Use a kitchen torch to toast the surface of each until the sugar is deeply golden and evenly caramelized. (If you do not have a torch, you can get similar results by placing the ramekins on a baking sheet and broiling them until the sugar melts and turns golden, about 4 minutes.) Let the custards rest for 10 minutes to allow the sugar to harden, then serve.

CARAMEL FLANS
WITH FRESH FIGS

Cool, eggy flan is one of Latin America's most iconic sweets. These saucy little custards are inspired by ones that Avani from Season 5 fell in love with during a family trip to Mexico. Topped with just a spoonful of honey-dressed fresh figs, they make a beautiful late-summer dessert—but when fresh figs are out of season, delicate suprêmed orange slices (see Tip) or tender dried figs would also be delicious options.

MAKES 6 INDIVIDUAL FLANS

3 large eggs

2 large egg yolks

1½ cups granulated sugar, divided

2 cups whole milk

1 teaspoon pure vanilla extract

⅛ teaspoon kosher salt

1 tablespoon honey

9 fresh black or green figs, halved lengthwise

TIP The term *suprême* refers to a technique of slicing citrus (often oranges or grapefruits) to separate the fruit segments cleanly and delicately from the pith and surrounding membranes.

1. Preheat the oven to 325°F.

2. In a medium bowl, whisk together the whole eggs and egg yolks until combined. Set aside.

3. In a small saucepan, combine 1 cup of the sugar and ⅓ cup water. Bring to a low simmer over medium heat, stirring just until the sugar dissolves, then cook, without stirring, until the sugar bubbles and turns a deep amber color, about 8 minutes. Quickly and carefully pour the caramel into six 6-ounce ramekins, tilting them to coat the bottoms evenly. (It will harden almost immediately.)

4. In a clean saucepan, combine the milk and remaining ½ cup sugar and cook over low heat, stirring, until the sugar has dissolved and the milk is warm but not boiling, 1 to 2 minutes. Whisking constantly, very slowly drizzle the warm milk mixture into the beaten eggs. (This process is called "tempering"; see MasterChef Lesson, page 210.) Add the vanilla and salt and whisk to combine. Divide the mixture among the prepared ramekins.

5. Bring a teakettle of water almost to a boil. Fold a kitchen towel so that it fits neatly inside a 9 × 13-inch baking dish and place the filled ramekins on top of it. (The towel will keep the ramekins from sliding as you move the pan.) Transfer the pan to a pulled-out rack in the oven. Pour enough hot water from the teakettle into the baking dish to come halfway up the sides of the ramekins. Bake until the custards are set but still wobble slightly when the pan is tapped, 45 to 50 minutes.

6. Carefully transfer the ramekins out of the water bath and onto a wire rack to cool for 30 minutes, then cover each ramekin with plastic wrap and refrigerate until chilled, at least 3 hours or for up to 3 days.

7. Just before serving, in a large skillet, warm the honey over medium-high heat until runny, about 1 minute. Add the figs, cut-side down, and cook until soft and caramelized, about 5 minutes.

8. To unmold the flans, run a knife around the rim of each ramekin, then invert it onto a plate. The caramel syrup will come out, too—make sure you allow it all to spill out and over the flan. Garnish each plate with some of the caramelized figs and serve.

BUTTERSCOTCH BUDINO
WITH SALTED CARAMEL AND CRÈME FRAÎCHE WHIPPED CREAM

These chic Italian pudding parfaits that Ivy prepared during the Season 7 finale contain three separate components: a plush butterscotch custard; a sweet-and-sticky salted caramel sauce; and a zippy cloud of crème fraîche whipped cream. While each element is delicious on its own, layering them together creates a deeply decadent dessert that's even more outrageous than the individual parts. As for the name, *budino* is just the Italian word for "pudding."

MAKES 8 BUDINOS

BUTTERSCOTCH BUDINO

1 large egg

3 large egg yolks

¼ cup cornstarch

1 cup plus 2 tablespoons packed dark brown sugar

1¼ teaspoons kosher salt

4½ cups half-and-half

5 tablespoons unsalted butter, sliced

2 tablespoons pure vanilla extract

SALTED CARAMEL

3 tablespoons unsalted butter, melted

½ cup heavy cream

2 teaspoons pure vanilla extract

½ cup granulated sugar

2 tablespoons light corn syrup

½ teaspoon kosher salt

CRÈME FRAÎCHE WHIPPED CREAM

¼ cup heavy cream

¾ cup crème fraîche

1. Make the butterscotch budino: Prepare an ice bath by filling a large bowl with ice cubes and about 2 cups water. Set aside. In a medium bowl, whisk together the whole egg, egg yolks, and cornstarch and set aside.

2. In a medium saucepan, whisk together the brown sugar, salt, and ½ cup water. Bring to a low simmer over medium heat, stirring just until the sugar has dissolved, then cook, without stirring, until the sugar bubbles and turns a deep amber color, about 8 minutes. Remove the pan from the heat and quickly whisk in the half-and-half. (Be very careful: The mixture will be very hot and bubble up a lot! You may want to ask an adult to help.) Whisk until smooth, about 1 minute.

3. With a long-handled spoon, very carefully scoop ¼ cup of the hot caramel out of the pan and, whisking constantly, slowly drizzle it into the egg mixture. (This is called "tempering"; see the MasterChef Lesson on page 210.) Stir the egg mixture into the saucepan with the remaining caramel.

4. Cook over medium heat, whisking constantly, until the mixture is thickened, about 2 minutes. Remove from the heat, add the butter and vanilla, and whisk until smooth. Submerge the bottom of the saucepan in the prepared ice bath and whisk the pudding until it is smooth and cool. Divide the pudding among eight 6-ounce ramekins or juice glasses. Cover each one with plastic wrap, pressing it against the surface of the puddings to prevent a skin from forming. Refrigerate until chilled, at least 3 hours or for up to 3 days.

5. Make the salted caramel: In a medium bowl, whisk together the melted butter, cream, and vanilla and set aside. In a medium saucepan, whisk together the granulated sugar, corn syrup, and 2 tablespoons water. Bring to a low simmer over medium heat, stirring just until the sugar has dissolved, then cook, without stirring, until the sugar bubbles and turns a deep amber color, about 8 minutes. Remove the pan from the heat and quickly and carefully whisk in the cream mixture. (Use caution: The mixture will bubble up.) Add the salt and whisk until smooth. Set aside.

6. Make the crème fraîche whipped cream: In a medium bowl, using an electric mixer fitted with the whisk attachment, beat the cream until thickened, about 1½ minutes. Add the crème fraîche and beat until soft peaks form, 1 to 2 minutes more.

7. To serve, top each budino with the salted caramel sauce and finish with a dollop of the crème fraîche whipped cream.

HIBISCUS-POACHED PEARS
WITH CIDER GRANITA

Poached pears is a classic French dessert that has made a few appearances on *MasterChef Junior*—and in the adult *MasterChef* kitchen, too! When Dara served them in Season 1, she took them in an Asian direction, using lemongrass and ginger. Here, tangy hibiscus syrup gives the pears a vibrant crimson color. Think of this version as a clever kid-friendly, alcohol-free twist on traditional red wine–poached pears. Infused with vanilla and cinnamon and paired with a sweet-tart apple cider granita, it's a light, seasonal dish that's full of big fall flavors. And should you have any poaching liquid left over, you can pour it over ice cubes and serve it as a yummy iced tea!

SERVES 6

CIDER GRANITA

4 cups apple cider

½ cup packed dark brown sugar

HIBISCUS-POACHED PEARS

2½ cups granulated sugar

⅓ cup dried hibiscus flowers (see Tip), or tea from 6 hibiscus tea bags (such as Red Zinger)

1 vanilla bean, split lengthwise

1 cinnamon stick

6 Forelle or small Bosc pears, peeled, stems attached

TIP Dried hibiscus flowers, also called *flores de Jamaica*, have an intense magenta color and a bright, sweet-tart flavor that's super refreshing. In Mexico and the Caribbean, they're a popular ingredient in punches called *aguas frescas*, and in the United States they're the main component in many teas, like Celestial Seasonings' Red Zinger.

1. Make the cider granita: In a medium saucepan, combine the cider and brown sugar. Cook over medium heat, stirring, until the sugar has dissolved. Remove from the heat and let the mixture cool to room temperature, then pour it into an 8-inch square metal baking pan. Transfer the pan to the freezer and freeze until firm, about 4 hours, scraping the surface with a fork every hour to create a flaky texture. (If well covered, the granita will keep for up to 1 week.)

2. Make the hibiscus-poached pears: In a large saucepan, combine the granulated sugar, hibiscus flowers, vanilla bean, cinnamon stick, and 4 cups water. Bring the mixture to a simmer over medium-low heat, stirring to dissolve the sugar, 8 to 10 minutes. Add the pears, cover with a round of parchment paper (see Tip, page 151), and simmer, turning the pears every 5 minutes so they are evenly cooked, until the flesh is tender when pierced with a thin, sharp knife, 20 to 25 minutes. Remove the pan from the heat and let the pears cool to room temperature in the poaching liquid. (You can also store the pears in their liquid, covered, in the refrigerator for up to 4 days.)

3. Before serving, gently lift the pears out of the poaching liquid and set aside. Discard the vanilla bean and cinnamon stick. Transfer the poaching liquid to a small saucepan, bring to a simmer over medium-low heat, and cook until the syrup has thickened and reduced by half (about 1¾ cups), about 45 minutes. Remove from the heat, strain the poaching liquid, discard the hibiscus flowers, and set the reduced syrup aside to cool.

4. To serve, divide the granita among six wide, shallow bowls. Nestle a pear on top and drizzle with the hibiscus syrup.

EASY VANILLA ICE CREAM

Smooth and rich, this vanilla ice cream is so easy to make. Unlike French-style ice creams, which begin with a custard base, this version is made in the "Philadelphia style," using a simple base of sweetened milk and cream. But don't let the simplicity of the process fool you: Even without eggs to enrich it, this is still some seriously decadent stuff. It's great on its own or as an à la mode partner for homemade pies or fruit crumbles—or you can play around and use it as a base for all sorts of tempting mix-ins like peanut butter cups or graham crackers and marshmallows. Mikey from Season 6 likes to save some of his Halloween candy, chop it up, and stir it in to make a homemade batch of candy crunch (his advice: "Avoid Skittles!"). Or you could follow Evan's lead from Season 6: Around Christmastime, he adds chopped-up candy canes for a minty-fresh ice cream that is "so delicious and looks really fancy."

MAKES ABOUT 1 QUART

2 cups heavy cream
1 cup whole milk
⅓ cup sugar
1 tablespoon pure vanilla extract
¼ cup light corn syrup
¼ teaspoon kosher salt

TIP To get a bite of mix-ins in every scoopful of ice cream, plan to add between ¾ and 1 cup crushed candy, nuts, or other add-ins per batch of ice cream. We've included a few ideas for combos to try in the Variations (opposite), but feel free to let your imagination run wild!

1. In a medium saucepan, combine the cream, milk, sugar, vanilla, corn syrup, and salt and heat over medium heat, stirring occasionally, until the mixture is warmed through and the sugar has dissolved, about 3 minutes. (To test, give the mixture a stir and then taste a spoonful: It should be completely smooth, not grainy.) Pour the ice cream base into a medium bowl, cover, and refrigerate until completely chilled, at least 5 hours or for up to 2 days.

2. Transfer the ice cream base to the chilled canister of an ice cream maker and churn according to the manufacturer's instructions. Eat immediately, soft-serve style, or transfer to an airtight container and freeze until firm, at least 6 hours or up to overnight.

VARIATIONS

Peppermint Stick Ice Cream: Fold ¾ cup crushed peppermint candies into the churned base.

Peanut Butter Cup Ice Cream: Fold ¾ cup chopped peanut butter cups into the churned base.

Ginger-Peach Ice Cream: Fold ½ cup crushed gingersnaps and ½ cup peach jam into the churned base.

Cookies and Cream Ice Cream: Fold ¾ cup crushed chocolate sandwich cookies into the churned base.

Banana Pudding Ice Cream: Fold ½ cup pureed ripe bananas and ¾ cup crushed vanilla wafer cookies into the churned base.

NO-CHURN ICE CREAM

Thanks to the magic of "no churn" ice cream, you can still make delicious ice cream at home, anytime. Unlike traditional ice cream recipes (like Easy Vanilla Ice Cream, page 220), no-churn bases are made by folding whipped cream into a mixture of sweetened condensed milk and flavorings. The texture is smooth and mousse-like, more like gelato than conventional ice cream. Here are two classic recipes to help you learn the formula and get started.

MAKES 1 QUART

TIP Freeze-dried strawberries add a burst of concentrated flavor and color to the base, but if you can't source them, the recipe will work without them.

NO-CHURN STRAWBERRY ICE CREAM

1 pound fresh strawberries, hulled

1 (14-ounce) can sweetened condensed milk

1 teaspoon pure vanilla extract

¼ teaspoon kosher salt

2 cups heavy cream

1 ounce freeze-dried strawberries, finely ground (optional; see Tip)

1. In a blender or food processor, pulse the fresh strawberries until you have a chunky puree, about 30 seconds. Transfer the puree to a large bowl and stir in the condensed milk, vanilla, and salt until well combined (the mixture will be very thick). Set aside.

2. In a medium bowl, using an electric mixer fitted with the whisk attachment, beat the cream until stiff peaks form, 2 to 3 minutes. Using a rubber spatula, fold 1 cup of the whipped cream into the strawberry mixture to lighten it, then gently spoon the strawberry mixture into the whipped cream. Add the freeze-dried strawberries (if using) and fold until well blended. Pour the mixture into a metal loaf pan. Cover and freeze until solid, at least 6 hours. (Once frozen, the ice cream can be stored, covered, for up to 1 week.)

NO-CHURN CHOCOLATE ICE CREAM

1 (14-ounce) can sweetened condensed milk

½ cup unsweetened Dutch-process cocoa powder

1 teaspoon pure vanilla extract

¼ teaspoon kosher salt

2 cups heavy cream

1. In a large bowl, combine the condensed milk, cocoa powder, vanilla, and salt. Stir until smooth (the mixture will be very thick). Set aside.

2. In a medium bowl, using an electric mixer fitted with the whisk attachment, beat the cream until stiff peaks form, 2 to 3 minutes. Fold 1 cup of the whipped cream into the cocoa mixture to lighten it, then gently spoon the cocoa mixture into the whipped cream and fold until well blended. Pour into a metal loaf pan. Cover and freeze until solid, at least 6 hours. (Once frozen, the ice cream can be stored, covered, for up to 1 week.)

~ HOME CHALLENGE ~

BANANA SPLIT
ICE CREAM CAKE

When judge Christina Tosi introduced the young MasterChefs to the banana split challenge in Season 7, she called the combo of bananas, ice cream, whipped cream, and cherries an "American classic"—and one of her all-time favorite desserts! This colossal sliceable version of the iconic sundae is guaranteed to inspire oohs and ahhs—and is proof that when it comes to ice cream cakes, there's no such thing as too much of a good thing. Because the recipe involves quite a few steps, you do have to plan ahead if you want to pull it off. But the good news is that all the elements are really easy to make and nothing requires any fancy equipment.

SERVES 10 TO 12

SEASON 7

BANANA CAKE

Nonstick pan spray

1½ cups all-purpose flour

1½ teaspoons baking powder

1 teaspoon ground cinnamon

½ teaspoon kosher salt

4 ripe medium bananas, mashed (about 1½ cups)

½ cup extra-virgin olive oil

1½ cups packed light brown sugar

3 large eggs

2 teaspoons pure vanilla extract

COOKIE CRUMBLE

2 cups chocolate syrup

26 chocolate sandwich cookies (such as Oreos), finely crushed

ICE CREAM LAYERS

1 quart store-bought strawberry ice cream, softened slightly

1 quart store-bought chocolate ice cream, softened slightly

CHOCOLATE FUDGE SAUCE

1 cup bittersweet chocolate chips

½ cup heavy cream

1 tablespoon light corn syrup

VANILLA WHIPPED CREAM

1½ teaspoons unflavored powdered gelatin

2 tablespoons granulated sugar

1⅓ cups heavy cream

1 tablespoon pure vanilla extract

TOPPINGS

Rainbow sprinkles

Chopped honey-roasted peanuts

Maraschino cherries, with stems attached

TIP If you want to break the project into smaller tasks, the banana cake can be made ahead and frozen, well wrapped, for up to 2 weeks.

1. Make the banana cake (see Tip): Preheat the oven to 350°F. Coat a 9-inch round cake pan or springform pan with pan spray.

2. In a medium bowl, whisk together the flour, baking powder, cinnamon, and salt. In a large bowl, whisk together the mashed bananas, olive oil, brown sugar, eggs, and vanilla until

recipe continues

Step 1: Spread half of the cookie crumble over a layer of banana cake.

Step 2: Working quickly, spread softened strawberry ice cream over the cookie crumble.

Step 3: Add the second layer of cake and cookie crumble, then spread the softened chocolate ice cream on top in an even layer.

Step 4: Slowly pour fudge sauce over the chilled cake, letting some drips run down the side.

thick and smooth. Add the flour mixture to the banana mixture and stir until just combined.

3. Pour the batter into the prepared pan and bake until the cake has begun to pull away from the edges of the pan and a toothpick inserted into the center of the cake comes out clean, 45 to 50 minutes. Let the cake rest in the pan for 10 minutes, then invert it onto a wire rack to cool completely.

4. Make the cookie crumble: In a large bowl, stir together the chocolate syrup and crushed cookies until the mixture is sticky and spreadable. Set aside.

5. To assemble the cake, using a long serrated knife, slice the banana cake in half horizontally to create 2 thinner layers (see the MasterChef Lesson on page 146). Fit one layer snugly into the bottom of a 9-inch springform pan with extra-tall (at least 3-inch) sides. Spoon half the cookie crumble over the cake and use the back of a spoon or an offset spatula to work it into an even layer. Place the pan in the freezer to chill until the cookie crumble firms up, about 1 hour.

6. Working quickly, spoon the softened strawberry ice cream over the cookie crumble layer and smooth the top. Freeze until the strawberry ice cream firms up, about 2 hours. Place the remaining banana cake layer on top of the strawberry ice cream layer and spread the remaining cookie crumble evenly over the top. Place the pan in the freezer to chill until the cookie mixture firms up, about 1 hour.

7. Working quickly, spoon the softened chocolate ice cream over the cookie crumble layer and smooth out the top. Return the pan to the freezer and freeze until the cake is completely solid, at least 6 hours or for up to overnight.

8. Make the chocolate fudge sauce: Place the chocolate chips in a heatproof medium bowl. In a small saucepan, bring the cream and corn syrup to a simmer over medium heat, whisking to combine. Pour the hot cream mixture over the chocolate chips. Let sit for 1 minute, then stir until smooth. Let sit at room temperature until the sauce is cool, thick, and pourable, about 1 hour.

9. Unmold the cake and carefully transfer it to a rimmed platter or baking sheet. (If the cake sticks to the springform pan, warm a butter knife under hot water and gently run the knife around the inner edge of the pan to release the cake.) Slowly pour the fudge sauce over the top of the cake, letting some drips run down the sides. Freeze the cake until the fudge sauce is firm, about 30 minutes.

10. Make the vanilla whipped cream: Pour ⅓ cup cool water into a small saucepan and sprinkle with the gelatin. Let sit until the gelatin softens, about 5 minutes, then stir in the granulated sugar and bring to a simmer over medium-low heat, stirring to dissolve the sugar. Remove the pan from the heat and let the syrup cool completely, then transfer it to a large bowl and add the cream. Using an electric mixer fitted with the whisk, beat on medium-high speed until stiff peaks form, 2 to 3 minutes.

11. Remove the chilled cake from the freezer. Spoon the whipped cream on top and smooth it into decorative swirls. Sprinkle the top of the cake with sprinkles and chopped peanuts. Garnish with maraschino cherries. Slice and serve immediately.

BREADS, SNACKS,
AND SAVORY PASTRIES

"Everything Bagel" Tomato Tart with Smoked Salmon and Cream Cheese, **page 238**

PUFF PASTRY PINWHEELS
WITH SPINACH AND FETA

These whimsical spinach-and-cheese swirls are similar in flavor and texture to the rolled puff pastry treats known as palmiers (sometimes called elephant ears), but their spiral shape is simple enough for even beginners to master. Remy from Season 6 served them alongside a dish of cocoa-braised short ribs and a sweet potato mash, but they're definitely tasty enough to stand on their own as a hearty snack, or as part of a cheese plate or charcuterie (cured meat and salami) spread. For maximum crunch, just make sure you don't skip the step of squeezing and blotting the spinach before adding it to the filling.

MAKES 24 PINWHEELS

10 ounces frozen chopped spinach, thawed and drained

8 ounces crumbled feta cheese, at room temperature

¼ cup sour cream

2 tablespoons chopped fresh dill

2 teaspoons crushed red pepper flakes

½ teaspoon garlic powder

½ teaspoon kosher salt

2 tablespoons all-purpose flour

2 sheets frozen puff pastry, thawed (from one 16-ounce package)

1 large egg, beaten

1. Sandwich the spinach between two layers of paper towels and press out any excess water. In a medium bowl, combine the spinach, feta, sour cream, dill, red pepper flakes, garlic powder, and salt and mix to combine.

2. Dust a work surface with the flour and place the thawed puff pastry sheets on it. Divide the feta mixture in half and spoon it evenly over each pastry sheet, leaving a ½-inch border on all sides. Starting with a long side, roll each puff pastry sheet into a log. Wrap the logs tightly with plastic wrap and set them seam-side down on a baking sheet. Freeze until firm, about 30 minutes. (To store longer, transfer the logs to an airtight freezer bag and freeze; they will keep for up to 2 months.)

3. Preheat the oven to 400°F. Line two baking sheets with parchment paper.

4. Remove the pastry logs from the freezer, unwrap, and place them seam-side down on your work surface. Slice each log crosswise into twelve ¾-inch-thick rounds. Arrange the slices cut-side down on the prepared baking sheets. In a small bowl, mix the beaten egg with 1 tablespoon water to make an egg wash and brush it over the top and sides of each slice. Bake until the pinwheels are puffed and golden brown, 15 to 20 minutes. Serve warm or at room temperature.

JALAPEÑO
CHEESE TWISTS

Whether they're getting ready for a challenge or planning a menu for the big finale, one of the most important lessons the young cooks on *MasterChef Junior* learn is the importance of prepping ahead. Like a cross between a breadstick and a cheddar cracker, these homemade cheese twists look super professional but couldn't be simpler to make for afterschool snacking or your next family party. Adding minced jalapeño gives the twists a nice pop of heat, but they're not too spicy. Just be warned: You might want to bake a double batch—they're so delicious, they get gobbled up fast!

MAKES ABOUT 44 TWISTS

1 cup finely grated Parmesan cheese (about 4 ounces)

1⅓ cups shredded sharp cheddar cheese (about 4 ounces)

4 tablespoons (½ stick) unsalted butter, at room temperature

1¾ cups all-purpose flour, plus more for rolling

1½ teaspoons kosher salt

½ teaspoon freshly ground black pepper

1 jalapeño pepper, halved, seeded, and minced

¼ cup plus 1 tablespoon heavy cream

1. Line two baking sheets with parchment paper.

2. In a food processor, combine the Parmesan, cheddar, butter, flour, salt, black pepper, and jalapeño and pulse in 5-second bursts until the mixture is sandy, with a few pea-size pieces of butter still visible, about 45 seconds. Drizzle in the cream and process until the dough forms a ball, about 15 seconds.

3. On a lightly floured work surface, use a rolling pin to roll the dough into a 14-inch square about ⅛ inch thick. Halve the dough into two 7 × 14-inch rectangles, then cut each rectangle crosswise into strips ½ inch wide. In the end you will have about 50 (7 × ½-inch) strips. Working with one at a time, gently twist each strip into a spiral. Transfer the strips to the prepared baking sheets, leaving ½ inch between them. Gently press the ends of the strips against the baking sheets so that the spirals hold their shape. Transfer the baking sheets to the refrigerator to chill the twists for at least 20 minutes or cover with plastic wrap and refrigerate for up to 3 days.

4. Preheat the oven to 400°F.

5. Bake until the twists are firm and golden, about 15 minutes. Let the twists rest on the baking sheets for 5 minutes, then transfer to a wire rack to cool completely. The twists will keep in an airtight container at room temperature for up to 1 week.

SPICED
CEREAL SNACK MIX

Even MasterChefs crave a salty snack sometimes! Bursting with crunchy cereal, pretzels, and honey-roasted peanuts, this buttery, savory party mix will scratch that itch—and spoil the store-bought stuff for you! Pack it into snack bags for a treat after baseball or soccer practice or set it out instead of popcorn at your next family movie night. A spoonful of Old Bay seasoning gives it a gently spicy kick that's hard to resist, but feel free to customize it to your taste or add other mix-ins like corn nuts or pita chips.

MAKES ABOUT 12 CUPS

3½ cups corn squares cereal (such as Corn Chex)

3½ cups wheat squares cereal (such as Wheat Chex)

2 cups pretzel fish (such as Goldfish) or other bite-size pretzels

1 cup oyster crackers

1 cup unsalted dry-roasted peanuts

1 stick (4 ounces) unsalted butter, melted

⅓ cup Worcestershire sauce

1 tablespoon plus 2 teaspoons Old Bay seasoning

½ teaspoon garlic powder

⅛ teaspoon cayenne pepper

1. Preheat the oven to 300°F. Line a baking sheet with parchment paper.

2. In a large bowl, combine the cereals, pretzels, oyster crackers, and peanuts. In a 4-cup measuring cup, stir together the melted butter, Worcestershire sauce, Old Bay seasoning, garlic powder, and cayenne. Pour the butter mixture over the cereal mixture and stir gently with a rubber spatula until well combined.

3. Spoon the mixture onto the prepared baking sheet and spread it out into an even layer. Bake until the mixture looks lightly toasted and smells fragrant, about 1 hour, tossing the mixture every 15 minutes. Let the mix cool on the baking sheets, then transfer to an airtight container and store for up to 2 weeks.

PHILLY-STYLE
SOFT PRETZELS

Soft, buttery, Philadelphia-style soft pretzels are one of Quani's (from Season 6) favorite things to bake with his mom. A short ingredient list and a straightforward process make the recipe a fun introduction to working with yeast dough. Don't worry if your twists look a little lopsided at first—you'll get the hang of it eventually, and they'll still be delicious! While there's no need to dress the pretzels up, if you want to add a little something extra, a homemade honey-mustard dip (see Tip) is the perfect complement.

MAKES 6 PRETZELS

2¼ teaspoons instant (Rapid Rise) yeast

2 tablespoons honey

2 tablespoons unsalted butter, melted, plus more for serving

1 teaspoon kosher salt

2¾ cups all-purpose flour, plus more for dusting and shaping

1 tablespoon canola oil, for the bowl

3 tablespoons baking soda

1 large egg, beaten

Coarse kosher salt, for sprinkling

TIP Ready to do some dunking? Chances are you already have all the ingredients to make honey-mustard dip right in your pantry. In a small bowl, just whisk together ¼ cup honey, ¼ cup mayonnaise, ¼ cup Dijon mustard, and 1 tablespoon distilled white vinegar.

1. In a stand mixer fitted with the dough hook, whisk together 1 cup warm water, the yeast, honey, melted butter, and salt. Add the flour and knead on low speed until a smooth, elastic ball of dough forms, about 6 minutes. (If you don't have a stand mixer, you can also knead by hand; for more, see MasterChef Lesson, page 234.)

2. Place the dough in a lightly oiled large bowl and turn to coat the dough with oil. Cover the bowl with plastic wrap or a kitchen towel and set aside in a warm place to rise until the dough has doubled in size, 45 minutes to 1 hour. Punch down the dough, cover the bowl, and let rise until nearly doubled again, 30 to 40 minutes more.

3. Line two large baking sheets with parchment paper and dust the parchment lightly with flour. Divide the dough into 6 equal pieces. Starting at the center and rolling outward, use the palms of your hands to roll each piece into a 20-inch-long rope (flour your hands if the dough is sticky). Form the rope into a "U" shape, twist the ends of the rope around each other, then flip the twisted section down and press the ends lightly onto the bottom of the "U." Transfer the pretzel to the prepared baking sheets and repeat with the remaining dough pieces.

4. Position racks in the upper and lower thirds of the oven and preheat the oven to 450°F. At the same time, in a wide

saucepan or large Dutch oven, bring 6 cups water and the baking soda to a boil.

5. Working in batches, use a spatula to carefully lower 2 pretzels into the boiling water. Cook the dough for 30 seconds, then use a spatula or tongs to flip the pretzels over and cook for 30 seconds more. Use a slotted spoon to remove the pretzels from the water, letting any excess water drip off, and return them to the baking sheets. Repeat with the remaining pretzels in batches of 2.

6. Brush the pretzels with the beaten egg and sprinkle with coarse salt. Bake until the pretzels are deeply golden brown and shiny, 12 to 14 minutes, switching the pans from the top to bottom rack halfway through. Brush the pretzels with melted butter and serve warm. Store leftovers at room temperature for up to 2 days or freeze in zip-top freezer bags for up to 1 month.

HOW TO KNEAD YEAST DOUGH
WITHOUT A MIXER

Making bread and other yeasted baked goods from scratch can seem like a mystical process, but all it takes are flour, salt, water, and yeast to create a dough that literally comes alive, growing right in front of you. None of that would be possible without the action that starts it all: kneading. The process of kneading sets off a series of important actions within the dough, incorporating air, developing flavor, and—most crucially—building and strengthening the gluten, the protein that gives yeast doughs their structure and chewiness.

Because getting dough to the right smooth, supple consistency can take more than 15 minutes, kneading is easiest with a stand mixer fitted with a dough hook. That said, even if you don't have a stand mixer, you can get the job done—as long as you're willing to put in the time and the muscle power! Here's a step-by-step if you want to give it a try:

1. Clear a large work surface and sprinkle it lightly with flour. Turn the dough out of its bowl onto the surface.

2. Using the heels of your hands, push the dough down and out, stretching and lengthening it in front of you.

3. Bring the top half of the dough back toward you, folding it over the bottom of the dough and pressing it down. Then push it down and away from you again, stretching it with the heels of your hands. Continue this process, folding the top half of the dough toward you and then pressing it away with the heels of your hands, until it starts to get smooth, 6 to 10 minutes. If at any point the dough seems too sticky to handle, sprinkle it lightly with flour—though try not to use too much, as overflouring will make the dough bland and tough.

4. Continue kneading, folding the dough over and pushing it away in a long length, until the dough is supple, elastic, and smooth. This may take anywhere from 15 to 20 minutes.

5. When you think the dough is ready, do what's known as the "windowpane test" to double-check: Pull off a piece of the dough about the size of a Ping-Pong ball. Hold the dough between your thumbs and index fingers, then pull your hands apart so that the dough is stretched into a thin rectangle between them. You want to stretch the dough as thin as possible—until you can see through it, like a windowpane. If the dough stretches without breaking, it's properly kneaded and ready to rise. If it tears when you try to stretch it, keep kneading for a few minutes more before testing it again.

Step 1: Using the heel of your hand, push the dough down and away from you on your work surface.

Step 2: Bring the top half of the dough back toward you, folding it over itself and pressing down.

Step 3: Continue kneading the dough out and folding it over itself until it is smooth and elastic.

Step 4: Check whether the dough is ready for rising by doing a "window-pane test." If a small piece of dough stretches into a thin rectangle without breaking, then it has been properly kneaded.

GARLIC KNOTS

Channel your inner *pizzaiolo* with a piping-hot batch of golden, chewy, garlic knots sprinkled with parsley and Parmesan. These little pizzeria favorites are big on flavor and great for sharing. Though the recipe needs time for the dough to rise, the work is mostly hands-off and the results are sure to win raves. Cydney from Season 5 says make sure to serve plenty of warm marinara sauce for dipping alongside!

MAKES 12 GARLIC KNOTS

GARLIC BUTTER

8 tablespoons (1 stick/4 ounces) unsalted butter, divided

8 large garlic cloves, minced

DOUGH

2 cups all-purpose flour, plus more for shaping

1½ teaspoons instant (Rapid Rise) yeast

1 teaspoon garlic powder

1 tablespoon extra-virgin olive oil, plus more for the bowl

FOR SERVING

2 tablespoons minced fresh flat-leaf parsley

2 tablespoons finely grated Parmesan cheese, plus more as needed

½ teaspoon kosher salt

Extra-virgin olive oil, as needed

1 cup marinara sauce, warmed

1. Make the garlic butter: In a small saucepan, melt 2 tablespoons of the butter over medium heat. Stir in the garlic, reduce the heat to low, and cook, stirring often, until the garlic is soft and fragrant but not browned, about 3 minutes. Add the remaining 6 tablespoons butter and swirl the pan until the butter has melted, about 1 minute. Strain the garlic butter through a fine-mesh sieve into a large bowl. Reserve the garlic solids in a small bowl. Set both bowls aside.

2. Make the dough: In the bowl of a stand mixer, whisk together the flour, yeast, and garlic powder. In a small bowl, whisk together the oil, reserved garlic solids, and ¾ cup warm water. Attach the dough hook to the stand mixer and, with the mixer on medium-low speed, drizzle the oil-garlic mixture into the flour mixture and knead, scraping down the sides of the bowl as needed, until a sticky dough starts to come together, about 3 minutes. Increase the speed to medium-high and knead until the dough is smooth and shiny and pulling away from the side of the bowl, about 6 minutes more.

3. Transfer the dough to a lightly floured work surface and knead it once or twice. Turn the dough over, push, and shape it into a ball. Lightly grease a large bowl with oil, then place the dough in the bowl, seam-side down. Cover the bowl with plastic wrap and transfer it to a warm spot to rest until the dough is doubled in size, about 1½ hours.

4. Transfer the dough to a lightly floured work surface. Using your hands, lightly stretch it into a 7 × 12-inch rectangle. With a long side facing you, use a sharp knife or a pizza cutter to cut the dough crosswise into 12 (1-inch-wide) strips. Cover the strips lightly with plastic wrap.

5. Line a baking sheet with parchment paper. Working with one at a time, place a dough strip on a lightly floured work surface and roll it into a 12-inch rope. Tie the rope into a loose overhand knot, tucking the ends underneath. Transfer the knot to the prepared baking sheet and repeat with the remaining dough, leaving 2 inches of space between the knots. Lightly cover the baking sheet with plastic wrap or a kitchen towel and transfer it to a warm spot to rest until the knots have nearly doubled in size, about 1½ hours.

6. Preheat the oven to 475°F.

7. Measure out 2 tablespoons of the reserved garlic butter and brush it over the knots. Bake until deeply golden, about 12 minutes.

8. Meanwhile, whisk the parsley, Parmesan, and salt into the garlic butter remaining in the large bowl to combine,

9. While the knots are still warm, add them to the bowl with the garlic butter mixture and toss them until well coated (if the mixture looks a little dry, drizzle in a bit of oil). Serve immediately, with the marinara sauce on the side for dipping.

"EVERYTHING BAGEL"
TOMATO TART
WITH SMOKED SALMON AND CREAM CHEESE

Brooklyn native Donovan from Season 5 always orders an "everything" bagel with smoked salmon, tomatoes, and scallion cream cheese at the bagel shop. This rustic tart—basically a savory galette—reinvents those flavors in a clever, family-size package that's perfect for sharing at a weekend brunch or picnic. "Everything bagel" seasoning is just a mix of poppy seeds, sesame seeds, dried garlic, dried onion, and salt. You can find premixed packages of it at some grocery stores, but making it is easy, too. Try sprinkling the leftover seasoning on scrambled eggs, popcorn, or avocado toast—or even add it to the batter for savory waffles!

SERVES 4 • **See photograph on page 227**

CRUST
- 1½ cups all-purpose flour, plus more for dusting
- 1 stick (4 ounces) unsalted butter, cubed and frozen
- ½ teaspoon kosher salt
- 1 large egg, beaten
- 2 tablespoons ice water, plus more if needed

"EVERYTHING BAGEL" SEASONING
- 2 tablespoons poppy seeds
- 2 tablespoons toasted sesame seeds
- 2 tablespoons dried garlic
- 2 tablespoons dried onion
- 4 teaspoons kosher salt

FILLING
- 6 ounces scallion cream cheese, at room temperature
- 1 large egg
- ¼ teaspoon kosher salt
- ¼ teaspoon freshly ground black pepper
- 2 ounces smoked salmon, finely chopped (about ¼ cup)
- 2 large tomatoes (about 1½ pounds), thinly sliced

- 1 large egg

1. Make the crust: In a food processor, combine the flour, butter, and salt and pulse until the mixture is sandy, with a few pea-size pieces of butter still visible, about 1 minute. Add the egg and ice water and pulse until moistened and the dough is starting to pull away from the sides of the bowl, about 30 seconds. (If the dough is still dry, add more ice water 1 teaspoon at a time; do not overprocess.) Shape the dough into a 1-inch-thick disc and wrap it tightly with plastic wrap. Transfer to the refrigerator to chill for at least 30 minutes or up to 3 days.

2. Make the "everything bagel" seasoning: In a small jar, combine the poppy seeds, sesame seeds, dried garlic, dried onion, and salt. Seal the jar and shake until well combined. (Store for up to 3 months.)

3. Position a rack in the center of the oven and preheat the oven to 400°F.

4. Make the filling: In a large bowl, using an electric mixer with the whisk attachment, beat the cream cheese and egg on medium-high speed until smooth, about 1 minute. Stir in the salt and pepper.

5. Pull off a 15-inch-long piece of parchment paper and dust it lightly with flour. Remove the chilled dough from the freezer, unwrap it, and place it on the parchment. Using a rolling pin, roll the dough into a 12-inch-diameter round. Using the parchment as support, transfer the dough on the parchment to a baking sheet

6. Spoon the cream cheese mixture into the center of the dough and spread it into an even layer, leaving a 2-inch border around the edges. Scatter the smoked salmon over the cream cheese. Arrange the tomatoes on top, overlapping the slices slightly so the cream cheese mixture is completely covered. Fold the bare edges of the dough up and over the tomatoes.

7. In a small bowl, whisk together the egg and 2 tablespoons water to make an egg wash. Brush the egg wash onto the crust and, while still moist, sprinkle the crust with the 1½ tablespoons of "everything bagel" seasoning. (Reserve the rest of the jar for another use.)

8. Bake until the crust is deeply golden brown and the tomatoes are soft, about 40 minutes. Let the tart rest on the baking sheet for 10 minutes, then use the parchment to transfer it to a wire rack. Let cool to room temperature, about 20 minutes, before slicing and serving. Wrap any leftovers in plastic wrap and store in the refrigerator for up to 2 days.

TOMATO AND EGG
FOCACCIA

Crunchy on the outside and soft and chewy on the inside, focaccia is like a cross between deep-dish pizza and flatbread. Cydney from Season 5 loves how simple the dough is to prepare and how easy it is to transform with different spices and toppings.

MAKES ONE 13 × 18-INCH FOCACCIA (SERVES 8)

4¼ cups all-purpose flour

1 tablespoon kosher salt, plus more for seasoning

2½ teaspoons instant (Rapid Rise) yeast

1¾ cups warm water

5 tablespoons extra-virgin olive oil, divided, plus more for the bowl

2 pints multicolored cherry tomatoes, halved (about 3½ cups)

8 large eggs

1 cup finely grated Parmesan cheese

Freshly ground black pepper

1 tablespoon chopped fresh chives

1. In a food processor, pulse together the flour, salt, and yeast. Add the water and 2 tablespoons of the oil and pulse until a rough ball of dough forms, about 1 minute. The dough will be sticky.

2. Using a rubber spatula, transfer the dough to a clean work surface. Shape the dough into a ball, place it in a lightly oiled large bowl, and turn to coat the dough with oil. Cover the bowl with plastic wrap and let rest at room temperature until doubled in size, 1½ to 2 hours.

3. Drizzle the remaining 3 tablespoons oil onto a rimmed baking sheet. Punch down the dough and transfer it to the baking sheet, turning it to coat with oil. Stretch the dough to the edges of the baking sheet. Lightly cover the baking sheet with plastic wrap and let sit at room temperature until nearly doubled in size again, 1 to 1½ hours.

4. Position a rack in the center of the oven and preheat the oven to 450°F.

5. Use your fingertips to press 8 evenly spaced wells across the dough (these will hold the eggs later). Scatter the tomatoes over the dough (avoiding the wells) and season with salt.

6. Bake the focaccia until the edges are lightly golden brown, 20 to 25 minutes. Remove from the oven. Crack an egg into a small bowl, then carefully add it to one of the wells. Repeat with the remaining eggs. Sprinkle with Parmesan and season with pepper. Bake until the egg whites are just set and the yolks are soft, 8 to 10 minutes. Garnish with the chives. Let rest for 2 minutes in the pan, then slice into squares with a pizza cutter and serve.

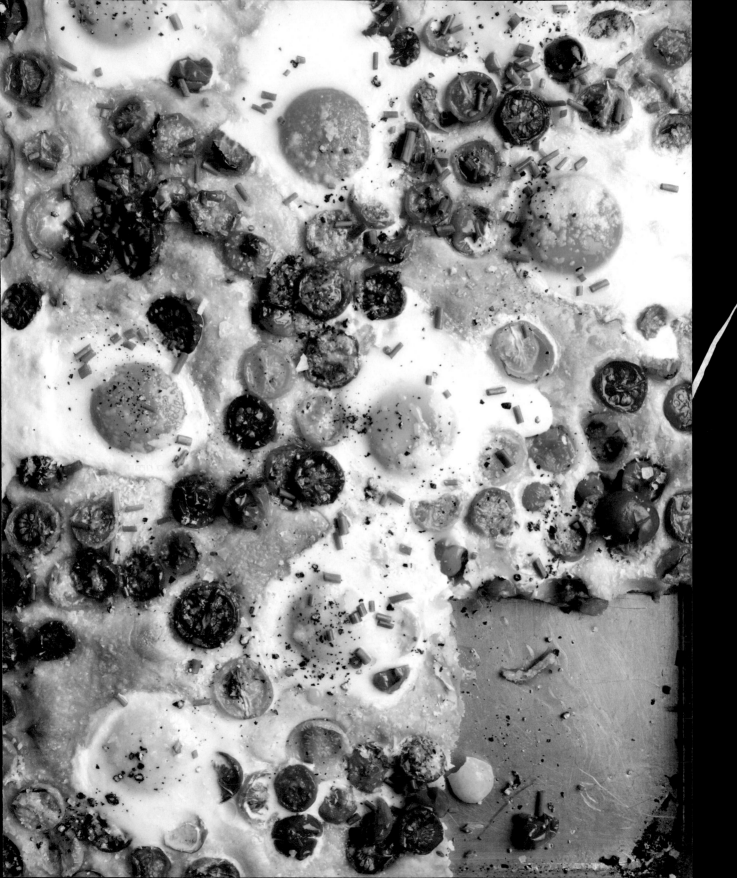

CORN, BACON, AND CHEDDAR
QUICHE

Digging into a warm cheddar-and-bacon-studded quiche is a holiday-morning tradition that Adam from Season 5 looks forward to all year long. Here corn kernels lend the creamy filling texture and a little pop of sweetness. Because there's nothing sadder than a quiche with a soggy crust, don't forget to blind bake the crust thoroughly before adding the filling.

SERVES 8

1½ cups all-purpose flour

1 stick (4 ounces) unsalted butter, cubed and frozen

½ teaspoon kosher salt

5 large eggs

2 tablespoons ice water, plus more as needed

6 slices bacon, coarsely chopped

1 cup fresh or frozen corn kernels

Nonstick pan spray

1½ cups half-and-half

1 teaspoon kosher salt

½ teaspoon freshly ground black pepper

¼ teaspoon nutmeg, preferably freshly grated

3 scallions, thinly sliced

2 cups shredded sharp cheddar cheese

1. In a food processor, combine the flour, butter, and salt and pulse until the mixture is sandy, with a few pea-size pieces of butter still visible, about 1 minute. Add 1 of the eggs and the ice water and pulse until the dough is moistened and starting to pull away from the sides of the bowl, about 30 seconds. (If the dough is still dry, add more ice water 1 teaspoon at a time; do not overprocess.) Shape the dough into a 1-inch-thick disc and wrap it tightly with plastic wrap. Transfer to the refrigerator to chill for at least 30 minutes or up to 3 days.

2. In a medium skillet, cook the bacon over medium-high heat, stirring often, until crisp, about 8 minutes. Using a slotted spoon, transfer the bacon to a paper towel to drain. Pour off and discard all but 1 tablespoon of the bacon drippings from the skillet. Add the corn to the skillet and cook over medium heat, stirring, until tender, 2 to 3 minutes. Set aside.

3. Preheat the oven to 400°F. Coat a 9½-inch deep-dish pie pan with pan spray.

4. Remove the chilled dough from the refrigerator and, using a rolling pin, roll it into a 12-inch round about ⅛ inch thick. Gently transfer the dough to the prepared pie pan and trim and crimp the edges. Place the pan in the freezer to chill for 10 minutes.

5. Remove the pie pan from the freezer and line the crust with parchment paper. Fill with dried beans or pie weights. Bake the crust until pale golden around the edges, about 20 minutes, then remove from the oven and carefully remove the parchment and the pie weights. Leave the oven on.

6. In a large bowl, whisk together the remaining 4 eggs, the half-and-half, salt, pepper, and nutmeg. Stir in the corn.

7. Sprinkle half the cheddar and the bacon over the bottom of the warm crust. Pour in the egg mixture and sprinkle with the remaining cheddar and bacon. Bake until a toothpick inserted into the center of the quiche comes out clean, about 45 minutes. (If the crust looks too brown before the filling is set, wrap some foil around the edges or use a pie crust shield to protect it.) Let the quiche cool for 30 minutes before slicing and serving.

CARAMELIZED FENNEL, HAM, AND GRUYÈRE
GRATIN

Inspired by the roasted Gruyère gratin that helped Nathan win the Season 3 finale, this warm savory bread pudding is the best kind of cozy comfort food. Custardy, soft, and ribboned with sweet caramelized onion and fennel between creamy layers of Italian bread, salty ham, and melted cheese, it tastes just like a giant bowl of French onion soup (minus the soup). It's very rich, so you don't need much to go along with it, other than a simple green salad.

SERVES 8 TO 10

SEASON **3**

4 tablespoons (½ stick) cold unsalted butter, plus 1 tablespoon at room temperature for the baking dish

2 tablespoons extra-virgin olive oil

2 medium yellow onions, thinly sliced

1½ teaspoons kosher salt, divided

Freshly ground black pepper

2 fennel bulbs, trimmed, halved, cored, and thinly sliced

3 tablespoons cider vinegar

1 (12-inch) loaf crusty Italian bread, cut into ⅓-inch-thick slices and lightly toasted

½ pound thinly sliced deli ham

1 tablespoon chopped fresh rosemary

12 ounces Gruyère cheese, grated (about 3 cups)

2 cups chicken stock or broth

2 cups heavy cream

1. Preheat the oven to 425°F. Use the 1 tablespoon room-temperature butter to grease an oblong 3-quart baking dish.

2. In a large skillet, melt the remaining 4 tablespoons butter with the oil over medium-low heat. Once the butter has melted, add the onions and 1 teaspoon of the salt. Cook, stirring occasionally, until the onions are soft and starting to color, 15 to 20 minutes. Season generously with pepper. Add the fennel and cook, stirring occasionally, until the fennel is soft and the onions are deeply golden, 15 to 20 minutes more. Remove from the heat. Immediately add the vinegar to the pan and stir to deglaze, using your spoon to scrape up any browned bits from the bottom of the pan. Spoon the onion-fennel mixture into a medium bowl and set aside.

3. Arrange half the bread slices over the bottom of the prepared baking dish in a single layer, tearing some into smaller pieces if needed to fill any gaps. Spoon half the onion-fennel mixture over the bread in an even layer and lay half the ham slices on top. Sprinkle half the Gruyère over the ham in an even layer. Repeat the layering with the remaining bread, onion-fennel mixture, ham, and cheese. Sprinkle the top with the rosemary and remaining ½ teaspoon salt, and season with pepper.

4. In a 4-cup measuring cup, combine the stock and cream. Starting at the edges of the baking dish and slowly working your way toward the center, pour the mixture over the layers of bread and cheese, pausing when needed to let it be absorbed. Continue until the dish is evenly saturated. Use the back of a spoon or a spatula (or your fingers) to press down on the gratin to compress it. Set aside for about 15 minutes to allow the bread to absorb the cream mixture, pressing it occasionally to compress it a bit more.

5. Cover the dish with foil and place it on a rimmed baking sheet. Bake for 30 minutes, then remove the foil and bake, uncovered, until the edges are bubbling, the cheese is melted, and the top is golden, about 15 minutes more. Let rest for 15 minutes before serving. Store leftovers, covered, in the refrigerator for up to 3 days.

CHICKEN POT PIE
WITH DILL BISCUITS AND GOLDEN BEETS

Combining traditionally Polish ingredients like beets and dill with elements of a classic British pot pie, a version of this warming, rustic take on chicken and biscuits was Beni's answer to the Season 6 heritage recipe challenge. Roasting the chicken and beets separately before combining them with the gravy amps up the caramelized flavors, and a pinch of smoked paprika lends the mixture subtle color and a smoky edge. Just remember: It's essential to use golden beets, not red ones, unless you want a pink pie!

SERVES 6

FILLING

2 pounds boneless, skinless chicken thighs

2 tablespoons extra-virgin olive oil, divided

Kosher salt and freshly ground black pepper

3 medium golden beets, peeled and diced

4 tablespoons (½ stick) unsalted butter

2 celery stalks, finely diced

1 medium yellow onion, diced

2 large garlic cloves, minced

10 ounces white mushrooms, stemmed and thinly sliced

1½ tablespoons chopped fresh thyme

¼ cup all-purpose flour

1¼ cups chicken stock

½ cup half-and-half

½ teaspoon smoked paprika

BISCUITS

2 cups all-purpose flour

1 tablespoon baking powder

1 teaspoon kosher salt

1 stick (4 ounces) unsalted butter, diced

¾ cup heavy cream

¼ cup chopped fresh dill

1. Make the filling: Preheat the oven to 375°F. Line two baking sheets with parchment paper.

2. Arrange the chicken thighs on one prepared baking sheet. Drizzle with 1 tablespoon of the oil and season with ¼ teaspoon each salt and pepper. Place the beets on the other prepared baking sheet and toss with the remaining 1 tablespoon oil, and season lightly with salt and pepper. Transfer both baking sheets to the oven. Roast the chicken thighs until cooked through, about 25 minutes. Remove the pan from the oven and set aside for about 10 minutes. Roast the beets until tender when pierced with a fork, about 30 minutes. Remove the pan from the oven and set aside. (If you are continuing on to bake the

pot pies, leave the oven on, but increase the oven temperature to 425°F.) When the chicken is cool enough to handle, cut it into coarse chunks and transfer it to a medium bowl, along with any juices from the pan.

3. In a large skillet or Dutch oven, melt the butter over medium heat. Add the celery and onion and sauté until they begin to soften, about 7 minutes. Add the garlic, mushrooms, and thyme and sauté until soft and fragrant, about 5 minutes more. Reduce the heat to medium-low, sprinkle in the flour, and cook, stirring constantly, until the flour is sticky and golden, about 2 minutes. Drizzle in the stock and bring to a simmer. Cook, stirring constantly, until thickened, 1 to 2 minutes. Stir in the half-and-half and smoked paprika and season with salt and pepper. Fold in the chicken and juices and the beets. Remove the pan from the heat and set aside as you prepare the biscuits.

4. Make the biscuits: In a large bowl, whisk together the flour, baking powder, and salt. Use your fingertips to cut the butter into the flour mixture until it is the texture of coarse crumbs and a few pea-size pieces of butter are still visible. Add the cream and dill and stir gently with a fork just until a shaggy dough forms.

5. If you haven't already, preheat the oven to 425°F. Divide the chicken mixture evenly among six 10-ounce casserole dishes or spoon it into one 9 × 12-inch baking dish. Divide the biscuit batter into 6 portions and scoop it on top of the chicken mixture. If using individual casserole dishes, transfer them to a rimmed baking sheet. Bake until the filling is bubbling at the edges and the biscuits are puffed and golden, 20 to 25 minutes. Let rest for 5 minutes before serving.

GLUTEN-FREE
SEEDY SODA BREAD

Moist, dense, and chewy, this tender loaf is inspired by one that Evan from Season 6 sometimes makes with his grandmother. Because the "dough" is made entirely of oats and seeds and sweetened only with a drizzle of molasses, it is not only Paleo-friendly but also gluten-free. But just because it's healthy doesn't mean it doesn't taste amazing! Try it sliced and topped with cream cheese and cucumbers or toasted and spread with blueberry jam.

MAKES ONE 8½ × 4½-INCH LOAF

Butter or nonstick pan spray

4 cups rolled oats

¼ cup chia seeds

2½ cups buttermilk

2 tablespoons extra-virgin olive oil

1½ tablespoons molasses

2 teaspoons baking soda

1 teaspoon kosher salt

⅓ cup plus 1 teaspoon flaxseeds

⅓ cup plus 1 tablespoon sunflower seeds

TIP If you'd like to make the recipe vegan, replace the buttermilk with an equal amount of almond milk and 1 tablespoon distilled white vinegar.

1. Preheat the oven to 400°F. Coat an 8½ × 4½-inch loaf pan with pan spray and line it with parchment paper, leaving a few inches of overhang on both of the long sides. (This will help you lift the loaf out of the pan after baking.)

2. In a large bowl, stir together the oats, chia seeds, and buttermilk until well combined. Set aside to allow the oats to soften and absorb the buttermilk, about 30 minutes. Stir in the oil, molasses, baking soda, salt, ⅓ cup of the flaxseeds, and ⅓ cup of the sunflower seeds.

3. Spoon the mixture into the prepared loaf pan, mounding it slightly in the center in a loaf shape. Scatter the top with the remaining 1 teaspoon flaxseeds and 1 tablespoon sunflower seeds. Bake until golden brown and a toothpick inserted into the center of the loaf comes out clean, about 45 minutes. Using oven mitts, use the parchment to lift the loaf out of the pan. (Be careful, as it will be very hot: You may want to ask an adult for help!) Return the parchment and the loaf to the oven without the pan, placing the parchment directly on the center rack. Bake until the exterior of the loaf is firm and dry, about 8 minutes more. Transfer the bread to a wire rack to cool completely before slicing. Store in a paper bag at room temperature for up to 3 days.

RUSTIC NO-KNEAD BREAD

Avani from Season 5 loves baking bread so much that she once designed a school project around studying the ideal water temperature to make dough rise! But you don't have to be a scientist like her to make crusty, chewy, artisan-quality loaves at home. This simple no-knead recipe is versatile, delicious, and almost impossible to screw up. (Though, in order to develop good flavor and structure, it does require a long time—18 hours!—to rise, so you'll need to plan ahead.) With a combo of whole wheat and white flour, it's perfect for morning toast or sandwiches, or buttered and served alongside a bowl of soup. Give it a try and you might get hooked!

MAKES ONE 10-INCH ROUND LOAF

2 cups all-purpose flour, plus more for shaping

2 cups whole wheat flour

2 teaspoons kosher salt

1 teaspoon active dry yeast

2 cups lukewarm water

2 tablespoons honey

TIP If your kitchen tends to be chilly and you need a spot to let your dough rise, try the top of the refrigerator. Because the appliance emits heat, it's usually a little warmer up there.

1. In a large bowl, whisk together the all-purpose flour, whole wheat flour, salt, and yeast. In a large measuring cup, combine the lukewarm water and honey and stir until the honey has dissolved. Pour the honey mixture into the flour mixture and stir with a fork until it forms a wet, sticky dough, about 2 minutes. Cover the bowl with plastic wrap and set it aside to rest in a warm spot until the dough has doubled in size, at least 18 hours. (One convenient way to time it is to prepare the dough in the afternoon, let the dough rest overnight, and then bake it the following morning.)

2. When you're ready to bake, place a lidded 6-quart enameled Dutch oven in the oven and preheat the oven to 475°F. Once the oven is preheated, continue to heat the pan in it for 45 minutes more, until it is scorching hot.

3. With floured hands, scoop the rested dough from the bowl and place it on a lightly floured large square of parchment paper. At this point the dough should look loose and puffy and contain pockets of small bubbles. Reflour your hands and lightly shape the dough into a round. Use a sharp knife to make two or three ¼-inch-deep slashes on the top of the loaf.

4. Carefully remove the Dutch oven from the oven and remove the lid. Always remember to use oven mitts when handling it—or ask a grown-up for help! Holding the edges of the parchment, lift the shaped dough and the parchment together. Lower them into the Dutch oven so the parchment lines the bottom and the dough sits inside it. Carefully cover the Dutch oven and return it to the oven. Bake for 30 minutes, then remove the lid and bake until the exterior of the bread is golden and firm and an instant-read thermometer inserted into the center reads 210°F, 15 to 20 minutes more.

5. Remove the Dutch oven from the oven and, using oven mitts, carefully lift the bread out using the parchment as a sling. Transfer the bread to a wire rack and let cool for at least 30 minutes before slicing. Store at room temperature in a paper bag for up to 2 days.

ACKNOWLEDGMENTS

First and foremost, a huge thank-you to all the kids who have shown that age doesn't matter in the kitchen. You inspire us and constantly surprise us with your passion, excitement, and humanity.

There are also a lot of people behind the scenes who deserve a special thanks for their work on this book. Thank you to the Endemol Shine North America team: Thomas Ferguson, Ross Caputo, Ryan Ullman, and Tamaya Petteway; and to our publishing partners at Clarkson Potter: Raquel Pelzel, Andrea Portanova, Stephanie Huntwork, Sonia Persad, Erica Gelbard, Stephanie Davis, Joyce Wong, and Heather Williamson.

To baker and writer extraordinaire, Sarah Karnasiewicz: You deftly executed our vision for this book down to every fine detail; we are lucky to have had you on this project. To the man behind the lens, photographer Evan Sung, and his talented team—Vivian Lui and Kira Corbin—as well as our wonderful hand models, Aili and Erkki Forster and Luisa and Lucas Malvar, thank you all for your energy, creativity, and nimbleness.

A heartfelt thank you to our entire TV network family at FOX and to our *MasterChef* judges: Gordon Ramsay, Christina Tosi, Graham Elliot, Joe Bastianich, and Aarón Sanchez, as well as all the production teams and crew—you may never see them on TV, but they are as central to the show as our young chefs and judges. Special thanks to Sandee Birdsong, Avery Pursell, Mary Keledjian, and the talent culinary teams they have led through the years.

To all the former *MasterChef Junior* contestants (and their families) who responded with such generosity when we reached out with questions: Thanks a million! Your imaginative spirits and clever ideas are on every page of this book.

And a special shout-out to *MasterChef Junior* views and fans. We enjoy working hard to bring this show to life—we do it for you!

Keep watching . . . and keep cooking!

INDEX

Note: Page references in *italics* indicate photographs.